Contact us: mathprep555@yahoo.com

Printed in the United States of America

C L E P:

COLLEGE MATHEMATICS

2020 Questions with Answers

Published: 07/01/2019

ISBN: 978-1673770438

Book design and interior formatting by Sahib Kazimov
e-mail: kazimli@hotmail.com

Tayyip Oral
Sheryl Knight

C L E P:

COLLEGE MATHEMATICS

2020 Questions with Answers

USA - 2020

555 Math Prep Book Series

1) 1000 Logic & Reasoning Questions for Gifted and Talented Elementary School Students

2) 555 SAT Math(555 Questions with Solution)

3) 555 GEOMETRY (555 Questions with Solution)

4) 555 GEOMETRY Problems for High School Students

5) 555 ACT Math (555 Questions with Solution)

6) 555 ACT Math (555 Questions with Answers)

7) 555 ADVANCED Math Problems - for Middle School Students

8) 555 MATH IQ Questions for High School Students

9) 555 MATH IQ Questions for Middle School Students

10) 555 MATH IQ Questions for Elementary School Students

11) 555 GEOMETRY Formula handbook for SAT, ACT, GRE

12) GEOMETRY Formula Handbook

13) ALGEBRA Handbook for Middle School Students

14) GEOMETRY for SAT&ACT (555 Questions with Answers)

15) 555 Gifted and Talented for Middle School Students

16) ALGEBRA for the New SAT (1111 Questions with Answers)

17) ALGEBRA for the ACT (1080 Questions with Answers)

18) 555 MATH IQ for Elementary School Students (Second Edition)

19) TSI MATH (Texas Success Initiative)

20) ACCUPLACERMATH PREP

21) CLEP College Algebra

22) MATH WORD Problems (540 Questions with Answers)

Table of Contents

Preface

CLEP COLLEGE MATHEMATICS book is a developmental practice questions text for all students who are getting ready for all test. It uses 1900 different types of College mathematics practice questions with over 50 topics included to develop and improve students' practical skills in College mathematics . Each test is composed of 12 questions. Students have a sufficient number of different types of questions to practice and prepare. This book functions as a practice questions text but also serves as a resource for both students and teachers. This book is adequate for students and teachers to use as an excellent resource for years to come. Authors utilized their extensive expertise and worked on each question of this book very diligently to provide students excellent practice to maximize their success in College Mathematics This selection of best quality questions inarguably is very similar to the questions of the CLEP College math Test, with all types of questions covered. It is the authors hope that this book helps all students in getting ready for the college mathematics test and serves as one of the best resources for wonderful educators.

Tayyip Oral
555 math book series author
oral_tayyip@yahoo.com

TEST – 1
Decimals

1. $(6.24 + 3.48) = ?$
   A) 9.62   B) 9.72
   C) 9.84   D) 8.72

2. $(13,721 + 3,621) = ?$
   A) 17.432   B) 17.342
   C) 16.232   D) 16.982

3. $(0.3^2 + 0.4^2) = ?$
   A) 0.22   B) 0.23
   C) 0.25   D) 0.28

4. $(6.44 + 3.56)^2 = ?$
   A) 10   B) 50   C) 20   D) 100

5. $(9.84 - 3.2 - 2.64)^2 = ?$
   A) 16   B) 25
   C) 36   D) 49

6. $3.47 + 1.37 + 7.16 = ?$
   A) 11   B) 12
   C) 11.72   D) 12.36

7. $\frac{3}{5} + \frac{3}{4} = a.bc, \; a + b + c = ?$
   A) 11   B) 10   C) 9   D) 8

8. $(-3^2 \cdot 1.2) + (9 \cdot 1.3) = ?$
   A) 3.3   B) 0.9   C) 4.3   D) 1.3

9. $|2.3 - 1| + |3.2 - 1.2| = ?$
   A) 3   B) 3.3   C) 3.2   D) 5.3

10. $(1.7) \times (12.4) = ?$
    A) 21.08   B) 22.08
    C) 24.06   D) 25.04

11. $(0.5) \times (6.25) = ?$
    A) 3.225   B) 3.45
    C) 4.125   D) 3.125

12. $(1.3) \times (1.3) - 1.69 + 1.64 = ?$
    A) 2.69   B) 3.69
    C) 4.34   D) 1.64

TEST – 2

Fraction and Decent Equivalencies

* Write each fraction as decimal.

1. $\dfrac{12}{25} = ?$
   A) 0.12 B) 1.2
   C) 0.48 D) 0.36

2. $\dfrac{6}{20} = ?$
   A) 1.2 B) 0.6
   C) 0.32 D) 0.30

3. $\dfrac{15}{25} = ?$
   A) 0.6 B) 0.7
   C) 0.8 D) 0.9

4. $\dfrac{48}{50} = ?$
   A) 0.48 B) 0.96
   C) 0.86 D) 9.6

5. $\dfrac{36}{20} = ?$
   A) 18 B) 1.8
   C) 0.18 D) 0.36

* Write each decimal as fraction.

6. $0.44 = ?$
   A) $\dfrac{11}{25}$ B) $\dfrac{11}{24}$ C) $\dfrac{11}{20}$ D) $\dfrac{44}{50}$

7. $0.72 = ?$
   A) $\dfrac{18}{20}$ B) $\dfrac{19}{20}$ C) $\dfrac{18}{25}$ D) $\dfrac{26}{20}$

8. $1.24 = ?$
   A) $1\dfrac{6}{25}$ B) $2\dfrac{6}{25}$
   C) $3\dfrac{1}{25}$ D) $2\dfrac{6}{20}$

* Write each decimal as a percent.

9. $0.23 = ?$
   A) 23% B) 2.3%
   C) 0.23% D) 230%

10. $0.423 = ?$
    A) 4.23% B) 42.3%
    C) 423% D) 4230%

11. $1.24 = ?$
    A) 1.24% B) 14.4%
    C) 124% D) 12%

12. $6.45 = ?$
    A) 6.45% B) 64.5%
    C) 645% D) 35%

TEST – 3
Mixed Numbers

1. $2\dfrac{1}{3} + 3\dfrac{1}{2} = ?$

   A) $\dfrac{35}{6}$ B) $\dfrac{35}{8}$ C) $\dfrac{32}{6}$ D) $5\dfrac{1}{6}$

2. $3\dfrac{1}{4} + 2\dfrac{1}{7} = ?$

   A) $\dfrac{151}{27}$ B) $\dfrac{151}{28}$ C) $\dfrac{161}{28}$ D) $\dfrac{141}{28}$

3. $7\dfrac{1}{2} + 6\dfrac{1}{3} + 4\dfrac{1}{4} = ?$

   A) $\dfrac{213}{11}$ B) $\dfrac{214}{12}$ C) $\dfrac{212}{12}$ D) $\dfrac{217}{12}$

4. $7\dfrac{1}{4} - 3\dfrac{1}{5} = ?$

   A) $\dfrac{81}{20}$ B) $\dfrac{81}{30}$ C) $\dfrac{41}{70}$ D) $\dfrac{21}{60}$

5. $3\dfrac{1}{3} - 2\dfrac{1}{2} = ?$

   A) $\dfrac{2}{6}$ B) $\dfrac{5}{7}$ C) $\dfrac{5}{6}$ D) $\dfrac{6}{5}$

6. $7\dfrac{1}{2} - 6\dfrac{1}{3} = ?$

   A) $\dfrac{7}{6}$ B) $\dfrac{1}{2}$ C) $\dfrac{1}{3}$ D) $\dfrac{1}{6}$

7. $3\dfrac{1}{4} \div 2\dfrac{1}{3} = ?$

   A) $\dfrac{39}{28}$ B) $\dfrac{39}{27}$ C) $\dfrac{29}{27}$ D) $\dfrac{29}{15}$

8. $9 \div \dfrac{1}{3}$

   A) 22   B) 27   C) 9   D) 3

9. 4.25×4

   A) 17   B) 16   C) 15   D) 14

10. $\left(2\dfrac{1}{6}\right) \cdot \left(4\dfrac{1}{5}\right) = ?$

    A) 6.1   B) 7.1   C) 8.1   D) 9.1

11. $7\dfrac{1}{7} \cdot 49 = ?$

    A) 250   B) 260   C) 280   D) 350

12. $\left(2\dfrac{1}{6}\right) \cdot \left(7\dfrac{4}{5}\right) = ?$

    A) 2.3   B) 16.9   C) 9.6   D) 28.9

TEST – 4

Changing Decimal to Fraction

1. 0.13 = ?

   A) $\dfrac{13}{10}$ B) $\dfrac{13}{100}$

   C) $\dfrac{13}{20}$ D) $\dfrac{13}{1000}$

2. 0.64 = ?

   A) $\dfrac{12}{9}$ B) $\dfrac{42}{80}$ C) $\dfrac{16}{22}$ D) $\dfrac{16}{25}$

Changing fraction to decimal

3. $\dfrac{13}{25} = ?$

   A) 1.2   B) 0.52   C) 0.9   D) 0.36

4. $\dfrac{15}{25} = ?$

   A) 0.3   B) 0.36   C) 0.6   D) 1.5

Changing decimal to percent

5. 0.32 =?

   A) 30%   B) 64%

   C) 32%   D) 3.2%

6. 2.17 = ?

   A) 217%   B) 21.9%

   C) 0.213%   D) 27%

7. 0.37 =?

   A) 3.7%   B) 37%

   C) 0.37%   D) 370%

8. 0.008 = ?

   A) 0.8%   B) 0.08%

   C) 8%   D) 80%

Changing percent to decimal

9. 22% = ?

   A) 0.22   B) 2.2

   C) 22   D) 0.212

10. 0.3% = ?

    A) 3   B) 0.3   C) 0.003   D) 30

Changing fraction to percent

11. $\dfrac{3}{5} = ?$

    A) 30%   B) 60%

    C) 70%   D) 80%

12. $\dfrac{3}{8} = ?$

    A) 37.5%   B) 36.5%

    C) 54.3%   D) 38.5%

TEST – 5

Changing Decimal to Fraction and Adding and Subtracting Decimals

1. $0.36 = ?$

   A) $\dfrac{9}{20}$ B) $\dfrac{9}{25}$ C) $\dfrac{8}{25}$ D) $\dfrac{8}{15}$

2. $0.12 = ?$

   A) $\dfrac{4}{25}$ B) $\dfrac{3}{20}$ C) $\dfrac{3}{25}$ D) $\dfrac{5}{23}$

3. $0.148 = ?$

   A) $\dfrac{27}{200}$ B) $\dfrac{27}{250}$ C) $\dfrac{37}{250}$ D) $\dfrac{37}{200}$

4. $\dfrac{4}{25} = ?$

   A) 0.20   B) 0.18   C) 0.19   D) 0.16

5. $\dfrac{3}{50} = ?$

   A) 0.3   B) 0.03   C) 0.6   D) 0.06

6. $\dfrac{3}{12} = ?$

   A) 0.12   B) 0.18   C) 0.20   D) 0.25

7. $6.442 + 7.824 = ?$

   A) 14.266   B) 13.266
   C) 15.266   D) 12.256

8. $12.842 + 21.988 = ?$

   A) 34.830   B) 33.830
   C) 34.840   D) 35.930

9. $13.721 - 9.872 = ?$

   A) 3.849   B) 4.849
   C) 3.789   D) 3.779

10. $8.27 + 9.77 \approx ?$

    A) 18.04   B) 19.04
    C) 18.05   D) 19.05

11. $2.12 \cdot 3.12 = ?$

    A) 6.6144   B) 6.5144
    C) 6.5134   D) 6.6244

12. $3^2 + 3.12 = ?$

    A) 12.12   B) 13.12
    C) 13.12   D) 12.13

13

TEST – 6

Rounding and Order of Operations

1. Round 246 to the nearest ten.
   A) 250   B) 240   C) 245   D) 200

2. Round 321 to the nearest ten.
   A) 300   B) 320   C) 322   D) 321

3. Round 3564 to the nearest hundred.
   A) 3600   B) 3560
   C) 3500   D) 4000

4. Round 7248 to the nearest hundred.
   A) 4000   B) 7265
   C) 7250   D) 7200

5. Round 64827 to nearest thousand.
   A) 65800   B) 65000
   C) 65430   D) 66720

6. Round off 43.248 to the nearest hundredth.
   A) 43.25   B) 43.35
   C) 43.45   D) 43.47

7. Round 6.378 to the nearest hundredth?
   A) 6.48   B) 6.38   C) 6.49   D) 6.30

8. Round 98.555 to nearest one.
   A) 48   B) 99   C) 100   D) 98.6

9. Estimate the numbers: 72+86+44+32=?
   A) 200   B) 210   C) 220   D) 230

10. Estimate the numbers:
    364+720+585+221=?
    A) 1600   B) 1800
    C) 1900   D) 2000

11. Round 199.872 to the nearest one.
    A) 199   B) 199.8   C) 199.7   D) 200

12. Round 217.217 to the nearest ten?
    A) 220   B) 221
    C) 223   D) 217.22

TEST – 7

Factors, Primes and Composites

1. Factors of 12.
   A) 1,2,3,6   B) 1,2,3,4,6,12
   C) 1,3,6,12   D) 1,3,6

2. Factor of 28.
   A) 1,2,7,14,28   B) 2,7,14
   C) 1,2,14,28   D) 7,14,28

3. Factor of 48.
   A) 3,4,6,8,12,16,24,48
   B) 3,4,6,8,12,16
   C) 1,2,3,4,6,8,12,16,24,48
   D) 6,8,12,16,24,48

4. Which is a prime number?
   A) 97   B) 87   C) 52   D) 27

5. Which is a prime number?
   A) 39   B) 71   C) 24   D) 69

6. Which is a prime number?
   A) 24   B) 23   C) 21   D) 22

7. Which is a composite number?
   A) 21   B) 23   C) 29   D) 31

8. Which is a composite number?
   A) 49   B) 31   C) 41   D) 61

9. Find the prime factorization of 24.
   A) 8×3   B) 6×4   C) 12×2   D) 2^3×3

10. Find the prime factorization of 80
    A) 2^4×5   B) 8×10   C) 16×5   D) 20×4

11. Find the prime factorization of 90.
    A) 9×10   B) 18×5
    C) 2×3^2×5   D) 2×5^2×3

12. Find the prime factorization of 122.
    A) 2×61   B) 2×63   C) 4×31   D) 4×32

TEST – 8
Order of Operations

1. $32 \div 8 + 4 = ?$
   A) 8   B) 12   C) 14   D) 16

2. $6 \times 3 + 7 - 5 = ?$
   A) 20   B) 19   C) 18   D) 17

3. $35 \div 5 + 2 * 3 = ?$
   A) 14   B) 13   C) 12   D) 11

4. $12^2 \div (18 \div 2) + 18 = ?$
   A) 30   B) 31   C) 32   D) 34

5. $36 - (36 \div 6)^2 + 36 = ?$
   A) 108   B) 72   C) 36   D) 10

6. $(36 - 30 \div 6) * 4 - 3^2 = ?$
   A) 111   B) 117   C) 119   D) 115

7. $44 - (44 \div 4)^2 + 4 * 3 = ?$
   A) 65   B) –65   C) 56   D) –56

8. $24 + (24 \div 4)^2 \cdot 6^0 - 24 = ?$
   A) 24   B) -24   C) 36   D) -36

9. $7x4 + 7 - 4 = ?$
   A) 31   B) 30   C) 29   D) 28

10. $3^3 \div (3^4 \div 3^2) + 3^3 = ?$
    A) 30   B) 31   C) 32   D) 34

11. $75 \div 25 + 5 + 2 = ?$
    A) 10   B) 11   C) 12   D) 13

12. $5^3 - 5^2 \div 5 + 3^5 \div 3^2 = ?$
    A) 50   B) 51   C) 147   D) 146

TEST – 9
Simplify, Rounding Numbers, Mixed Numbers

1. Simplify the fraction: $\frac{15}{25}$

   A) $\frac{3}{5}$ B) $\frac{3}{7}$ C) $\frac{5}{10}$ D) $\frac{4}{5}$

2. Simplify the fraction: $\frac{36}{48}$

   A) $\frac{1}{3}$ B) $\frac{2}{3}$ C) $\frac{3}{4}$ D) $\frac{3}{8}$

3. Simplify the fraction: $\frac{45}{75}$

   A) $\frac{2}{3}$ B) $\frac{4}{5}$ C) $\frac{3}{7}$ D) $\frac{3}{5}$

4. Rounding to the nearest hundred 27964
   A) 28000 B) 27900
   C) 27960 D) 28140

5. Rounding the numbers nearest to hundreds 7893.
   A) 7900 B) 7800 C) 7600 D) 7700

6. 480 rounded to the nearest hundred is....
   A) 490 B) 495 C) 500 D) 510

7. $4\frac{3}{5}=\frac{ab}{c}$, a+b+c=?
   A) 20 B) 21 C) 10 D) 23

8. $\left(2\frac{1}{3}\right)^2=\frac{ab}{c}$, a+b+c=?
   A) 20 B) 21 C) 22 D) 23

9. $4\frac{1}{3}-3\frac{1}{4}=?$
   A) $\frac{13}{12}$ B) $\frac{11}{12}$ C) $\frac{7}{12}$ D) $\frac{15}{13}$

10. $\frac{97}{8}=?$
    A) $12\frac{1}{8}$ B) $13\frac{1}{8}$ C) $7\frac{1}{12}$ D) $9\frac{1}{12}$

11. $4\frac{2}{3}-\frac{14}{3}+\frac{1}{3}=?$
    A) 0 B) $4\frac{3}{4}$ C) 1 D) $\frac{1}{3}$

12. $\left(2+\frac{1}{2}\right)+\left(3+\frac{1}{3}\right)=?$
    A) $\frac{35}{7}$ B) $\frac{35}{6}$ C) $\frac{35}{9}$ D) $\frac{34}{7}$

TEST – 10

Operations with Whole Numbers and Fractions

1. $\dfrac{2}{3} + \dfrac{4}{5} = ?$

   A) $\dfrac{22}{10}$ B) $\dfrac{22}{15}$ C) $\dfrac{6}{15}$ D) $\dfrac{8}{15}$

2. $\dfrac{1}{3} + \dfrac{1}{4} + \dfrac{1}{12} = ?$

   A) $\dfrac{1}{3}$ B) $\dfrac{2}{3}$ C) $\dfrac{3}{4}$ D) $\dfrac{5}{12}$

3. $\dfrac{2}{3} \cdot \dfrac{1}{4} \cdot \dfrac{7}{5} = ?$

   A) $\dfrac{6}{12}$ B) $\dfrac{7}{20}$ C) $\dfrac{7}{30}$ D) $\dfrac{8}{21}$

4. $\dfrac{4}{3} \div \dfrac{7}{9} = ?$

   A) $\dfrac{12}{7}$ B) $\dfrac{12}{9}$ C) $\dfrac{7}{12}$ D) $\dfrac{7}{19}$

5. $0.42 = \dfrac{ab}{cd}$, $a + b + c + d = ?$

   A) 10   B) 9   C) 8   D) 7

6. $6 \div \dfrac{1}{2} + 2 \div \dfrac{1}{6} = ?$

   A) 24   B) 12   C) 1   D) 0

7. $36 \div (36 \div 6)^2 + 6 = ?$

   A) 11   B) 10   C) 9   D) 7

8. $\left(9 \div 2\dfrac{1}{3}\right) + \left(4 \div 5\dfrac{2}{6}\right) = ?$

   A) $\dfrac{119}{15}$ B) $\dfrac{119}{14}$ C) $\dfrac{129}{28}$ D) $\dfrac{139}{28}$

9. Simplify the fraction: $\dfrac{87}{51}$

   A) $\dfrac{29}{19}$ B) $\dfrac{29}{18}$ C) $\dfrac{29}{17}$ D) $\dfrac{39}{17}$

10. $12 \cdot \left(4\dfrac{1}{3}\right) = ?$

    A) 52   B) 48   C) 42   D) 32

11. $9 \cdot \left(4\dfrac{5}{3}\right) = ?$

    A) 51   B) 53   C) 52   D) 54

12. $75 \cdot \dfrac{7}{15} = ?$

    A) 30   B) 32   C) 33   D) 35

TEST – 11
Common Factor (GCF and LCF)

1. Find the common factors of 14 and 21.
   A) {1,3}   B) {1,7}
   C) {7,21}   D) {14,3}

2. Find the common factors 12 and 20.
   A) {1,3,5}   B) {1,2,4}
   C) {4,5,12}   D) {3,5,12}

3. Find the factors of 18
   A) {1,3,4,6,18}   B) {1,2,3,4,5,9}
   C) {1,2,3,6,9,18}   D) {1,2,3,9,18}

4. Find the common factors of 15 and 20.
   A) {4,5,8}   B) {1,3,5}
   C) {2,3,5}   D) {1,5}

5. Find the Greatest common factor of 15 and 25.
   A) 5   B) 10   C) 15   D) 30

6. Find the GCF of 18 and 24.
   A) 12   B) 9   C) 8   D) 6

7. Find the GCF of 30 and 75.
   A) 10   B) 15   C) 20   D) 30

8. Find the least common factor of 12 and 21.
   A) 80   B) 82   C) 84   D) 80

9. Find the least common factor of 15 and 25.
   A) 70   B) 75   C) 80   D) 125

10. Find the LGF of 16 and 48.
    A) 42   B) 44   C) 48   D) 60

11. Find the GCF of 13 and 39
    A) 13   B) 26   C) 39   D) 64

12. Find the LCF of the 15 and 60
    A) 15   B) 30   C) 45   D) 60

TEST – 12

Prime and Composite Numbers

1. Which number is prime?
    A) 30   B) 31   C) 32   D) 33

2. Which number is prime ?
    A) 39   B) 40   C) 41   D) 49

3. How many prime numbers are less than 28?
    A) 9   B) 10   C) 11   D) 12

4. How many composite numbers are less than 23?
    A) 10   B) 11   C) 12   D) 13

5. Which number is prime and even ?
    A) 19   B) 22   C) 15   D) 2

6. How many prime numbers are between 10 and 30?
    A) 9   B) 8   C) 7   D) 6

7. How many composite numbers are between 19 and 29?
    A) 9   B) 8   C) 7   D) 6

8. Find the largest two digit prime number.
    A) 95   B) 96   C) 97   D) 91

9. Find the smallest two digit prime number
    A) 11   B) 13   C) 17   D) 19

10. Which is correct?
    A) 1 is prime
    B) 1 is composite
    C) 1 is not prime and not composite
    D) 1 is even

11. Which number is prime?
    A) 37   B) 96   C) 94   D) 42

12. Which number is composite ?
    A) 101   B) 61   C) 71   D) 72

TEST – 13
Radical Equations

1. Solve for x: $\sqrt{x+5}=5$
   A) 19   B) 20   C) 21   D) 25

2. Solve for x: $\sqrt{3x+3}=4$
   A) $\dfrac{13}{3}$ B) $\dfrac{13}{4}$ C) $\dfrac{1}{3}$ D) $-\dfrac{1}{3}$

3. Solve for x: $\sqrt{2x+1}+4=7$
   A) 1   B) 2   C) 3   D) 4

4. Solve for x: $\sqrt{x^2+7}-4=0$
   A) ±3   B) ±2   C) 3   D) 2

5. Solve for x: $\sqrt[3]{3x+3}=3$
   A) 8   B) 7   C) 6   D) 5

6. Solve for x: $\sqrt[3]{4x-4}=4$
   A) 16   B) 17   C) 18   D) 19

7. Solve for x: $x+2=\sqrt{3x+24}$
   A) 4   B) 5   C) 6   D) 7

8. Solve for x: $\sqrt{4x+3}=\sqrt{3x+5}$
   A) 1   B) 2   C) 3   D) 4

9. $\sqrt{x^2+4x+4}=\sqrt{x^2+3x+5}$
   A) 1   B) 1/2   C) 2   D) $\dfrac{1}{3}$

10. Solve for x: $\sqrt{5x+1}=5$
    A) $\dfrac{24}{7}$ B) $\dfrac{24}{9}$ C) $\dfrac{24}{5}$ D) $\dfrac{5}{24}$

11. Solve for x: $\sqrt{2x+3}=4$
    A) 6   B) 6.5   C) 7   D) 7.5

12. Solve for x: $\sqrt{6x+6}=6$
    A) 4   B) 5   C) 6   D) 7

TEST – 14
Square Roots

1. $\sqrt{150} - \sqrt{125} = ?$

   A) 25   B) 5   C) $\sqrt{5}$ D) $2\sqrt{5}$

2. $\sqrt{75} \div \sqrt{5} + \sqrt{60} = ?$

   A) $\sqrt{15}$ B) $3\sqrt{15}$ C) $4\sqrt{15}$ D) 5

3. $\sqrt{20} + \sqrt{40} - 2\sqrt{5} = ?$

   A) $2\sqrt{10}$ B) $2\sqrt{3}$ C) $2\sqrt{5}$ D) $4\sqrt{5}$

4. $\sqrt{9} + \sqrt{16} + \sqrt{169} = ?$

   A) 12   B) 16   C) 20   D) 19

5. $\sqrt{9x^2} + \sqrt{16x^2} + \sqrt{\dfrac{x^2}{4}} = ?$

   A) 15x   B) $\dfrac{15x}{2}$ C) 7x   D) 8x

6. $\sqrt{0.04} + \sqrt{0.09} + \sqrt{0.25} + \sqrt{1.69} = ?$

   A) 2.5   B) 2.4   C) 2.3   D) 2.2

7. $\sqrt{3} \cdot \sqrt{2} \cdot \sqrt{6} \cdot \sqrt{144} = ?$

   A) 62   B) 72   C) 82   D) 86

8. $\sqrt{\dfrac{24}{6}} + \sqrt{\dfrac{48}{6}} + \sqrt{\dfrac{1}{81}} = ?$

   A) $\dfrac{19}{9}$ B) $\dfrac{19}{9} + \sqrt{2}$

   C) $\dfrac{19}{9} + 2\sqrt{2}$ D) $2\sqrt{2}$

9. $\sqrt{\dfrac{1}{100}} + \sqrt{\dfrac{1}{25}} + \sqrt{\dfrac{3}{75}} = ?$

   A) $\dfrac{1}{2}$ B) $\dfrac{1}{3}$ C) $\dfrac{1}{4}$ D) $\dfrac{1}{6}$

10. $\sqrt{\dfrac{48}{3}} + \sqrt{\dfrac{24}{6}} + \sqrt{\dfrac{144}{16}} = ?$

    A) 8   B) 9   C) 10   D) 11

11. $\sqrt[3]{8} + \sqrt[3]{27} + \sqrt{1} = ?$

    A) 4   B) 5   C) 6   D) 7

12. $\sqrt[3]{1000} + \sqrt[3]{64} + \sqrt{125} = ?$

    A) 11   B) 12   C) 16   D) 19

TEST – 15
Data (Mean, Median, Mode, Range)

Use the following numbers:
6, 12, 14, 14, 14, 18, 20

1. Find the mean.
   A) 12   B) 14   C) 15   D) 18

2. Find the median.
   A) 6   B) 12   C) 14   D) 18

3. Find the mode.
   A) 20   B) 18   C) 6   D) 14

4. Find the range.
   A) 10   B) 12   C) 13   D) 14

Set A:{4,6,2,8,4,7,10}

5. Find the mean.
   A) $\frac{31}{3}$ B) $\frac{31}{4}$ C) $\frac{41}{7}$ D) $\frac{32}{7}$

6. Find the range.
   A) 2   B) 4   C) 6   D) 8

7. Find the mode.
   A) 4   B) 2   C) 8   D) 10

8. Find the median.
   A) 6   B) 2   C) 8   D) 4

Set B:{-4,6,3,8,5,10,3}

9. Find the mode.
   A) 8   B) 5   C) 10   D) 3

10. Find the range.
    A) 14   B) 5   C) 9   D) 10

11. Find the median.
    A) -4   B) 3   C) 5   D) 10

12. Find the mean.
    A) $\frac{31}{3}$ B) $\frac{31}{4}$ C) $\frac{31}{7}$ D) $\frac{32}{5}$

TEST – 16
Composition of Two Functions

1. $f(x)=2x + 1$, $f(1) + f(3) =?$
   A) 10   B) 11   C) 12   D) 13

2. $f(x)=3x+2$, $g(x)=x-1$ find $f(g(x))=?$
   A) $3x + 1$ B) $3x$
   C) $3x - 1$ D) $3x + 4$

3. $f(x)=x^2+1$, $h(x)=x+1$. Find $h(f(x))=?$
   A) $x^2 + 1$ B) $x^2 - 1$
   C) $x^2 + 3$ D) $x^2 + 2$

4. $f(x)=3x^2 + 4x + 2$, $f(1) - f(0) =?$
   A) 0   B) 1   C) 2   D) 7

5. $f(x)=x^2+4x+4$, $g(x)=(x+2)$.
   Which is correct?
   A) $f(x)=g(x)$ B) $f(x)=g(x)^2$
   C) $f(x)=2g(x)$ D) $g(x) = f(x)^2$

6. $f(x) = x^2 + 6x + 10$, $g(x)=(x+3)^2$.
   Which is correct?
   A) $f(x)=g(x)$ B) $f(x)=g(x)+1$
   C) $f(x)=g(x)-1$ D) $f(x) -g(x)=0$

7. $f(x)=3x^2 + 4x + 1$. Find the $f(3x)=?$
   A) $27x^2 + 12x + 1$ B) $27x^2+10x+ 12$
   D) $9x^2 +12x+1$ D) $30x^2 +10x$

8. $f(x)=3x+1$, $g(x)=3+x$, $f(x) - g(x)=?$
   A) $2x$ B) $3x$
   C) $2x-2$ D) $2x-3$

9. $f(x)=x^2$, $g(x)=x+1$ find $f(g(2))=?$
   A) 8   B) 9   C) 16   D) 25

10. $f(x) = 3x+7$, $g(x)=3x$, $f(g(0))=?$
    A) 0   B) 7   C) 9   D) 16

11. $f(x)=3x$, $g(x) = \dfrac{x}{3}$, find $f(g(x))=?$
    A) x B) $3x$ C) $\dfrac{x}{3}$ D) x^2

12. $f(x)=2x+3$, $g(x)=3x+2$, $g(f(x))=?$
    A) $6x+11$ B) $5x + 5$
    C) $6x^2 + 12$ D) $5x^2-4$

TEST – 17
Percent

1. Find the 30% of 40.
   A) 120   B) 60   C) 40   D) 12

2. Find the 40% of 40.
   A) 160   B) 120   C) 80   D) 16

3. Find the 80% of 900.
   A) 720   B) 620   C) 610   D) 330

4. Find the 90% of 9.
   A) 81   B) 8.1   C) 27   D) 2.7

5. Convert to fraction in the simplest form: 0.24.
   A) $\frac{6}{25}$ B) $\frac{12}{25}$ C) $\frac{6}{50}$ D) $\frac{18}{25}$

6. Convert to fraction in the simplest form: 0.35.
   A) $\frac{7}{100}$ B) $\frac{7}{50}$ C) $\frac{7}{25}$ D) $\frac{7}{20}$

7. 22% convert to decimal.
   A) 2.2   B) 22   C) 0.224   D) 0.22

8. 28% convert to decimal.
   A) 28   B) 2.8   C) 0.28   D) 0.028

9. $\frac{1}{4}$ fraction convert to percent (%).
   A) 4%   B) 10%   C) 20%   D) 25%

10. $\frac{7}{20}$ fraction convert to percent (%).
    A) 7%   B) 14%   C) 21%   D) 35%

11. $\frac{11}{25}$ fraction convert to percent (%).
    A) 11%   B) 25%   C) 22%   D) 44%

12. $\frac{3}{20}$ fraction convert to percent (%).
    A) 3%   B) 20%   C) 12%   D) 15%

TEST – 18
Terminating and Repeating Decimals

1. Which is a terminating decimal?

   A) $\frac{1}{3}$ B) $\frac{3}{20}$ C) $\frac{2}{3}$ D) $\frac{3}{9}$

2. Which is a terminating decimal?

   A) $\frac{1}{9}$ B) $\frac{2}{9}$ C) $\frac{3}{9}$ D) $\frac{6}{50}$

3. Which is a terminating decimal?

   A) $\frac{9}{27}$ B) $\frac{27}{81}$ C) $\frac{2}{9}$ D) $\frac{12}{10}$

4. Which is a terminating decimal?
   A) 0.34   B) 0.1111
   C) 0.99999...   D) 0.6666...

5. Which is a repeating decimal?

   A) $\frac{2}{5}$ B) $\frac{3}{5}$ C) $\frac{8}{10}$ D) $\frac{1}{9}$

6. Which is a repeating decimal?
   A) 0.30   B) 0.$\overline{3}$ C) 0.60   D) 0.75

7. Which is repeating number?

   A) $\frac{10}{3}$ B) $\frac{10}{2}$ C) $\frac{1}{5}$ D) $\frac{1}{8}$

8. Which is a repeating number?

   A) $\frac{11}{9}$ B) $\frac{11}{10}$ C) $\frac{22}{20}$ D) $\frac{25}{35}$

9. Which is a repeating number?

   A) $\frac{7}{10}$ B) $\frac{7}{11}$ C) $\frac{8}{10}$ D) $\frac{2}{5}$

10. Which is a repeating number?

   A) $\frac{1}{4}$ B) $\frac{16}{20}$ C) $\frac{4}{6}$ D) $\frac{3}{20}$

11. Which is a repeating number?

   A) $\frac{9}{10}$ B) $\frac{12}{31}$ C) $\frac{8}{12}$ D) $\frac{5}{8}$

12. Which is a terminating number?

   A) 0.$\overline{22}$ B) 0.3   C) 0.$\overline{66}$ D) $\frac{1}{3}$

TEST – 19

Simplify Fraction and Mixed Fraction

1. Simplify the fraction: $\dfrac{10}{15}$

    A) $\dfrac{2}{5}$ B) $\dfrac{3}{2}$ C) $\dfrac{5}{3}$ D) $\dfrac{2}{3}$

2. Simplify the fraction: $\dfrac{25}{35}$

    A) $\dfrac{5}{6}$ B) $\dfrac{5}{7}$ C) $\dfrac{5}{8}$ D) $\dfrac{2}{5}$

3. Simplify the fraction: $\dfrac{45}{75}$

    A) $\dfrac{2}{3}$ B) $\dfrac{1}{3}$ C) $\dfrac{5}{7}$ D) $\dfrac{3}{5}$

4. Simplify the fraction: $\dfrac{16}{44}$

    A) $\dfrac{4}{11}$ B) $\dfrac{11}{4}$ C) $\dfrac{4}{10}$ D) $\dfrac{5}{11}$

5. Simplify the fraction: $\dfrac{9}{144}$

    A) $\dfrac{1}{12}$ B) $\dfrac{1}{16}$ C) $\dfrac{1}{18}$ D) $\dfrac{2}{9}$

6. Simplify the fraction: $\dfrac{18}{75}$

    A) $\dfrac{6}{25}$ B) $\dfrac{15}{16}$ C) $\dfrac{16}{17}$ D) $\dfrac{16}{25}$

7. Convert mixed fraction to improper fraction: $4\dfrac{3}{7}$

    A) $\dfrac{30}{7}$ B) $\dfrac{31}{7}$ C) $\dfrac{29}{7}$ D) $\dfrac{28}{7}$

8. Convert mixed fraction to improper fraction: $12\dfrac{3}{5}$

    A) $\dfrac{61}{5}$ B) $\dfrac{62}{5}$ C) $\dfrac{63}{5}$ D) $\dfrac{64}{5}$

9. Convert mixed fraction to improper fraction: $8\dfrac{8}{9}$

    A) $\dfrac{22}{9}$ B) $\dfrac{78}{9}$ C) $\dfrac{79}{9}$ D) $\dfrac{80}{9}$

10. $\dfrac{25}{8} = a\dfrac{b}{c}$, $a + b + c = ?$

    A) 10   B) 11   C) 12   D) 13

11. $\dfrac{37}{12} = ?$

    A) $3\dfrac{2}{12}$ B) $2\dfrac{1}{24}$ C) $3\dfrac{1}{12}$ D) $3\dfrac{2}{14}$

12. $\left(4\dfrac{3}{4}\right)^2 = ?$

    A) $\dfrac{251}{16}$ B) $\dfrac{361}{16}$ C) $\dfrac{127}{17}$ D) $\dfrac{351}{17}$

TEST – 20
Complex Numbers

1. $x=3+4i$, $y=2+5i$, $x + y =?$
    A) 5+7i   B) 5+9i
    C) 6+20i   D) 5+12i

2. $x=2+3i$, $y=4+2i$, $x - y=?$
    A) -2+i   B) -2+i
    C) 2i-1   D) 2i+2

3. $f(x)=x^2+4x+1$, $f(i)=?$
    A) 4i   B) 4i+1
    C) 4i-1   D) 2

4. What is the distance of the point (5; -12i) from the origin?
    A) 13i   B) 14i   C) 13   D) 14

5. $(i)^2 + (i)^4 + (i)^6 + (i)^8 =?$
    A) 1   B) 2   C) 4   D) 0

6. $(1+2i)^2 - 3=?$
    A) 3   B) 4i–6   C) 4i   D) –4–4i

7. $(4+4i) + (1 +i)=?$
    A) 1   B) 5i+5   C) -4   D) -i

8. $z = \dfrac{2-i}{3-i} = ?$
    A) $\dfrac{1+i}{5}$ B) $\dfrac{7-i}{10}$
    C) $\dfrac{1+i}{10}$ D) $\dfrac{1+2i}{10}$

9. $x=6-8i$, $y=12+4i$, $y-x=?$
    A) 6+6i   B) 6i-12
    C) 12i-6   D) 12i+6

10. $m=2-3i$, $n=3+2i$, $m \times n=?$
    A) 5+12i   B) 13
    C) 12-5i   D) 12+5i

11. $\dfrac{2}{3+2i} = ?$
    A) $\dfrac{6-4i}{13}$ B) $\dfrac{6+4i}{13}$
    C) $\dfrac{4+6i}{6}$ D) $\dfrac{4+6i}{5}$

12. $\dfrac{5-4i}{1-i} = ?$
    A) $\dfrac{9+i}{2}$ B) $\dfrac{9-i}{2}$
    C) $\dfrac{3-i}{2}$ D) $\dfrac{3+2i}{4}$

TEST – 21
Scientific Notation

1. Convert 83000 to scientific notation.
   A) $8.3×10^4$ B) $83×10^5$
   C) $8.3×10^5$ D) $0.83×10^2$

2. Convert 42000000 to scientific notation.
   A) $4.2×10^7$ B) $4.2×10^6$
   C) $0.42×10^{10}$ D) $0.42×10^3$

3. Convert 24000 to scientific notation.
   A) $24×10^4$ B) $2.4×10^5$
   C) $0.24×10^8$ D) $2.4×10^4$

4. Convert $3.2×10^{-6}$ to decimal notation.
   A) 0.000032   B) 0.0000032
   C) 0.00000032   D) 0.000000032

5. Write using scientific notation 650 000.
   A) $6.5×10^5$ B) $0.65×10^3$
   C) $0.65×10^2$ D) $6.5×10^{-4}$

6. Converting to scientific notation 2430000.
   A) $2.43×10^{-6}$ B) $0.24×10^4$
   C) $2.43×10^7$ D) $2.43×10^6$

7. Write the number scientific notation:
   $(0.24)×(0.0003)=?$
   A) $72×10^{-3}$ B) $7.2×10^{-5}$
   C) $72×10^{-5}$ D) $72×10^{-6}$

8. Write the number scientific notation:
   $(7×10^{-7}) × (7×10^{-17})=?$
   A) $17×10^{-23}$ B) $49×10^{-24}$
   C) $7×10^{-25}$ D) $4.9×10^{-23}$

9. Convert number from scientific notation to real $3.624×10^5$.
   A) 3624000   B) 36240
   C) 362400   D) 3624

10. Convert number from scientific notation to real $8.143×10^6$.
    A) 814300000   B) 81430
    C) 814300   D) 8143000

11. Convert 960000to scientific notation.
    A) $96×10^4$ B) $9.6×10^7$
    C) $9.6×10^3$ D) $9.6×10^6$

12. Convert number from scientific notation scientific to real: $7.421×10^6$.
    A) 74210000   B) 7421000
    C) 742100   D) 742100

TEST – 22
Probability

1. There are 14 marbles in a box, 6 red and 8 blue. Two marbles are drawn from the box, one at a time and without replacement. What is the probability that the first marble is blue and second one red?

   A) $\dfrac{24}{91}$ B) $\dfrac{12}{49}$ C) $\dfrac{13}{48}$ D) $\dfrac{13}{49}$

2. Numbers from 1 to 80 are written on cards separately and put into a box. One of the cards is selected randomly. What is the probability of selecting either an even number or an odd number under 10?

   A) $\dfrac{9}{17}$ B) $\dfrac{9}{16}$ C) $\dfrac{8}{19}$ D) $\dfrac{8}{17}$

3. Each team plays another only once in a soccer league consisting of 16 teams. How many combinations are there for the first match?

   A) 90   B) 100   C) 110   D) 120

4. If there are 12 American,18 French and 8 German passengers in a plane, what is the probability of the first two passengers disembarking both being American?

   A) $\dfrac{33}{405}$ B) $\dfrac{44}{501}$ C) $\dfrac{55}{603}$ D) $\dfrac{66}{703}$

5. There are 11 red balls numbered from 5 to 15 and 11 green balls numbered from 7 to 17 in a bag. What is the probability of drawing a ball with an even number on it?

   A) $\dfrac{11}{5}$ B) $\dfrac{6}{11}$ C) $\dfrac{5}{9}$ D) $\dfrac{5}{11}$

6. Some cards are numbered from 1 to 12 and put in a box. What is the probability of a card drawn being a prime number or a number smaller than 7 on it?

   A) $\dfrac{1}{4}$ B) $\dfrac{3}{4}$ C) $\dfrac{2}{3}$ D) $\dfrac{1}{3}$

7. Marbles numbered from 1 to 12 are put in a bag. If marbles are not put back into the bag after being drawn, what is the probability of drawing two prime numbers in a row?

   A) $\dfrac{5}{21}$ B) $\dfrac{5}{17}$ C) $\dfrac{4}{33}$ D) $\dfrac{5}{33}$

8. A class has a total of 44 students of which 24 are girls. 12 of the girls and 13 of the boys have blonde hair. What is the probability that a randomly chose student will be a blonde girl or a boy that is not blonde?

   A) $\dfrac{19}{44}$ B) $\dfrac{19}{43}$ C) $\dfrac{17}{44}$ D) $\dfrac{44}{17}$

9. There are 6 yellow marbles, 5 red marbles and 7 green marbles in a box. What is the probability that a randomly choosen marble will be green?

   A) $\dfrac{16}{17}$ B) $\dfrac{5}{18}$ C) $\dfrac{7}{18}$ D) $\dfrac{8}{19}$

10. A gumball machine has 7 red gumballs, 7 yellow gumballs and 4 green gumballs. If two gumballs are selected from the machine at random, what is the probability that they are both yellow?

    A) $\dfrac{2}{19}$ B) $\dfrac{1}{19}$ C) $\dfrac{6}{19}$ D) $\dfrac{7}{51}$

11. There are 5 green, 8 yellow and 6 blue marbles in a box. If one marble is randomly chosen what is the probability it will be green?

    A) $\dfrac{5}{19}$ B) $\dfrac{4}{19}$ C) $\dfrac{8}{19}$ D) $\dfrac{7}{19}$

12. There are 6 green and 9 yellow marbles in a box. If one marble is randomly chosen, what is the probability it will be yellow?

    A) $\dfrac{2}{7}$ B) $\dfrac{4}{5}$ C) $\dfrac{3}{5}$ D) $\dfrac{1}{3}$

TEST – 23
Probability

1. Numbers from 1 to 80 are written on cards separately and put into a box .One of the cards is selected randomly. What is the probability of selecting either an even number or an odd number under 10?

   A) $\dfrac{9}{16}$ B) $\dfrac{9}{17}$ C) $\dfrac{8}{17}$ D) $\dfrac{8}{19}$

Please answer the questions 2–3 according to the information below.

The table below shows the results of a survey about future professions conducted with 11th graders of a school.

	Doctor	Comp. Eng.	Accoun tant	Teacher
Girl	20	12	18	18
Boy	10	18	16	10
Total	30	30	34	28

2. What is the probability of a student chosen being a male or a future computer engineer?

   A) $\dfrac{3}{4}$ B) $\dfrac{3}{5}$ C) $\dfrac{4}{5}$ D) $\dfrac{11}{20}$

3. What is the probability of a student chosen being a female or a future teacher?

   A) $\dfrac{11}{70}$ B) $\dfrac{11}{60}$ C) $\dfrac{11}{30}$ D) $\dfrac{12}{51}$

4. If there are 12 American, 18 French and 8 German passengers in a plane, what is the probability of the first two passengers disembarking both being American?

   A) $\dfrac{66}{703}$ B) $\dfrac{64}{701}$ C) $\dfrac{54}{703}$ D) $\dfrac{11}{604}$

5. The following table shows the number of books and faulty books printed by a publishing company within 3 months. What is the probability of a randomly selected book being a faulty book printed in February?

	January	February	March
Number of published books	900	1200	1500
Number of faulty books	18	20	30

   A) $\dfrac{1}{90}$ B) $\dfrac{1}{80}$ C) $\dfrac{5}{181}$ D) $\dfrac{1}{180}$

6. The following table shows the number of passengers and their nationalities in an airplane. What is the probability of the first passenger disembarking being a German or a male?

	American	German	Italian
Female	30	40	25
Male	20	30	15
Total	50	70	40

   A) $\dfrac{19}{27}$ B) $\dfrac{17}{32}$ C) $\dfrac{21}{31}$ D) $\dfrac{21}{32}$

7. Tables at a picnic area are for 6 and 8, while there are 18 tables total. If the area can seat 128 people, how many 6–seater tables are there?

   A) 6   B) 7   C) 8   D) 10

8. Marbles numbered from 1 to 12 are put in a bag. If marbles are not put back into the bag after being drawn, what is the probability of drawing two prime numbers in a row?

   A) $\dfrac{5}{21}$ B) $\dfrac{5}{17}$ C) $\dfrac{4}{33}$ D) $\dfrac{5}{33}$

9. How many games are played in a basketball league which consists of 8 teams, if teams play each other only once?

A) 30   B) 28   C) 26   D) 24

10. There are 4 yellow, 7 red, 5 green, and 4 blue marbles in one box. What is the probability of a randomly chosen marble to be green?

A) $\frac{1}{2}$ B) $\frac{1}{3}$ C) $\frac{1}{4}$ D) $\frac{1}{5}$

11. There are 5 yellow, 8 red, 6 green, and 5 blue marbles in one box. What is the probability of a randomly chosen marble to be red?

A) $\frac{1}{3}$ B) $\frac{1}{2}$ C) $\frac{1}{5}$ D) $\frac{1}{7}$

12. There are 6 yellow, 9 red, 7 green, and 6 blue marbles in one box. What is the probability of a randomly chosen marble to be blue ?

A) $\frac{1}{8}$ B) $\frac{3}{14}$ C) $\frac{3}{11}$ D) $\frac{4}{11}$

TEST – 24
Combining Like Terms

1. Simplify by combining like terms:
   $2(7x–3y + 3x + y + 2)$
   A) $20x + 4y + 4$ B) $20x – 4y + 4$
   C) $10x + 8y + 8$ D) $20x + 8y + 4$

2. Combine like terms:
   $4a^2 – 2a + 4 –2a^2 + 6a + 6$
   A) $a^2 + 2a + 3$ B) $(a+3)^2$
   C) $2(a^2+2a+3)$ D) $2a^2+4a+10$

3. Simplify: $6y + 4y^2 – 8 + 3y + 12$
   A) $3y^2 + 4y + 4$
   B) $4y^2 + 9y + 4$
   C) $4y^2 + 8y + 4$
   D) $2y^2 +6y + 3$

4. Simplify: $6a^3 – 2ab^2 + 8a^3 – 14$
   A) $14a^3 – 2ab^2 – 14$
   B) $14a^3 + 3ab + 14$
   C) $14a^3 – 2b^2a – 14$
   D) $2a^3 – 3ab^2 + 14$

5. Simplify: $5x – 4 + 2y + 3(y–x)=$?
   A) $2y + 5x + 4$ B) $5x + 2y – 4$
   C) $2x + 5y – 4$ D) $5x – 2y – 4$

6. $4(x + y + 2) – 3(y – x – 2)=$?
   A) $7x + y + 14$ B) $7x – y + 14$
   C) $6x + y + 14$ D) $7x – y + 12$

7. Simplify: $6y + 3 – 6x – 2y – 7$
   A) $4y – 8x + 4$ B) $4y – 6x – 4$
   C) $4x + 4y + 4$ D) $4y + 8x – 8$

8. Simplify: $mn + 4m – 6mn + 6m – 10n$
   A) $5mn + 10n – 10m$
   B) $5mn + 10n + 8m$
   C) $–5mn + 10m – 10n$
   D) $–5mn + 10n – 10m$

9. Simplify: $2(a+b)^2–3(b–a)^2$
   A) $–a^2 + 10ab – b^2$
   B) $a^2 + 10ab + b^2$
   C) $–a^2 + 10ab + b^2$
   D) $2a^2 + 10ab + b^2$

10. Simplify: $3(a+b) +3(a–b) – 4b$
    A) $6a+7b+10$ B) $6a+7b–14$
    C) $7a+6b+10$ D) $6a–4b$

11. Find the perimeter of rectangle.

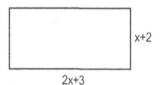

    A) $6x + 10$ B) $5x + 10$
    C) $3x + 5$ D) $6x + 8$

12. Find the perimeter of rectangle.

    x-3
    x+4

    A) $2(2x+2)$ B) $2(2x+1)$
    C) $3(x+2)$ D) $4(x+3)$

TEST – 25
Distance and Midpoint

1. What is the distance between (-4, -7) and (7, 3)?

   A) $\sqrt{221}$ B) $\sqrt{121}$ C) 11   D) 22

2. What is the distance between (6, 2) and (3, 7)?

   A) 6   B) $\sqrt{32}$ C) $\sqrt{34}$ D) $\sqrt{37}$

3. What is the distance between (8, 1) and (6, 4)?

   A) 8   B) 10   C) $\sqrt{112}$ D) $\sqrt{13}$

4. What is the midpoint between points (-4, 8) and (12, -14)?

   A) (4, -3)   B) (-4, -3)
   C) (-3, 4)   D) (2, 6)

5. What is the midpoint for points (-6, 8) and (10, 16)?

   A) (4, 12)   B) (6, 12)
   C) (2, 2)   D) (2, 12)

6. C is the midpoint of AB. AC=5x + 18 and BC=7x + 8, find AB.

   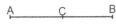

   A) 50   B) 51   B) 54   D) 86

7. Find the distance between A and B.

   A) $\sqrt{32}$
   B) $\sqrt{33}$
   C) $\sqrt{34}$
   D) 34

   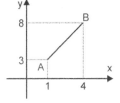

8. What is the midpoint for AB for above figure.

   A) (3,5)   B) $\left(\dfrac{5}{2};\dfrac{11}{2}\right)$

   C) $\left(\dfrac{5}{3};\dfrac{11}{3}\right)$ D) $\left(\dfrac{5}{2};\dfrac{13}{2}\right)$

9. Find the midpoint for AB .

   A) $\left(2;\dfrac{1}{2}\right)$ B) $\left(1;\dfrac{1}{2}\right)$

   C) (3; 2)   D) $\left(2;\dfrac{1}{3}\right)$

   B(6; 4)
   A(-2; -3)

10. Find the distance between A and B.

    A) 113   B) $\sqrt{113}$ C) 112   D) $\sqrt{112}$

11. Find the midpoint between the two point (-7, 4) and (3, 6).

    A) (2,5)   B) (5,2)
    C) (-2,5)   D) (5,6)

12. What is the distance between (8, 4) and (12,9)?

    A) $\sqrt{61}$ B) $\sqrt{71}$ D) $\sqrt{41}$ D) $\sqrt{31}$

TEST – 26

Arithmetic Mean

1. Find the arithmetic average of 6, 3, 4, 2 and 5.

   A) 4   B) 5   C) 6   D) 7

2. Find the arithmetic mean of -6, 4, 2, 3, 9 and 1.

   A) $\dfrac{13}{7}$ B) $\dfrac{13}{6}$ C) $\dfrac{13}{5}$ D) 4

3. Find the arithmetic mean of -3^2, 4, 6, 8 and 12.

   A) 4   B) 4.1   C) 4.2   D) 4.5

4. Find the mean of the decimal numbers 7.2, 3.4, 5.1 and 6.9.

   A) 5.56   B) 5.72   C) 5.65   D) 5.8

5. Find the mean of the first six prime numbers.

   A) $\dfrac{38}{6}$ B) $\dfrac{39}{6}$ C) $\dfrac{40}{6}$ D) $\dfrac{41}{6}$

6. Find the mean of the first five composite numbers.

   A) $\dfrac{37}{5}$ B) $\dfrac{37}{6}$ C) $\dfrac{33}{5}$ D) $\dfrac{32}{5}$

7. If the mean of 6, 3, 5, 4, x and 10 is 14. Find the x value.

   A) 36   B) 46   C) 56   D) 64

8. Find the arithmetic mean of (3m+4) and (5m+6).

   A) 4m+2   B) 3m+5
   C) 4m+5   D) 2m+3

9. Find the arithmetic mean of $\sqrt{12}$, $\sqrt{27}$ and $\sqrt{48}$.

   A) $2\sqrt{3}$ B) $3\sqrt{3}$ C) $3\sqrt{2}$ D) $4\sqrt{2}$

10. Evaluate the arithmetic mean of the first six positive even integers.

    A) 7   B) 8   C) 9   D) 10

11. Calculate the average of the first 8 prime numbers.

    A) $\dfrac{77}{8}$ B) $\dfrac{77}{9}$ C) $\dfrac{75}{8}$ D) $\dfrac{74}{8}$

12. Calculate the sum of the first four prime numbers cube.

    A) 210   B) 432   C) 503   D) 532

TEST – 27
Logarithms

1. $\log_3 81 - \log_3 9 = ?$
   A) 1   B) 2   C) 3   D) 4

2. $\log_7 2 + \log_2 32 - \log_7 2 = ?$
   A) 3   B) 4   C) 5   D) 6

3. $\log_2 a = 4$, $\log_3 b = 2$, $\dfrac{a+b}{a-b} = ? = ?$

   A) $\dfrac{25}{6}$ B) $\dfrac{25}{9}$ C) $\dfrac{24}{7}$ D) $\dfrac{25}{7}$

4. $\log_5 25 + \log_{\frac{1}{3}} 27 = ?$

   A) 0   B) -1   C) 1   D) 2

5. $7^{\log_7 (x+4)} = 7$, $x = ?$
   A) 0   B) 7   C) 3   D) 4

6. $\log_4 x = -2$, $x = ?$
   A) -16   B) 16   C) $\dfrac{1}{16}$ D) $-\dfrac{1}{16}$

7. $\log 400 - \log 4 = ?$
   A) 100   B) 25   C) 20   D) 2

8. $\log(2a+3b) = \log a + \log b$, $b = ?$

   A) $3a+2b$ B) $\dfrac{2a}{a+3}$

   C) $\dfrac{2a}{a-3}$ D) $\dfrac{a}{a+3}$

9. $\log_3(2x+1) = 2$, $x = ?$
   A) 4   B) 5   C) 6   D) 7

10. $\log_2 3 + \log_2 a = 4$, $a = ?$

    A) $\dfrac{8}{3}$ B) $\dfrac{16}{3}$ C) $\dfrac{4}{3}$ D) $\dfrac{3}{4}$

11. $\log_{\frac{1}{5}} 25 + \log_{\frac{1}{3}} 27 + \log_2 16 = ?$

    A) -1   B) -2   C) 1   D) 2

12. $\log_{\frac{1}{8}} \dfrac{1}{64} = x$, $x = ?$

    A) -2   B) 2   C) $\dfrac{1}{2}$ D) $-\dfrac{1}{2}$

TEST – 28
Inverse Function

1. Find the inverse of f(x)=7x-5.
   A) 7x+4
   B) 4-7x
   C) $\frac{x-4}{7}$
   D) $\frac{x+5}{7}$

2. $f(x) = \frac{2x+7}{4}$, $f^{-1}(x)=?$
   A) $\frac{2x-7}{4}$
   B) $\frac{4x-7}{2}$
   C) $\frac{4x+7}{2}$
   D) $\frac{x+4}{7}$

3. f(x)=4x²-3, $f^{-1}(x)=?$
   A) $\sqrt{\frac{x+3}{4}}$
   B) $\sqrt{\frac{x-3}{4}}$
   C) $\sqrt{\frac{x-4}{3}}$
   D) 4x²+3

4. f(x)=7x³+2, $f^{-1}(x)=?$
   A) $\sqrt[3]{\frac{x+2}{7}}$
   B) $\sqrt[3]{\frac{x-2}{7}}$
   C) $\sqrt[3]{\frac{x+3}{7}}$
   D) $\sqrt[3]{\frac{x-2}{3}}$

5. $f(x) = \frac{x-11}{3}$, $f^{-1}(x)=?$
   A) 3x -11
   B) $x - \frac{3}{11}$
   C) $\frac{11-x}{3}$
   D) 3x + 11

6. f(x)=7x, $f^{-1}(x)=?$
   A) $-\frac{x}{7}$
   B) $\frac{x}{7}$
   D) $\frac{7}{x}$
   D) -7x

7. f(x)=x²-49, $f^{-1}(x)=?$
   A) $\sqrt{x^2+49}$
   B) $\sqrt{49-x^2}$
   C) $\sqrt{x+49}$
   D) x + 7

8. f(x)=x+6, $f^{-1}(x)=?$
   A) $\frac{1}{x+6}$
   B) $\frac{1}{x-6}$
   C) 6x + 1
   D) x – 6

9. $f(x) = \frac{8x-6}{3}$, $f^{-1}(x)=?$
   A) $\frac{3x+6}{8}$
   B) $\frac{3x-6}{8}$
   C) $\frac{6x-3}{8}$
   D) $\frac{8x-6}{3}$

10. $f(x) = \frac{1}{x} - 6$, $f^{-1}(x)=?$
    A) $\frac{1}{x+6}$
    B) $\frac{1}{x-6}$
    C) 6x + 1
    D) 6x - 1

11. f(x)=6x + 9, $f^{-1}(2)=?$
    A) $\frac{7}{6}$
    B) $-\frac{7}{6}$
    C) $\frac{6}{7}$
    D) $-\frac{6}{7}$

12. $f(x) = \frac{7x+5}{3x-4}$, $f^{-1}(x)=?$
    A) $\frac{4x-5}{3x+7}$
    B) $\frac{4x+5}{3x-7}$
    C) $\frac{5x+7}{4x-3}$
    D) $\frac{7x-5}{4-3x}$

TEST – 29
Parabolas

1. What is the vertex of the parabola with the equation $y=x^2 - 6x + 8$?

   A) (3, -1)   B) (-1, 3)
   C) (4, 3)   D) (2, 3)

4. Find the parabola equation.

   A) $y=x^2 - 5x + 4$ B) $y=x^2 + 5x + 4$
   C) $y=x^2 + 4x + 4$ D) $y=x^2 + 5x - 4$

2. Which parabola opens up?

   A) 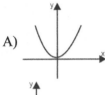   B)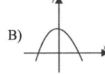

   C)    D)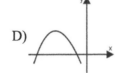

5. $y=(x-2)^2 + 2$
   Find the parabola vertex.

   A) (1; 2)   B) (2; 1)
   C) (2; 2)   D) (3; 2)

3. $y=2x^2 + 11x + 12$
   Find the parabola vertex.

   A) $\left(\dfrac{-11}{4}; \dfrac{-25}{8}\right)$ B) $\left(\dfrac{-11}{4}; \dfrac{27}{8}\right)$

   C) $\left(\dfrac{25}{8}; \dfrac{11}{4}\right)$ D) $\left(\dfrac{-27}{4}; \dfrac{11}{4}\right)$

6. $y=(x-3)^2 + 1$
   Find the graph of equation.

   A) 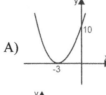   B)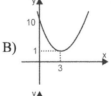

   C) 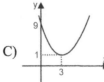   D)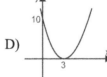

7. $y=2(x-4)^2+3$. Find the vertex.
   A) (4; -3)   B) (-3; 4)
   C) (4; 3)   D) (-4; 3)

8. $y=x^2-9x+14$. a+b+c=?

   A) 20   B) 21   C) 22   D) 23

9. $y=(x+3)^2 - 4$
   What is the graph of this parabola?

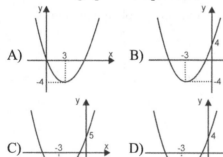

10. Which is the vertex for this parabola?
    $y=(x+5)^2+4$
    A) (5; 4)   B) (4; -5)
    C) (-5; 4)   D) (-5; -4)

11. What is the vertex of parabola
    $y=4(x-5)^2+4$. Does the parabola open
    upward or downward?

    A) The vertex (5, 4) downward
    B) The vertex (-5, 4) up or down
    C) The vertex (-4, -5) up or down
    D) The vertex (5, 4) its opens upward

12. What is the graph of the following
    parabola $y=(x+4)^2-5$?

    A) 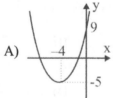   B)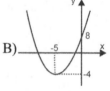

    C) 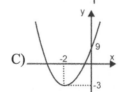   D)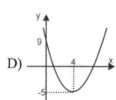

TEST – 30
Fractions

1. $\dfrac{m}{6} + \dfrac{6}{m} = ?$

   A) $\dfrac{m-36}{6m}$ B) $\dfrac{6-m^2}{m}$

   C) $\dfrac{36+m^2}{6m}$ D) $\dfrac{6m^2}{6-m}$

2. $\dfrac{4}{7} - \dfrac{4}{5} = ?$

   A) 0 B) $-\dfrac{8}{35}$ C) $\dfrac{48}{35}$ D) $\dfrac{8}{35}$

3. $\dfrac{\pi}{8} + \dfrac{8}{\pi} = ?$

   A) $\dfrac{\pi^2+64}{8}$ B) $\dfrac{\pi^2-16}{8}$

   C) $\dfrac{\pi^2+64}{8\pi}$ D) $\dfrac{\pi-64}{8\pi}$

4. $\dfrac{-8^2+4^3+3}{-4^2+2^4-3} = ?$

   A) -1 B) 1 C) 3 D) -3

5. $\dfrac{3}{4} + \dfrac{4}{5} = ?$

   A) $\dfrac{7}{20}$ B) $\dfrac{1}{20}$ C) $\dfrac{31}{20}$ D) $\dfrac{34}{20}$

6. $\dfrac{n}{7} + \dfrac{3}{14} = ?$

   A) $\dfrac{2n+3}{7}$ B) $\dfrac{2n+3}{14}$ C) $\dfrac{2n-3}{7}$ D) $\dfrac{2n}{14}$

7. $\dfrac{m}{9} + \dfrac{n}{4} - \left(\dfrac{m}{9} - \dfrac{n}{4}\right) = ?$

   A) $\dfrac{m}{4}$ B) $-\dfrac{m}{3}$ C) $-\dfrac{n}{4}$ D) $\dfrac{n}{2}$

8. $\dfrac{m\cdot(7-5)^2}{8m^2} \cdot \dfrac{4n^2}{n\cdot(7-3)^2} = ?$

   A) $\dfrac{2n^2}{3m}$ B) $\dfrac{n}{8m}$ C) $\dfrac{m}{8n}$ D) $\dfrac{n^2}{16}$

9. $-\dfrac{2}{7} - \dfrac{3}{4} = ?$

   A) $-\dfrac{5}{7}$ B) $\dfrac{5}{7}$ C) $\dfrac{29}{28}$ D) $-\dfrac{29}{28}$

10. $\dfrac{m\cdot x^2}{11} \cdot \dfrac{121}{x\cdot m^2} = ?$

   A) $\dfrac{11m}{x}$ B) $\dfrac{11x}{m}$ C) $\dfrac{x}{m}$ D) $\dfrac{m}{x}$

11. $-\dfrac{4}{15} \cdot 60 = ?$

   A) -20 B) 20 C) -16 D) 16

12. $\dfrac{3}{9} + \dfrac{2}{7} - \left(\dfrac{2}{7} - \dfrac{6}{9}\right) = ?$

   A) $\dfrac{1}{21}$ B) $-\dfrac{1}{21}$ C) 1 D) -1

TEST – 31
Simplifying Expressions

1. $(-5x-y)+2 \cdot (y+3x)=?$
   A) $2x+3y$ B) $3x+2y$
   C) $-x-y$ D) $x+y$

2. $(-4)^2 \cdot (y+1)+3 \cdot (2-y)=?$
   A) $13y$ B) $-13y$
   C) $13y+22$ D) $13y-6$

3. $-2^2+4(y+2)-2(3-y)=?$
   A) $-2+6y$ B) $-3+6y$
   C) $-15+6y$ D) $15-6y$

4. $-(3m+5)+5 \cdot (2m+1)=?$
   A) $10m$ B) $7m+10$
   C) $7m$ D) $13m$

5. $3(5k+2)+2 \cdot (3-7k)=?$
   A) $2k+12$ B) $2k+13$
   C) $-k+12$ D) $k+12$

6. $-(4m+5)-(5+4m-3)=?$
   A) -8 B) $-8m-13$
   C) $-8m-7$ D) $-8m-3$

7. $-n^2+n+(n)^2+3n+2=?$
   A) $2+2n$ B) $2+3n$
   C) $4n$ D) $4n+2$

8. $3y+4 \cdot (y-2)-2 \cdot (y-3)=?$
   A) $9y+14$ B) $9y-2$
   C) $5y-11$ D) $5y-2$

9. $\dfrac{3x}{2}+\dfrac{7y}{3}-\left(\dfrac{7y}{3}-\dfrac{3x}{2}\right)=?$
   A) $3x$ B) $2x$ C) $\dfrac{14y}{3}$ D) $4y$

10. $5(4-n)-4(n-5)=?$
    A) $9n$ B) $40-9n$ C) 40 D) 0

11. $-x(4+x)+x(2+x)=?$
    A) $2x$ B) $-2x$ C) $x-4$ D) $-2+x$

12. $4y+4\left(\dfrac{10y}{2}+\dfrac{4}{8}\right)=?$
    A) $20y$ B) $\dfrac{44y+16}{8}$
    C) $20y+4$ D) $24y+2$

TEST – 32
Solving Equations

1. $7m = (m + 2)\cdot 3$, m=?

   A) 3   B) $\frac{2}{3}$ C) $\frac{3}{2}$ D) –3

2. $-5^2(x - 1) = 11x + 7$, x = ?

   A) 3   B) 2   C) $\frac{1}{2}$ D) $\frac{1}{3}$

3. $\frac{x^2}{3} = 4$, $x^2 - 1 = ?$

   A) 10   B) 11   C) 12   D) 14

4. $-8 = x + 4$, $x^2 + 1 = ?$

   A) 122   B) 144   C) 145   D) 146

5. $\frac{m - 8}{4} = 3$, $\frac{m}{4} - 1 = ?$

   A) 2   B) 3   C) 4   D) 5

6. $2x - 4 = 36$,   x=?

   A) 10   B) 12   C) 15   D) 20

7. $9n - 3 = 4n + 32$, n=?

   A) 5   B) 6   C) 7   D) 8

8. $5(x - 4) = -15$, x=?

   A) 1   B) –1   C) -2   D) 2

9. $5x + 3(12 + x) = 12$,   x = ?

   A) -2   B) -3   C) 5   D) 6

10. $3m + 5(m + 3) = 5m + 24$, m=?

    A) 9   B) 6   C) 3   D) 2

11. $-4^2(n+1) = 5(5 - 3n)$, n =?

    A) 32   B) -41   C) -13   D) -17

12. $2n + 7 = 13$, n=?

    A) 8   B) 6   C) 4   D) 3

TEST – 33
Solving Inequalities

1. Solve the inequality: $3y + 5 > -10$
   A) y=3   B) y>5
   C) y > 3   D) y >-5

2. Solve the inequality: $3x - 4 < -13$
   A) x<–3   B) x>–3
   C) x< 4   D) x < -9

3. Solve the inequality: $3(2x + 1) \leq -6$
   A) $x \geq \dfrac{3}{2}$ B) $x \leq -\dfrac{3}{2}$

   C) $x \geq \dfrac{3}{4}$ D) $x \leq \dfrac{3}{4}$

4. Solve the inequality: $6x < 2(x - 2)$
   A) x < 1   B) x>2
   C) x<-1   D) x>-2

5. Solve the inequality: $\dfrac{x-5}{2} \leq 5$

   A) x > 15   B) x ≥ 15
   C) x ≤ –15   D) x ≤ 15

6. Solve the inequality: $t + 3 > 5$
   A)
   B)
   C)
   D)

7. Solve the inequality: $7x +2 \geq 6x + 3$
   A)
   B)
   C)
   D)

8. Solve the inequality: $7x - 5 \geq 9$
   A)
   B)
   C)
   D)

9. $x \leq -3$. Choose the graph.
   A)
   B)
   C)
   D)

10. Solve the inequality: $4x + 4 < 3x + 5$
    A)
    B)
    C)
    D)

11. $5x+3>13$. Solve the inequality as shown on a number line.
    A)
    B)
    C)
    D)

12. Solve the inequality: $5x - 10 \geq 0$
    A)
    B)
    C)
    D)

TEST – 34

Slope and y–Intercept

1. $2y = 4x + 8$. Find the slope.

   A) $\dfrac{1}{4}$ B) -2 C) $-\dfrac{1}{4}$ D) 2

2. $6x - 5y = 20$. Find the y-intercept.

   A) $\dfrac{6}{5}$ B) $\dfrac{20}{6}$ C) 4 D) –4

3. $y = 9 + 3x$. Find the slope.

   A) 9 B) –9 C) 3 D) –3

4. $4y + 3x = 36$. Find the y– intercept.

   A) 12 B) 9 C) $\dfrac{1}{3}$ D) $\dfrac{3}{4}$

5. $8x + 6y = 12$. Find the y– intercept.

   A) 5 B) $\dfrac{4}{3}$ C) –2 D) 2

6. $x + 4y = 16$. Find the y-intercept.

   A) 4 B) 16 C) 15 D) $\dfrac{4}{3}$

7. $y = \dfrac{3}{4}x - \dfrac{4}{3}$. Find the slope.

   A) $\dfrac{4}{3}$ B) $\dfrac{3}{4}$ C) $-\dfrac{4}{3}$ D) $-\dfrac{3}{4}$

8. $y = -5x + 6$. Find the slope.

   A) 8 B) 6 C) –5 D) 1

9. $ax - by = 14$. If slope is 4, find $\dfrac{a}{b}$.

   A) –4 B) $\dfrac{1}{4}$ C) $-\dfrac{1}{4}$ D) 4

10. $3x + 4y + c = 0$. y-intercept is 2, find the c.

    A) 8 B) -8 C) –3 D) $\dfrac{3}{4}$

11. $\dfrac{3x}{4} - \dfrac{5y}{3} = 12$. Find the slope.

    A) $\dfrac{5}{4}$ B) $\dfrac{4}{5}$ C) $\dfrac{9}{20}$ D) $-\dfrac{9}{20}$

12. $-2x - 5y = 10$. Find the slope.

    A) $\dfrac{2}{5}$ B) $-\dfrac{2}{5}$ C) $\dfrac{5}{2}$ D) $-\dfrac{5}{2}$

TEST – 35

Choose the Expression

1. The sum of 7 and a number b.

   A) $\dfrac{7}{b}$ B) $\dfrac{b}{7}$ C) 7b   D) 7+b

2. Four times the number a plus five.

   A) 4a+5   B) 5a+4
   C) 4a–4   D) 5a+3

3. 5 less than six times a number.

   A) 5+6x   B) 5–6x
   C) 6x–5   D) 6(a-5)

4. John has 12 pens. His brother has n times as many pens as John has. Write an expression for how many pens his brother has.

   A) 12   B) $\dfrac{12}{n}$ C) 12n   D) 12-n

5. Jack has 40 Math books. If he sells x math books per day for 5 days, how many math books will he have left?

   A) 40x   B) 40+5x
   C) 40–5x   D) 5x–40

6. The quotient of a number and 8.

   A) 8x   B) 8–x   C) $\dfrac{8}{x}$ D) $\dfrac{x}{8}$

7. Seven times a number plus the sum of six times a number and –5.

   A) 7(6x–5)   B) 7x+(6x–5)
   C) 6(7x–5)   D) 6x+(7x–6)

8. 7 more than three times a number.

   A) 7x+2   B) 7x+3
   C) 3x–7   D) 3x+7

9. 9 decreased by the quotient of a number and 7.

   A) $9+\dfrac{x}{7}$ B) 9+7x

   C) $9-\dfrac{x}{7}$ D) $7-\dfrac{x}{9}$

10. 15 increased by a number is 45.

    A) 15n=45   B) 15–n=45
    C) 15n+45=0   D) 15+n=45

11. The product of $\dfrac{1}{3}$ and a number is 12.

    A) $\dfrac{2n}{3}=12$ B) $\dfrac{n}{3}=12$

    C) $\dfrac{3n}{3}=12$ D) $\dfrac{1+n}{3}=12$

12. Two times the sum of x and 4.

    A) 4(x + 2)   B) 2(x + 4)
    C) 2(x – 4)   D) 4(x – 2)

TEST – 36
Factoring Polynomials

1. $(x + 2)(x + 4)=?$
   A) $x^2 + 6x + 6$ B) $x^2 + 2x -8$
   C) x^2+2x+8 D) x^2+6x+8

2. $x^2 – 9x + 20=?$
   A) $(x–5)(x+4)$ B) $(x–2)(x–10)$
   C) $(x–5)(x- 4)$ D) $(x–10)(x+2)$

3. $x^2– 5x + 4=?$
   A) $(x–2)(x+1)$ B) $(x–2)(x+3)$
   C) $(x + 2)(x - 2)$ D) $(x–4)(x–1)$

4. $x^2 + 4x – 12=?$
   A) $(x+2)(x+6)$ B) $(x+2)(x-6)$
   C) $(x+6)(x–2)$ D) $(x+4)(x–3)$

5. $2x^2+8x+6=?$
   A) $(2x+2)(x+3)$ B) $(2x–3)(x + 1)$
   C) $(x+3)^2$ D) $(2x+6)(x+1)$

6. $x^2 + 5x – 6 = ?$
   A) $(x+1)(x+6)$ B) $(x - 1)(x+6)$
   C) $(x+2)(x+3)$ D) $(x–2)(x+3)$

7. $14x^2–9x+1=?$
   A) $(7x–1)(2x+1)$ B) $(2x+1)(7x+1)$
   C) $(14x-1)(x–1)$ D) $(2x-1)(7x-1)$

8. $(x–3)·(x+7)=x^2+ax–b$, $3a–b=?$
   A) 27   B) 31   C) 33   D) 35

9. $x^2+7x+12=(x+a)(x+b)$
   $a>b$, $a + 3b=?$
   A) 10   B) 11   C) 12   D) 13

10. $x^2+5x–24=(x–a)(x+b)$, $3b–a=?$
    A) 16   B) 8   C) 21   D) 27

11. $(x–3)(x+5)=?$
    A) $x^2+2x–15$ B) $x^2-3x+15$
    C) $x^2+2x+15$ D) $x^2+8x–15$

12. $x^2 + x(\sqrt{5} + \sqrt{3}) + \sqrt{15} = ?$
    A) $(x + \sqrt{5})(x + \sqrt{3})$
    B) $(x + \sqrt{5})(x – \sqrt{3})$
    C) $(x – \sqrt{5})(x + \sqrt{3})$
    D) $(x – \sqrt{5})(x – \sqrt{3})$

TEST – 37
Simplifying Radical Expressions

1. $\sqrt{108} - \sqrt{27} = ?$

   A) 9   B) $\sqrt{3}$ C) $3\sqrt{3}$ D) 3

2. $\sqrt{3} \cdot \sqrt{6} \cdot \sqrt{18} = ?$

   A) 3   B) 9   C) 18   D) $\sqrt{18}$

3. $\sqrt{45} + \sqrt{20} = ?$

   A) $4\sqrt{5}$ B) $2\sqrt{5}$ C) $5\sqrt{5}$ D) $3\sqrt{5}$

4. $\sqrt{75} + \sqrt{12} = ?$

   A) $7\sqrt{3}$ B) $8\sqrt{3}$ C) $6\sqrt{3}$ D) $2\sqrt{3}$

5. $\sqrt{3} \cdot \sqrt{27} \cdot 4 = ?$

   A) 81   B) 12   C) $12\sqrt{3}$ D) 36

6. $\sqrt{75} : \sqrt{25} = ?$

   A) $\sqrt{5}$ B) $\sqrt{10}$ C) $\sqrt{3}$ D) 3

7. $\sqrt{25x} \cdot \sqrt{36x} = ?$

   A) 20x   B) 11x   C) 30x   D) $30x^2$

8. $\sqrt{\dfrac{60}{15}} = ?$

   A) 5   B) $\sqrt{5}$ C) 2   D) $\sqrt{7}$

9. $\sqrt{80} + \sqrt{5} = ?$

   A) $5\sqrt{5}$ B) $4\sqrt{5}$

   C) 10   D) $\sqrt{3} + \sqrt{5}$

10. $\sqrt{48} - \sqrt{3} + \sqrt{27} = ?$

    A) $5\sqrt{3}$ B) $6\sqrt{3}$ C) $\sqrt{72}$ D) $8\sqrt{3}$

11. $\sqrt{32} + \sqrt{8} + \sqrt{4} = ?$

    A) $2 + 4\sqrt{2}$ B) $6\sqrt{2}$

    C) $\sqrt{2}$ D) $2 + 6\sqrt{2}$

12. $\sqrt{1} + \sqrt{4} + \sqrt{9} = ?$

    A) 5   B) 6   C) 7   D) 8

TEST – 38
Exponents

1. $7^8 \cdot 7^7 \cdot 7 = ?$
    A) 7^{19} B) 7^{18} C) 7^{16} D) 7^{15}

7. $\dfrac{b^{14}}{a^{14}} \cdot \dfrac{a^{16}}{b^{12}} = ?$
    A) ab B) a^2b C) ab^2 D) $(ab)^2$

2. $(16)^{\frac{1}{2}} + (25)^{\frac{1}{2}} + (256)^{\frac{1}{2}} = ?$
    A) 26   B) 25   C) 24   D) 21

8. $(3x^2)^2 \cdot (2y^2)^3$
    A) $36\ x^4y^6$ B) $54x^4y^6$
    C) $72x^4y^6$ D) $6\ x^4y^6$

3. $a^7 \cdot a^8 = ?$
    A) a^{56} B) a^{15} C) a^1 D) a^{14}

9. $(2a)^3 \cdot (2b)^2 = ?$
    A) $8ab^3$ B) $16a^2b^2$
    C) $32a^3b^2$ D) $64a^2b^3$

4. $\dfrac{x^{36}}{x^{12}} = ?$
    A) x^3 B) x^{48} C) x^{24} D) x^{27}

10. $(1000)^{\frac{1}{3}} + (10000)^{\frac{1}{2}} = ?$
    A) 100   B) 110   C) 10   D) 20

5. $4^{-1} + 3^0 + 4^1 = ?$
    A) 1   B) 3   C) 4.25   D) 5.25

11. $\dfrac{10^{28}}{7^6} \cdot \dfrac{7^{16}}{10^{18}} = ?$
    A) 17^{10} B) 70^{10} C) 70^{39} D) 70^{19}

6. $5^{-1} + 5^0 + 5^1 = ?$
    A) $\dfrac{31}{5}$ B) $\dfrac{26}{5}$ C) 1   D) $\dfrac{41}{5}$

12. $(2x)^3 \cdot (3y)^2 = ?$
    A) $72x^3y^2$ B) $108x^2y^3$
    C) $54x^2y^3$ D) $36x^5y^4$

TEST – 39
Graphing Absolute Value Equations

1. Which graph shows the function y=2-|x|?

A) 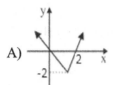 B)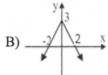

C) 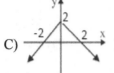 D)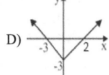

2. Which graph shows the function y=|x|-5?

A) 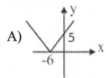 B)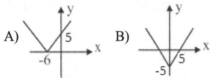

C) 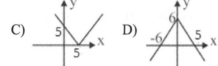 D)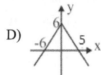

3. Which graph shows the function y=|-x|?

A) 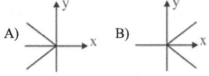 B)

C) 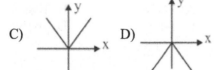 D)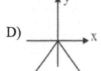

4. Which graph shows the function y=|x–2|–2?

A) 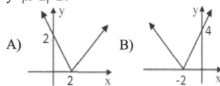 B)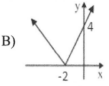

C) 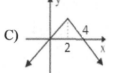 D)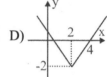

5. Which graph shows the function y=|x+5|?

A) 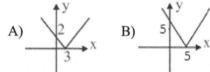 B)

C) 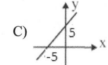 D)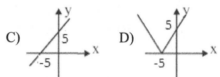

6. Which graph shows the function y=|x-1|?

A) 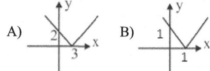 B)

C) 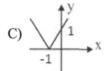 D)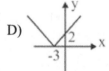

7. Which graph shows the function y=-2-|x|?

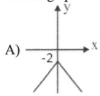

A)   B)

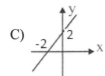

C)   D)

10. Which is the equation of line shown in the graph?
    A) y=|x|– 3
    B) y=|x|+3
    C) y=|x + 3|
    D) y=|x–3|

8. Which is the equation of line shown in the graph?
    A) y=|x+1|
    B) y=|x-2|+ 2
    C) y=|x+2|+2
    D) y=|x- 1| - 3

11. What is the equation of the line shown in the graph?
    A) y=|5x|
    B) y=5x
    C) y=-|x|-5
    D) y=|x|+5

9. Which is the equation of line shown in the graph?
    A) y=|x+5|+2
    B) y=|x–2|+5
    C) y=|x+2|+5
    D) y=|x–1|+ 1

12. Which graph shows the function y=|x–2|?

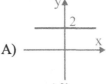
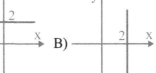

A)   B)

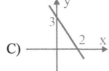
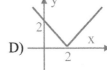

C)   D)

TEST – 40
Algebra Equations

1. Solve: $x - \dfrac{5}{6} = \dfrac{5}{6} - \dfrac{x}{6}$

   A) $-\dfrac{5}{12}$ B) $\dfrac{10}{7}$ C) $-\dfrac{10}{7}$ D) $\dfrac{7}{10}$

2. Solve: $8\left(\dfrac{x}{4} + \dfrac{1}{4}\right) = 9\left(\dfrac{x}{3} + \dfrac{1}{6}\right)$

   A) $-\dfrac{1}{12}$ B) $-\dfrac{1}{2}$ C) $-\dfrac{1}{2}$ D) $\dfrac{1}{2}$

3. Solve for x: $2x + 4 = 28$

   A) 10   B) 11   C) 12   D) 13

4. Solve for x: $8(x-3) - x = 2(3x+1) - 4$

   A) 22   B) 20   C) 18   D) 16

5. Solve for x: $x - \dfrac{12}{11} = \dfrac{10}{11}$

   A) 1   B) 2   C) $\dfrac{2}{11}$ D) $\dfrac{15}{2}$

6. Solve for x: $x - \dfrac{1}{5} = \dfrac{10}{20}$

   A) 2   B) $\dfrac{11}{20}$ C) $\dfrac{7}{10}$ D) $\dfrac{3}{10}$

7. Solve: $\dfrac{5x}{3} = \dfrac{4}{12}$

   A) $\dfrac{1}{12}$ B) $\dfrac{15}{12}$ C) $\dfrac{5}{12}$ D) $\dfrac{1}{5}$

8. Solve: $k - 2 + \dfrac{k}{3} = \dfrac{5}{3}$

   A) $\dfrac{4}{11}$ B) $\dfrac{11}{4}$ C) $-\dfrac{4}{3}$ D) $-\dfrac{5}{3}$

9. Solve: $5(x-3) = 3(3-x)$

   A) 1   B) 2   C) 3   D) 4

10. Solve: $\dfrac{1}{3} - x = \dfrac{x}{5} + \dfrac{5}{6}$

    A) $-\dfrac{15}{24}$ B) $-\dfrac{5}{12}$ C) $\dfrac{24}{15}$ D) $-\dfrac{24}{25}$

11. Solve: $8(x-2) + 6 = 6(3-x)$

    A) $-\dfrac{20}{7}$ B) 2   C) -2   D) $\dfrac{20}{7}$

12. Solve: $x - 4^2 = 4^2 - x$

    A) 0   B) 8   C) 16   D) 32

TEST – 41
Rational Exponents

1. Which is the simplified form for $\left(\dfrac{2x^{\frac{1}{2}}}{3x^{\frac{1}{3}}}\right)^4 = ?$

   A) $\dfrac{81}{10}x^2$ B) $\dfrac{16}{81}x^{\frac{2}{3}}$ C) $\dfrac{27}{10}x^{\frac{4}{3}}$ D) $\dfrac{16}{27}x^{\frac{3}{4}}$

2. $\sqrt{3m^3} \cdot \sqrt{9m^3} \cdot \sqrt{4m^4} = ?$

   A) $6m^5\sqrt{3}$ B) $6m^6\sqrt{3}$
   C) $6m^4\sqrt{2}$ D) $6m^6\sqrt{2}$

3. Evaluate: $\left(\dfrac{27}{125}\right)^{\frac{1}{3}} + \left(\dfrac{16}{25}\right)^{\frac{1}{2}} = ?$

   A) 0.80   B) 0.75   C) 1.4   D) 1.75

4. Which is equivalent to $\sqrt[4]{16m^4} = ?$
   A) $4m^4$ B) $2m^4$ C) $2m$ D) $4m$

5. Which is equivalent to $k^{\frac{5}{7}} = ?$
   A) $\sqrt[4]{k^7}$ B) $\sqrt[2]{k^7}$ C) $\sqrt[5]{k^7}$ D) $\sqrt[7]{k^5}$

6. Which is equivalent to $27^{\frac{1}{3}} \cdot 32^{\frac{1}{5}} \cdot 64^{\frac{1}{3}} = ?$
   A) 4   B) 6   C) 18   D) 24

7. Which is equivalent to $\left[\left(x^6\right)^{\frac{1}{2}}\right]^{\frac{4}{3}} = ?$

   A) x   B) $\sqrt{x}$ C) x^4 D) $x^{\frac{1}{4}}$

8. Which is equivalent to
   $\left(x^8\right)^{\frac{1}{2}} + \left(x^6\right)^{\frac{1}{2}} + \left(\sqrt[2]{x}\right)^8 = ?$

   A) $2x^4+x^3$ B) $2x^2+x$
   C) $3x^3+x^2$ D) $2x^2+x^3$

9. Evaluate: $8^{-\frac{1}{3}} + 16^{-\frac{1}{2}} + 81^{-\frac{1}{4}} = ?$

   A) $\dfrac{13}{12}$ B) $\dfrac{12}{13}$ C) $\dfrac{5}{8}$ D) $\dfrac{8}{5}$

10. $\left[\left(\sqrt{5}\right)^{\sqrt{2}}\right]^{\sqrt{2}} + \left[\left(\sqrt{3}\right)^{\sqrt{2}}\right]^{\sqrt{2}} = ?$

    A) 6   B) 5   C) 8   D) $2\sqrt{2}$

11. $(27)^{-\frac{1}{3}} + (243)^{-\frac{1}{5}} = ?$

    A) 1   B) $\dfrac{1}{2}$ C) $\dfrac{1}{3}$ D) $\dfrac{2}{3}$

12. Which is the simplified form to
    $\sqrt[3]{64x^6y^9} = ?$

    A) $28x^3y^2$ B) $8y^3x^2$ C) $4y^3x^2$ D) $5xy^3$

TEST – 42

Solving Quadratic Equations

1. Solve the equation: $8x^2+64x=0$

   A) x=0 and x=8
   B) x=0 and x=–8
   C) x=1 and x=–8
   D) x=4 and x=0

2. Solve the equation: $(x–5)^2=16$

   A) x=1 and x= -5
   B) x=1 and x=9
   C) x= -1and x= -9
   D) x=1 and x=4

3. Solve the equation: $x^2+13x+30=0$

   A) {–10, –3}
   B) {10, 3}
   C) {–6, –3}
   D) {6, 5}

4. Solve the equation: $(x–2)^2=3$

   A) $\sqrt{5}\pm3$
   B) $5\pm\sqrt{3}$
   C) 22
   D) $2\pm\sqrt{3}$

5. Solve the equation: $(x–2)^2=5$

   A) $2\pm\sqrt{5}$
   B) $\sqrt{5}\pm2$
   C) 3
   D) 9

6. Solve the equation: $x^2-9x=-18$

   A) {–6, 3}
   B) {–3, 6}
   C) {–3, –6}
   D) {3, 6}

7. Solve the equation: $x^2–3x–28 = 0$

   A) {–7, –4}
   B) {4, 7}
   C) {–4, 7}
   D) {–5, 4}

8. Solve the equation: $(x–5)^2=7$

   A) $5\pm\sqrt{7}$
   B) $-5\pm\sqrt{7}$
   C) $-7\pm\sqrt{5}$
   D) $7\pm\sqrt{5}$

9. Solve the equation: $144=64x^2$

   A) $x=-\dfrac{2}{3}$, $x=\dfrac{2}{3}$
   B) $x=\dfrac{3}{2}$
   C) $x=-\dfrac{3}{2}$, $x=\dfrac{3}{2}$
   D) x=8

10. Solve the equation: $x^2–30=x$

   A) {–5, –6}
   B) {5, 6}
   C) {–5, 6}
   D) {–6, 5}

11. Solve the equation: $x^2+4x+3=0$

   A) {–10, –3}
   B) {10, 3}
   C) {–6, –5}
   D) {–3, –1}

12. Solve the equation: $1=49x^2$

   A) $x=\dfrac{1}{7}$, $x=7$
   B) $x=\dfrac{1}{7}$, $x=-7$
   C) $x=\dfrac{1}{7}$, $x=-\dfrac{1}{7}$
   D) $x=\dfrac{1}{7}$, $x=-\dfrac{1}{3}$

TEST – 43
Algebraic Expressions

1. Which expression is equivalent to $5(-3x^2 + 2y^2 + 2x^2)$?
   A) $5x^2+10y^2$
   B) $5y^2-10x^2$
   C) $10y^2-5x^2$
   D) $10x^2-5y^2$

2. Simplify: $(2x-5) + 4(3-x) - x$
   A) 14
   B) $4x-4$
   C) $3x +19$
   D) $7-3x$

3. Which is $x^7 \cdot x^8$ in simplified form?
   A) x^1
   B) x^{56}
   C) x^{15}
   D) x^8

4. Simplify: $\left(\dfrac{2y^2x}{3x^2y^4}\right)^3 = ?$

   A) $\dfrac{6y^6x^3}{9x^6y^{12}}$
   B) $\dfrac{8y^5x^3}{27x^5y^{12}}$
   C) $\dfrac{8y^6x^3}{27}$
   D) $\dfrac{8}{27x^3y^6}$

5. $(4^{20})^0+(4^0)^3+(4^1)^2=?$
   A) 18
   B) 28
   C) 79
   D) 16

6. Simplify: $\dfrac{3}{4}m^3n^5 \cdot \dfrac{8}{9}m^{-3}n^3$

   A) $\dfrac{3}{2}m^8n^8$
   B) $\dfrac{2}{3}n^8$
   C) $\dfrac{3}{2}n^8$
   D) $\dfrac{3}{2}m^5n^5$

7. Simplify: $7m^3+3n^4+2m^3-n^4$
   A) $9m^3+3n^4$
   B) $5m^3+4n^4$
   C) $9m^3+2n^4$
   D) $5m^3-3n^4$

8. Which is $y^{-17} \cdot y^8$ in simplified form?
   A) y^{-25}
   B) y^9
   C) y^{-136}
   D) y^{-9}

9. Simplify: $3(x - 5) + 5(3 - x) + 7 + 2x$
   A) 7
   B) $2x-7$
   C) 2
   D) $4x+37$

10. Evaluate x^2y^3 for $x = \sqrt{4}$, $y = \sqrt{8}$
    A) $64\sqrt{2}$
    B) $16\sqrt{8}$
    C) $24\sqrt{8}$
    D) $32\sqrt{2}$

11. Evaluate $\sqrt{9x^2yz^3}$ for $x=3$, $y=4$, $z=1$.
    A) 24
    B) 18
    C) 12
    D) 8

12. Evaluate $\dfrac{m^7n^4}{m^5n^2}$ for $m=3$, $n=2$.
    A) 6
    B) 12
    C) 54
    D) 36

TEST – 44
Polynomial Expressions

1. Add the polynomials:
   $(5x^3-x-x^2) + (2x^3+4x+2x^2)$
   A) $7x^3+x^2+3x$ B) $7x^3+2x^2+2x$
   C) $7x^3-x^2+3x$ D) $3x^3-2x^2+2x$

2. Find the difference of the polynomials:
   $(7x^2+3x-4)-(2x^2+4x+5)$
   A) $5x^2 - 7x - 9$ B) $5x^2 - x - 9$
   C) $7x^2 + x + 1$ D) $5x^2 + 7x + 1$

3. Find the product: $(3m^2+1) \cdot (1-m)$
   A) $-3m^3 - m^2 + 4m + 1$
   B) $-3m^3 + 3m^2 - m + 1$
   C) $-3m^3 + 3m^2 + m$
   D) $-3m^3 + 3m^2 + 1$

4. Which of the following is not a polynomial?
   A) $2x^3+5x-2$ B) $-11x^5+6x$
   C) $9x+3^x$ D) $7x^2+\sqrt{5}x$

5. Simplify: $(5a-2) \cdot (5a+2)$
   A) $25a - 4$ B) $25a^2-4$
   C) $4-25a^2$ D) $4+25a^2$

6. Simplify: $(3m-6) - (7-3m)$
   A) -13 B) $6m+13$
   C) $6m-13$ D) $6m-1$

7. A square's side is $(3m+2)$. Find its area.
   A) $9m^2+4$ B) $6m^2+6m+4$
   C) $6m^2+12m+4$ D) $9m^2+12m+4$

8. What is the quotient of
   $(y^2+9y+18)\div(y^2+3y)$?
   A) $\dfrac{y+6}{y}$ B) $\dfrac{y+3}{y}$ C) $\dfrac{y+9}{y}$ D) $\dfrac{y+2}{y}$

9. $10x^3y^5+3xy^5+xy+2$
   Find the polynomial degree.
   A) 10   B) 8   C) 5   D) 2

10. What is the quotient of
    $(y^2 + 17y + 42) \div (y^2 + 12y - 28)$?
    A) $\dfrac{y+3}{y-2}$ B) $\dfrac{y+7}{y-2}$ C) $\dfrac{y+6}{y-7}$ D) $\dfrac{y+6}{y-7}$

11. The triangle base is $(4x+1)$ and height is $(4x-1)$. Find the triangle area.
    A) $\dfrac{8x^2-1}{2}$ B) $\dfrac{16x^2-1}{4}$
    C) $\dfrac{16x^2+8x-1}{2}$ D) $\dfrac{16x^2-1}{2}$

12. Find the ABCD rectangle area.
    A) $12x-6$
    B) $12x^2+x-6$
    C) $12x^2-x-6$
    D) $12x^2-x+6$

TEST – 45
Linear Equations

1. Solve: $\dfrac{3}{5}(2x + 4) = 6$

   A) 2   B) 3   C) $\dfrac{15}{2}$ D) 7

2. Solve: $-7(x+5)=3x+5$

   A) 2   B) –2   C) 4   D) –4

3. $0.9x-4(0.2x+2.5)= -0.1x+20$

   A) 90   B) 2   C) 150   D) 100

4. Solve: $9 = \dfrac{4x}{5} - 3$

   A) $\dfrac{15}{2}$ B) 15   C) 12   D) 10

5. Solve: $5^2 \cdot m - 7 = 4^2 \cdot m + 23$

   A) $\dfrac{16}{9}$ B) $\dfrac{9}{16}$ C) $\dfrac{10}{3}$ D) $\dfrac{15}{2}$

6. Solve: $9(x - 4) = 8(4 - x)$

   A) 4   B) 5   C) 6   D) 7

7. Solve: $\dfrac{m + 4}{5} = 3$

   A) 8   B) 9   C) 10   D) 11

8. Solve: $\dfrac{3(m - 4)}{5} = \dfrac{9}{4}$

   A) 5   B) 6.75   C) 6   D) 7.75

9. Solve: $\dfrac{m + 4}{5} = \dfrac{m - 3}{4}$

   A) 31   B) 25   C) 24   D) 20

10. $\dfrac{0.6x + 4}{3} = \dfrac{1}{5}$

    A) $-\dfrac{23}{3}$ B) $-\dfrac{17}{3}$ C) $\dfrac{17}{3}$ D) $\dfrac{3}{23}$

11. Solve: $0.9x-4(0.2x+2.5)=0.1x+10$

    A) $\emptyset$ B) 10   C) $\dfrac{17}{10}$ D) $-\dfrac{17}{10}$

12. Solve: $13+8y=4(2y+3)$

    A) y=10
    B) y=2
    C) There is no solution
    D) The solution is all real numbers

TEST – 46
Absolute Value Equations and Inequalities

1. Solve: $|4y+2|=10$

   A) $\{2, 3\}$ B) $\{-2, 3\}$

   C) $\{2\}$ D) $\{-3, 2\}$

2. Solve: $|3m+3|=15$

   A) $\{4\}$ B) $\{-4, 6\}$

   C) $\{-6, 4\}$ D) $\{-6\}$

3. Solve: $|7n+5|=26$

   A) $\{3\}$ B) $\{-\dfrac{31}{7}, 3\}$

   C) $\{-3, 4\}$ D) $\{-6, -\dfrac{31}{7}\}$

4. Solve: $|5-3y|=15$

   A) $\left\{-\dfrac{10}{3}, \dfrac{20}{3}\right\}$ B) $\left\{\dfrac{10}{3}, \dfrac{20}{3}\right\}$

   C) $\left\{-\dfrac{3}{10}, \dfrac{3}{20}\right\}$ D) $\{-5, 6\}$

5. Solve: $|2x + 5| < 7$

   A) $0<x<1$ B) $-5<x<1$

   C) $-6<x<1$ D) $-6<x<3$

6. Solve: $|4y+4|<12$

   A) $-4<y<2$ B) $-4<y<-2$

   C) $-4<y<1$ D) $4<y<2$

7. Solve: $|n+3|+3<4$

   A) $3<n<1$ B) $-4>n>-2$

   C) $-3<n<0$ D) $-4<n<-2$

8. Solve: $|x-3|+4=0$

   A) $\{-1, 3\}$ B) $\{-1\}$

   C) $\varnothing$ D) $\{-4, 3\}$

9. Solve: $|m+3|=2m-2$

   A) $\left\{\dfrac{1}{3}, 5\right\}$ B) $\{5\}$

   C) $\left\{-\dfrac{1}{3}, 5\right\}$ D) $\left\{-\dfrac{1}{3}\right\}$

10. Solve: $|4y|=1$

    A) $\left\{\dfrac{1}{4}\right\}$ B) $\left\{-\dfrac{1}{2}, \dfrac{1}{2}\right\}$

    C) $\{-1, 1\}$ D) $\left\{-\dfrac{1}{4}, \dfrac{1}{4}\right\}$

11. Solve: $\left|\dfrac{3x-2}{4}\right|=1$

    A) $\{2\}$ B) $\left\{-\dfrac{2}{3}, \dfrac{1}{2}\right\}$

    C) $\left\{-\dfrac{2}{3}, 2\right\}$ D) $\left\{-\dfrac{2}{3}, -\dfrac{1}{2}\right\}$

12. Solve: $\left|\dfrac{2y-2}{5}\right|=2$

    A) $\{-4, 6\}$ B) $\{6\}$

    C) $\{-6, 4\}$ D) $\{4, 6\}$

TEST – 47
Graphing Linear Equations

1. Which graph shows the function x+3y=6?

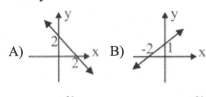

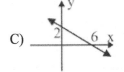

2. Which graph shows the function x-3y= -6?

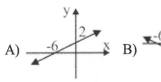

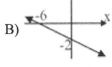

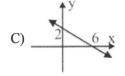

3. Which graph shows the function
    $3y = x - 3$?

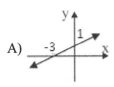

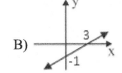

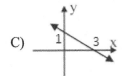

4. Which graph shows the function x-y=3

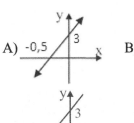

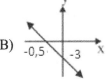

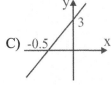

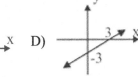

5. Which graph shows the function y=2-x?

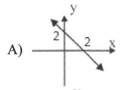

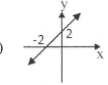

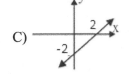

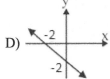

6. Which graph shows the function
    -4x-6y=24?

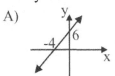

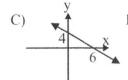

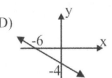

7. What is the equation of the line shown in the graph below?

A) 2x+3y=4
B) 2x+2y=4
C) 5x–2y=10
D) -5x-2y= -10

10. What is the equation of the line shown in the graph below?

A) –5x+2y=2
B) 5x–2y=– 5
C) 3x - 2y = 6
D) 2y+5x=10

8. What is the equation of the line shown in the graph below?

A) 4x+y=5
B) x+5y=4
C) -2x + 5y=10
D) 4x–5y=-10

11. Find the possible value of a+b+c=?

A) –11
B) –31
C) –21
D) –22

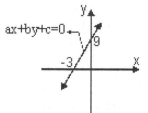

9. What is the equation of the line shown in the graph below?

A) x + 2y = -4
B) –x - 2y =-2
C) x - y = 1
D) –x-y=–1

12. What is the equation of the line shown in the graph below?

A) $y = \frac{x}{2}$
B) y = 2x
C) y = x
D) y = –x

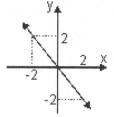

TEST – 48
Absolute Value of Numbers

1. $|7^2\text{-}7| - |-2^3\text{-}5| - |\text{-}5\text{-}4|=?$
   A) 64   B) 20   C) 38   D) 46

2. $-|-7| + |5| - |-6| + |-6|=?$
   A) 0   B) -2   C) 12   D) 24

3. $\dfrac{|5|+|-4|+|-9|}{|-10|-|-1|} = ?$
   A) 2   B) –2   C) –1   D) 1

4. $|-5|+|5|+\left|-\dfrac{2}{3}\right|+\left|-\dfrac{7}{3}\right| = ?$
   A) 9   B) 11   C) 13   D) -3

5. $|2y+3|=11$, y=?
   A) $\{7, 4\}$ B) $\left\{\dfrac{11}{2}, -\dfrac{9}{2}\right\}$
   C) $\{-7, 4\}$ D) $\left\{\dfrac{11}{3}, -\dfrac{9}{3}\right\}$

6. $|x - 4| = 2$
   A) $\{-3, 6\}$ B) $\{2, 6\}$
   C) $\{-2, 5\}$ D) $\{-2, -6\}$

7. $5|2y+3|\text{-}25=0$, y=?
   A) $\left\{\dfrac{15}{2}, -\dfrac{9}{2}\right\}$ B) $\left\{-\dfrac{15}{2}, \dfrac{9}{2}\right\}$
   C) $\{1, -4\}$ D) $\{-1, 4\}$

8. If $|4y\text{-}4|=16$ what is the smallest possible value of y?
   A) –5   B) –3   C) 3   D) 5

9. $5|y+3|+4=3|y+3|+6$, y=?
   A) $\{2, 4\}$ B) $\{-4, 2\}$
   C) $\{-2, 4$ D) $\{-2, -4\}$

10. $|3y+3|<16$
   A) $\left(-\dfrac{19}{3}<y<\dfrac{13}{3}\right)$ B) $\left(-\dfrac{16}{3}<y<\dfrac{13}{3}\right)$
   C) $\left(-\dfrac{16}{3}<y<\dfrac{19}{3}\right)$ D) $\left(\dfrac{13}{3}<y<\dfrac{19}{3}\right)$

11. $|7^2 - 4|-7| - |13|=?$
   A) 25   B) 64   C) 8   D) 29

12. $\dfrac{|5|\cdot|-4|}{|-4|+|5|} = ?$
   A) -20   B) 20   C) $-\dfrac{20}{9}$ D) $\dfrac{20}{9}$

TEST – 49
Signed Numbers

1. $7 - (-3) + 8 + (-4) + 9 - (+5) =$?

    A) 11   B) 18   C) 26   D) 14

2. $-4 - (+3) - 8 - (-4) - 9 - (-5) = $?

    A) 10   B) -12   C) 14   D) -15

3. $\dfrac{-4 \cdot (+3) + 8 \cdot (-4)}{(-3) - (-4)}$

    A) $-\dfrac{20}{7}$ B) $\dfrac{20}{7}$ C) –44   D) 44

4. What is the value of $(-4.24) \cdot (-5.05)$?

    A) 21.412   B) 20.412
    C) 21.312   D) 20.312

5. The number of the students enrolled in the school math club decreased by 300 students over a 5 year period. What was the average decrease in students enrolled per year?

    A) 40   B) 50   C) 60   D) 75

6. What is the quotient of $-7.6 \div 1.9$?

    A) 3   B) –3   C) 4   D) –4

7. Jacob's family spent $10,500 for one year's home rental. What is the average amount that Jacob's family spent per month?

    A) $1500   B) $105   C) $875   D) $975

8. Kevin wants to buy an Algebra book for $83 and a Geometry book for $58. If Kevin currently has $95, how much more money does he need to buy the two books?

    A) $7   B) $46   C) $12   D) $18

9. Jason solved 120 math questions in 80 minutes. What is the average number of questions he solves per minute?

    A) 1.3   B) 1.2   C) 1.4   D) 1.5

10. Brian and his five friends are eating out for lunch. The bill was $120. How much did each person pay to share the payment equally?

    A) $24   B) $23   C) $20   D) $25

11. Which of the following fractions has a decimal equivalent that is a repeating decimal?

    A) $\dfrac{2}{5}$ B) $\dfrac{4}{5}$ C) $\dfrac{3}{4}$ D) $\dfrac{4}{6}$

12. Susan bought a new Geometry book that was on sale for $\dfrac{3}{4}$ of the original price. If the original price was $60, what was the price that Susan paid?

    A) $20   B) $ 45   C) $40   D) $ 36

TEST – 50

Percent

1. 84 is what percent of 1400?
    A) 5   B) 6.5   C) 6   D) 6.6

2. 39 is what percent of 130?
    A) 15%   B) 20%   C) 30%   D) 35%

3. 5 is 15% of what number?
    A) 33.3   B) 33   C) 75   D) 75.5

4. Find 25% of 30.
    A) 4   B) 6   C) 7   D) 7.5

5. Find $13\frac{1}{4}$% of 200.
    A) 26   B) 26.5   C) 26.25   D) 25

6. How much interest is earned in 4 years on an investment of $40000 at 20%?
    A) $3200   B) $32000
    C) $16000   D) $8000

7. Find 120% of 70.
    A) 84   B) 94   C) 104   D) 50

8. 65 is 140% of what number?
    A) $\dfrac{200}{3}$ B) $\dfrac{300}{7}$ C) $\dfrac{325}{7}$ D) $\dfrac{350}{3}$

9. Write 0.7% as a decimal.
    A) 7   B) 0.7   C) 0.07   D) 0.007

10. The new math book's original price is $80. It is sold for $60. What is the rate of discount?
    A) 10%   B) 15%   C) 20%   D) 25%

11. James has a job working 12 hours per day. If he only worked 40% of his work day, how many minutes did he work?
    A) 350 min   B) 280 min
    C) 300 min   D) 288 min

12. A book's original price is $60. Markdown is 25%. Find the sale price.
    A) $45   B) $40   C) $35   D) $25

TEST – 51
Exponents

1. Which of the given expressions is equal to $x^8 \cdot y^7 \cdot x^{-5} \cdot y^5 =$?
   A) $x^{13} \cdot y^{12}$ B) $x^{13} \cdot y^2$
   C) $x^3 \cdot y^2$ D) $x^3 \cdot y^{12}$

2. $\dfrac{(a^3 b^{-4})^5}{\left(a^{-2} b^{\frac{4}{3}}\right)^{-9}} =$?

   A) $a^{33} b^{-56}$ B) 1
   C) $a^{-3} b^{-8}$ D) $a^{-8} b^{-6}$

3. $n^5 \cdot n^4 \cdot n =$?
   A) n^9 B) n^{10} C) n^{11} D) n^{12}

4. $(x^3 y^4)^5 =$?
   A) $x^8 y^9$ B) $x^{15} y^{20}$
   C) $x^{20} y^{15}$ D) $x^9 y^8$

5. $m^{13} n^{17} \div (m^4 n^8) =$?
   A) $m^{17} n^{25}$ B) $m^8 n^8$
   C) $(nm)^9$ D) $(mn)^8$

6. $x^{-4} \cdot y^{-2} \cdot x^{-5} \cdot y^{-7}$
   A) $\dfrac{1}{(xy)^9}$ B) $(xy)^9$ C) $(xy)^2$ D) xy

7. $x^{\frac{1}{3}} \cdot x^{\frac{2}{3}} \cdot x^3 =$?
   A) x^3 B) x^4 C) x^5 D) x^6

8. $n^{-7} \cdot n^7 \cdot n =$?
   A) 0 B) 1 C) n D) n^{-1}

9. If $x>0$ and $y>0$, $x^2 = 144$, $y^2 = 225$ then what is the value of $2x - y =$?
   A) -1 B) 9 C) 39 D) -6

10. If a, b and c are positive integers. $a^2 = 144$, $b^2 = 625$, $c^2 = 100$ then what is the value of $(a + b + c)^2 =$?
    A) 2400 B) 2500 C) 3000 D) 2209

11. $a^2 = 100$, $b^2 = 196$ and $c^2 = 289$ What is the greatest value of $2a + 4b + 3c =$?
    A) 600 B) 721 C) 127 D) 943

12. Which of the following expressions is equal to $\dfrac{a^3 b^5 c^3}{ab^{-3} c^1}$
    A) $\dfrac{1}{(abc)^2}$ B) $(abc)^2$
    C) $(ab^3 c)^2$ D) $a^2 b^8 c^2$

TEST – 52
Exponents and Roots

1. $a^7 \cdot a^2 \cdot a^3 \cdot b^4 \cdot b^{-2} \cdot b^3 = ?$
   A) $a^{12}b^9$ B) $a^{12}b^5$
   C) $(ab)^5$ D) $(ab)^3$

2. If $2^x = 16$, what is the value of $4^{\frac{x}{4}+2} = ?$
   A) 16 B) 32 C) 64 D) 128

3. $8^3 \cdot 8^{-3} = ?$
   A) 8 B) 1 C) 0 D) –8

4. $6^7 \cdot 6^{-5} = ?$
   A) 42 B) 12 C) 36 D) 6

5. $-7^{-2} + \dfrac{1}{49} = ?$
   A) $\dfrac{2}{49}$ B) $\dfrac{1}{49}$ C) 1 D) 0

6. $13^5 \cdot 13^8 \cdot 13^7 = ?$
   A) 13^{280} B) 13^{56} C) 13^{22} D) 13^{20}

7. $7^7 \cdot 7^2 \div 7^6 = ?$
   A) 7 B) 49 C) 7^3 D) 7^4

8. $19^0 \div 19^{-1} + 19^1 = ?$
   A) 36 B) 38 C) 20 D) 19

9. Which of the following expressions is equal to $\dfrac{a^{\frac{4}{3}}b^{-\frac{1}{3}}}{a^2 b^1} = ?$
   A) $\dfrac{1}{\sqrt[3]{a^2 b^4}}$ B) $\dfrac{1}{\sqrt[3]{a^4 b^2}}$ C) $\dfrac{a\sqrt{a}}{b\sqrt{b}}$ D) $\dfrac{\sqrt{a}}{\sqrt{b}}$

10. $800 + 40 + 1 = ?$
    A) 19^2 B) 29^2 C) 21^2 D) 31^2

11. Which of the following expressions is equal to $\dfrac{x^{\frac{5}{2}}y^{\frac{1}{2}}}{xy^{\frac{-3}{2}}}$
    A) $x^{\frac{3}{2}}y^2$ B) $\dfrac{x^2\sqrt{x}}{y\sqrt{y}}$ C) $y\sqrt{x^3}$ D) $\sqrt{x^3 y^3}$

12. $(33^{-3})^0 + (11^0)^3 = ?$
    A) 44 B) 11 C) 0 D) 2

TEST – 53
Radical Expressions

1. $\sqrt{72} - \sqrt{128} + \sqrt{98} = ?$

   A) $\sqrt{42}$ B) $5\sqrt{2}$ C) $4\sqrt{2}$ D) $7\sqrt{2}$

2. What is the sum of
   $\sqrt{144} + \sqrt{64} + \sqrt{16} + \sqrt{8} + \sqrt{4} = ?$

   A) $15 + 15\sqrt{2}$ B) $26 + 4\sqrt{2}$
   C) $26 + 2\sqrt{2}$ D) $5 + 15\sqrt{2}$

3. $\sqrt{1} + \sqrt{4} + \sqrt{9} + \sqrt{16} = ?$

   A) 30   B) 20   C) 15   D) 10

4. $\sqrt{\dfrac{144}{4}} + \sqrt[4]{\dfrac{81}{16}} = ?$

   A) 7.5   B) 7   C) 6   D) 4

5. $\dfrac{\sqrt{80x^4 y}}{\sqrt{5y}} = ?$

   A) $4xy$ B) $4x$ C) $4y$ D) $4x^2$

6. $3\sqrt{2n} + 5\sqrt{n} + 3\sqrt{n} = ?$

   A) $11\sqrt{5n}$ B) $11\sqrt{2n}$
   C) $3\sqrt{2n} + 8\sqrt{n}$ D) $8\sqrt{2n} + 3\sqrt{n}$

7. $\sqrt{(-3)^2} - \sqrt{(-5)^2} - \sqrt{(-8)^2} = ?$

   A) -16   B) 16   C) 8   D) -10

8. $\sqrt{50} + \sqrt{242} + \sqrt{200} = ?$

   A) $21\sqrt{2}$ B) $24\sqrt{2}$
   C) $6\sqrt{2}$ D) $26\sqrt{2}$

9. $\sqrt{0.01} + \sqrt{0.36} + \sqrt{0.81} = ?$

   A) 1.6   B) 1   C) 0.2   D) 2.6

10. Which expression is equivalent to
    $\sqrt[4]{256y} + \sqrt[4]{625y}$

    A) $9\sqrt{y}$ B) $9\sqrt[4]{y}$ C) $9y$ D) $9y^4$

11. Solve for x: $\dfrac{5\sqrt{4y^2}}{3} = \sqrt{300}$

    A) $\dfrac{3}{5}$ B) $\dfrac{3\sqrt{3}}{5}$ C) $3\sqrt{3}$ D) $\dfrac{9\sqrt{3}}{5}$

12. If $\dfrac{2}{3a} = \sqrt{0.36}$, what does a equal?

    A) $\dfrac{3}{5}$ B) $\dfrac{5}{3}$ C) $\dfrac{9}{10}$ D) $\dfrac{10}{9}$

TEST – 54
Polynomials

1. Simplify: $(3x^3 + 4) - (x^3 - 5)$
   A) $2x^3 - 1$ B) $2x^3 + 9$
   C) $3x^6 + 9$ D) $3x^6 - 1$

2. Find the polynomial degree:
   $15x^5 - 4x^{10} - 6x^{12} + 20x$
   A) 20   B) 15   C) 12   D) 10

3. Which of the following is not a polynomial?
   A) $5x^2 + 4x - 6$ B) $3x^3 + 4x$
   C) $\sqrt{7}x^7$ D) $3x^3 + 4x - 4^x$

4. Simplify: $(4b^2 - 5b + 8) + (-3b^2 + 6b + 7)$
   A) $b^2 + b + 15$ B) $7b^2 - b + 15$
   C) $b^2 - 11b + 15$ D) $7b^2 + b + 15$

5. Simplify: $7(y^2 - 2) + 6(y^2 + 3)$
   A) $13y^2 + 1$ B) $y^2 + 1$
   C) $13y^2 + 4$ D) $y^2 + 4$

6. What is sum of the polynomials?
   $(-8x^2 + 3x - 8)$ and $(-2x^2 + 2x - 2)$.
   A) $-6x^2 + x - 6$ B) $-6x^2 + 5x - 6$
   C) $-10x^2 - x - 6$ D) $-10x^2 + 5x - 10$

7. What is the difference of the polynomials below?
   $(a^2 + 5b) - (-2a^2 - 4 - 4b)$
   A) $3a^2 + 9b + 4$ B) $3a^2 + b - 4$
   C) $3a^2 + b + 4$ D) $a^2 + 9b + 4$

8. Which polynomial gives the area of the square in square centimeters?
   A) $16n^2 + 4n + 4$
   B) $16n^2 + 4$
   C) $16n^2 + 16n + 4$
   D) $8n^2 + 4n + 4$

   4n+2
   4n+2

9. Find the polynomial degree:
   $7ab^3 + 10a^2b^3 + 17ab^2 - 7a^7b^1$
   A) 17   B) 10   C) 8   D) 5

10. What is the quotient of $(x^2 + 12x + 36) \div (x + 6)$?
    A) $x - 3$ B) $x + 6$ C) $x - 6$ D) $x^2 - 6$

11. $6(x - 3) + 5(x + 5) = ?$
    A) $11x + 7$ B) $11x - 3$
    C) $11x + 1$ D) $x + 11$

12. What is the quotient of $(y^2 + 9y + 20) \div (y^2 + 12y + 35)$?
    A) $\dfrac{y - 4}{7}$ B) $\dfrac{y + 4}{7}$ C) $\dfrac{y + 4}{y + 7}$ D) $\dfrac{y + 7}{y + 4}$

TEST – 55

Solving Quadratic Equations

1. Solve for x: $2x^2 - 8x = 0$

   A) 0 or -4   B) $\frac{1}{4}$ or $-\frac{1}{4}$

   C) 0 or 4   D) 4

2. Solve for x: $x^2 + \frac{1}{4} = x$

   A) –2   B) 1   C) $\frac{1}{2}$ D) $\frac{1}{4}$

3. Solve for x: $x^2 + x - 6 = 0$

   A) –1 or 6   B) –3 or 2

   C) 3 or –2   D) -6 or 1

4. Solve for x: $4x^2 = 5x$

   A) $\left\{-\frac{\sqrt{5}}{2}, 0\right\}$ B) $\left\{\frac{\sqrt{5}}{2}, 0\right\}$

   C) $\left\{\frac{5}{4}, 0\right\}$ D) $\left\{\frac{4}{5}, 0\right\}$

5. Solve for x: $x^2 - 2x - 4 = 0$

   A) $x = \frac{1+\sqrt{5}}{4}, x = \frac{1-\sqrt{5}}{4}$

   B) $x = 1+\sqrt{5}, x = 1-\sqrt{5}$

   C) $x = \frac{1+\sqrt{5}}{2}, x = \frac{1-\sqrt{5}}{2}$

   D) $x = -1+\sqrt{5}, x = -1-\sqrt{5}$

6. Solve for x: $x^2 + 36 = 12x$

   A) 3   B) –6   C) 6   D) -3

7. Solve for x: $-9x^2 = -27$

   A) $\sqrt{7}$ B) $-\sqrt{7}$ or $\sqrt{7}$

   C) $-\sqrt{3}$ or $\sqrt{3}$ D) $-\sqrt{7}$ or $\sqrt{3}$

8. Find the product of the roots of the equation: $3x^2 - 9x - 12 = 0$

   A) 3   B) -4   C) -3   D) 4

9. Find the sum of the roots of the equation: $5x^2 - 9x - 4 = 0$

   A) $-\frac{9}{5}$ B) -13   C) $\frac{9}{5}$ D) –14

10. Solve for x: $3x^2 + x - 5 = 0$

    A) $x = \frac{-3+\sqrt{61}}{3}, x = \frac{-3-\sqrt{61}}{3}$

    B) $\frac{1+\sqrt{61}}{6}, x = \frac{1-\sqrt{61}}{6}$

    C) $x = \frac{-1+\sqrt{61}}{3}, x = \frac{-1-\sqrt{61}}{3}$

    D) $x = \frac{-1+\sqrt{61}}{6}, x = \frac{-1-\sqrt{61}}{6}$

11. Solve for x: $9x^2 - 1 = 0$

    A) $\frac{1}{9}$ and $-\frac{1}{4}$ B) –3 and 3

    C) $\frac{1}{3}$ D) $\frac{1}{3}$ and $-\frac{1}{3}$

12. Solve for x: $x^2 + 3x = 28$

    A) –7 or 4   B) 7 or –4

    C) 3 or 0   D) –3 or 0

TEST – 56
Inequalities

1. What is the value of m in the inequality?
   $-13 < 3m+2 < 26$
   A) $-2 \leq m \leq 6$ B) $5 < m < 8$
   C) $-5 < m < 8$ D) $-2 < m < 6$

2. $5(x-3) < 5$
   A) x>4   B) x<4   C) x<5   D) x>5

3. Solve the inequality: $3 - 5y \leq -22$
   A) y≥5   B) y≤4   C) y≤5   D) y≥4

4. If $6y - 6 \geq 7y$, then
   A) y≤ –6   B) y≤–7   C) y≥–6   D) y≥7

5. Solve the inequality: $0 < 2x-6 < 12$
   A) 3<x<9   B) 1<x<3
   C) 3<x<6   D) 2<x<5

6. Which of the following graphs shows
   the solutions of the given inequality?
   $5x-3 \leq 4x+3$
   A)
   B)
   C)
   D)

7. Solve the inequality: $\dfrac{4x - 5}{7} < 9$
   A) x <11   B) x<15   C) x>17 D) x<17

8. What is the solution set for the
   inequality? $\dfrac{-3x}{4} + 5 \geq 11$
   A) $x > 4$ B) $x \leq -8$
   C) $x \geq 6$ D) $x \leq -12$

9. What is the value of x in the inequality?
   $7x - 12 > 3x + 4$
   A) x>7   B) x<6   C) x>4   D) x>8

10. Which of these graphs represents the
    solution set of $5x+4 \geq -26$?
    A)
    B)
    C)
    D)

11. What is the value of x in the inequality?
    $7x-3-3x < 9$
    A) x>3   B) x<3   C) x>-3   D) x<–3

12. What is the solution of the inequality?
    $\dfrac{x-1}{3} > \dfrac{2x+4}{7}$
    A) x>7   B) x>16   C) x<18   D) x>19

TEST – 57
Rational Expressions

1. Simplify: $6a\left(\dfrac{b+3}{2a}\right) + 9b\left(\dfrac{c+3}{3b}\right)$

 A) 3b+3c   B) b+c+9
 C) 3b+3c+6   D) 3b+3c+18

2. Simplify: $\dfrac{4a^7}{3} \cdot \dfrac{27}{24a^5}$

 A) $\dfrac{1}{2}$ B) $\dfrac{3a}{2}$ C) $\dfrac{3a^2}{2}$ D) $\dfrac{9a^2}{4}$

3. Simplify: $\dfrac{24a^8}{7b} \cdot \dfrac{35b^4}{32a^5}$

 A) $\dfrac{10a^3b^3}{7}$ B) $\dfrac{15a^3b^3}{4}$

 C) $\dfrac{15a^3b^3}{14}$ D) $\dfrac{4a^3b^3}{15}$

4. Simplify: $\dfrac{3a^4}{21} \cdot \dfrac{7}{2a^5}$

 A) $\dfrac{1}{2a}$ B) $\dfrac{1}{18a}$ C) $\dfrac{a}{18}$ D) $\dfrac{a}{12}$

5. $\dfrac{2m-3}{m+2} - \dfrac{1}{m+2} - \dfrac{m}{m+2} = ?$

 A) 3m+1   B) $\dfrac{m-4}{m+2}$ C) 1   D) $\dfrac{1}{m+2}$

6. $\dfrac{x^2-2x+1}{x^2-4x+4} \div \dfrac{x-1}{x-2} = ?$

 A) $\dfrac{x-1}{2x+1}$ B) $\dfrac{2x-1}{x-2}$

 C) $\dfrac{x-1}{x-2}$ D) $\dfrac{x-1}{x+2}$

7. $\dfrac{3y}{y-6} - \dfrac{18}{y-6} = ?$

 A) 3   B) m – 6
 C) $\dfrac{2}{m-6}$ D) $\dfrac{6}{m-6}$

8. Simplify: $\dfrac{x^2+11x+24}{x+3} - \dfrac{x^2-2x-15}{x+3}$

 A) 2x+13   B) 13   C) 2x –3   D) 3

9. $\dfrac{3a}{12m} + \dfrac{2a}{4m} + \dfrac{a}{4m} = ?$

 A) $\dfrac{a}{m}$ B) 4a   C) $\dfrac{2a}{m}$ D) $\dfrac{a}{2m}$

10. $\dfrac{7}{5x} + \dfrac{10}{3x} = ?$

 A) $\dfrac{61}{15x}$ B) $\dfrac{14}{3x}$ C) $\dfrac{70}{15x}$ D) $\dfrac{71}{15x}$

11. $(x-7) \div \left(\dfrac{x^2-10x+21}{3}\right)$

 A) $\dfrac{x-3}{3}$ B) 1   C) $\dfrac{3}{x-3}$ D) x–3

12. $\dfrac{1}{-2+m} - \dfrac{1}{m+2} = ?$

 A) $\dfrac{m}{m^2-4}$ B) $\dfrac{m-1}{m^2+4}$

 C) $\dfrac{2m+1}{m^2}$ D) $\dfrac{4}{m^2-4}$

69

TEST – 58

Solving Systems of Equations

1. $\left.\begin{array}{l}3x + 2y = 13 \\ 3x - 2y = 5\end{array}\right\}$, $x = ?$

   A) 4   B) 3   C) 2   D) 1

2. $\left.\begin{array}{l}3x + 2y = 13 \\ 3y - 3x = 12\end{array}\right\}$, $y = ?$

   A) 5   B) 3   C) 6   D) 1

3. Which of the following expressions is equivalent to x?

   $\left.\begin{array}{l}x + 2y = 3b \\ -2y + x = 5b\end{array}\right\}$

   A) a   B) 2a   C) 3a   D) 4b

4. $\left.\begin{array}{l}3x + 2y = 12 \\ 3y + 2x = 8\end{array}\right\}$, $x + y = ?$

   A) 2   B) 3   C) 4   D) 5

5. Which of the following expressions is equivalent to x?

   $\left.\begin{array}{l}x - 2y = 3k + 5 \\ x + 2y = 3k + 1\end{array}\right\}$

   A) 3k + 3   B) 2k + 2
   C) 3k + 4   D) 6k + 6

6. $\left.\begin{array}{l}3a + b = 12 \\ b - 2a = -8\end{array}\right\}$, $ab = ?$

   A) 4   B) –1   C) 2   D) 0

7. Which of the following expressions is equivalent to a?

   $\left.\begin{array}{l}a + b = 3^x \\ a - b = 3^y\end{array}\right\}$

   A) 3^{2x} B) 3^x C) 3^{x+y} D) $\dfrac{3^x + 3^y}{2}$

8. $\left.\begin{array}{l}4a + 2b = 12 \\ b - a = 9\end{array}\right\}$, $a + b = ?$

   A) 6   B) 7   C) 8   D) 9

9. $\left.\begin{array}{l}4a + 2b = 12 \\ 5a + 4b = 12\end{array}\right\}$, $3a + 2b = ?$

   A) 8   B) 12   C) 10   D) 4

10. $\left.\begin{array}{l}a = 2b - 7 \\ 5a + 4b = 14\end{array}\right\}$, $b = ?$

    A) $\dfrac{7}{2}$ B) $-\dfrac{7}{2}$ C) 1   D) -1

11. Which of the following expressions is equivalent to *a*?

    $\left.\begin{array}{l}3a + 5b = 5\pi \\ a + 2b = \pi\end{array}\right\}$

    A) π B) 3π C) 4π D) 5π

12. What is the *b* value of the given system below?

    $\left.\begin{array}{l}\dfrac{a}{b} = 3 \\ 5(a + 7) = b\end{array}\right\}$

    A) –12   B) $-\dfrac{5}{2}$ C) $-\dfrac{7}{2}$ D) $\dfrac{7}{2}$

TEST – 59
Functions

1. $f(x)=x+4$, $g(x)=x^2+8x$, $h(x)=x^2+8x+16$
   Which is correct?

   A) $g(x)=2f(x)$ B) $h(x)=f(x)^2$
   C) $h(x)=g(x)^2$ D) $h(x)=2f(x)^2$

2. Which equation represents a direct variation?

   A) $y=\dfrac{3}{x}$ B) $y=7x$

   C) $y=4x^2+3$ D) $y=x^2+5$

3. $f(x)=7x^2+5x-2$, $g(x)=3x^2-5$.
   Find $f(x)+g(x)$.

   A) $10x^2+7$
   B) $10x^2+5x-7$
   C) $10x^2+5x+7$
   D) $4x^2-7$

4. Which function opens down?

   A) $y=5x^2+3$ B) $y=\dfrac{2}{3}x^2+5$

   C) $y=-x^2+2$ D) $y=8x^2+8$

5. $f(x)=\dfrac{3x}{2}-k$. k is constant in the function above. If $f(8)=4$, what is the value of $f(10)$?

   A) 7   B) 5   C) 9   D) 6

6. $f(x)=2x^2-10$

   A)   B)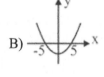

   C)   D)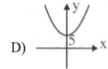

7. If $f(x)=2x^2+5$ and $g(x)=(-x)^2+7$ what is the value of $f(2)-g(2)=$?

   A) 1   B) 2   C) 3   D) 4

8. Which equation is equivalent to
   $$y=\frac{3x}{4}-7$$

   A) $4y=3x-7$ B) $4y+3x=-7$
   C) $4y=3x+28$ D) $4y=3x-28$

9. Which function represents this graph?

   A) $y=x-3$
   B) $y=x+3$
   C) $y=6-2x$
   D) $y=2x+6$

   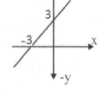

10. $f(x)=|x-3|$

    A) 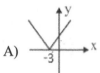   B)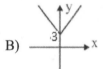

    C) 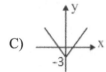   D)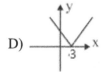

11. Which equation represents a linear function?

    A) $y=x^2+4$ B) $y=x^3+8$

    C) $y=\dfrac{1}{2}x+4$ D) $y=x^2+16$

12. $f(x)=x^2+6x$, $g(x)=(x+3)^2$.
    Which is correct?

    A) $f(x)=g(x)$ B) $f(x)=g(x)+3$
    C) $f(x)-g(x)=9$ D) $g(x)=f(x)+9$

TEST – 60
Law of Exponents

1. $(10^0)^5 + (9^0)^4 + (2)^2 + (1^0)^1 = ?$
   A) 7   B) 8   C) 9   D) 10

2. $3^4 \times 48 \times 225 = 2^x \cdot 3^y \cdot 5^z$. $x + y + z = ?$
   A) 12   B) 13   C) 14   D) 15

3. Simplify: $\left(\dfrac{3a^3b^5}{4ab}\right)^2$

   A) $\dfrac{3a^5b^9}{4}$ B) $\dfrac{3a^4b^8}{4}$

   C) $\dfrac{9a^4b^8}{16}$ D) $\dfrac{9a^5b^9}{16}$

4. What is the value of the expression 3^{-5} ?
   A) $\dfrac{1}{15}$ B) $\dfrac{1}{125}$ C) $\dfrac{1}{243}$ D) $\dfrac{1}{81}$

5. Simplify the expression: $(xy^2z^3)^3$
   A) $x^5y^7z^6$ B) $x^6y^{12}z^{27}$
   C) $x^3y^6z^9$ D) $x^8y^4z^9$

6. Which is $(-3a^2b^3)^4$ in simplified form?
   A) $-3a^8b^{12}$ B) $-81a^8b^{12}$
   C) $81a^8b^{12}$ D) $3a^8b^{12}$

7. $5^{-2} + 5^{-1} + 5^0 = ?$
   A) $\dfrac{6}{25}$ B) $\dfrac{25}{6}$ C) $\dfrac{25}{31}$ D) $\dfrac{31}{25}$

8. What is the result when $a^5b^{-6}c^8$ is divided by $a^{-3}b^6c^4$?
   A) a^2c^4 B) $a^8b^{-12}c^4$
   C) $a^2b^{-12}c^{12}$ D) $a^8b^{-6}c^{12}$

9. Simplify the expression: $\left(\dfrac{a^7b^8c^9}{a^4b^5c^6}\right)^2$
   A) $a^3b^3c^3$ B) $a^{22}b^{26}c^{30}$
   C) $a^6b^8c^{10}$ D) $a^6b^6c^6$

10. Simplify the expression: $\left(a^{12}b^9c^3\right)^{\frac{1}{3}}$
    A) $a^4b^3c^1$ B) $a^{12}b^9c^1$
    C) $a^3b^4c^3$ D) $a^4b^3c^9$

11. If $32 \times 27 \times 72 = 2^x \times 3^y$, then find $(x+y)$.
    A) 10   B) 11   C) 12   D) 13

12. $\left(\left(ab^3c^2\right)^8\right)^{\frac{3}{4}} = ?$
    A) $a^2b^{12}c^{11}$ B) $a^6b^9c^{10}$
    C) $a^6b^{18}c^{12}$ D) $a^2b^{18}c^9$

TEST – 61
Literal Equations

1. The volume of a rectangular parallelepiped can be found using the formula $V = lwh$. Solve for h.

   A) $\dfrac{2V}{lw}$ B) $\dfrac{V}{lw}$ C) $\dfrac{Vl}{w}$ D) $\sqrt{\dfrac{V}{lw}}$

2. The volume of a rectangular pyramid can be found using the formula $V = \dfrac{1}{3}lwh$. Solve for $\dfrac{h}{2}$.

   A) $\dfrac{3V}{lw}$ B) $\dfrac{V}{3lw}$ C) $\dfrac{2V}{3lw}$ D) $\dfrac{3V}{2lw}$

3. Standard form of a linear equation $Ax + By + C = 0$. Solve for y.

   A) $\dfrac{C - Ax}{B}$ B) $\dfrac{Ax - C}{B}$

   C) $\dfrac{-C - Ax}{B}$ D) $\dfrac{Ax + C}{B}$

4. Graph function of the form $f(x) = ax^2 + bx + c$. Solve for x.

   A) $\dfrac{f(x) - (ax^2 - c)}{b}$ B) $\dfrac{f(x) - (ax^2 + c)}{b}$

   C) $\dfrac{f(x)}{ax^2 + \dfrac{c}{b}}$ D) $\dfrac{f(x) - c}{\dfrac{a}{b}x^2}$

5. Trapezoid area formula is $A = \dfrac{1}{2}h(b + d)$. Solve for $\dfrac{h}{2}$.

   A) $\dfrac{A}{b + d}$ B) $\dfrac{2A}{b - d}$ C) $\dfrac{4A}{b + d}$ D) $\dfrac{b + d}{4A}$

6. Solve formula for V: $PV = vRT$

   A) $\dfrac{vRT}{P}$ B) $\dfrac{RP}{Tv}$ C) $\dfrac{pV}{RT}$ D) $\dfrac{RT}{pv}$

7. The volume of a sphere can be found using the formula $v = \dfrac{4}{3}\pi r^3$. Solve for r.

   A) $\sqrt{\dfrac{3v^3}{4\pi^3}}$ B) $\sqrt[3]{\dfrac{3v^3}{4\pi^3}}$ C) $\sqrt{\dfrac{27v^3}{64\pi^3}}$ D) $\sqrt[3]{\dfrac{3v}{4\pi}}$

8. Solve formula for 2R: $g = \dfrac{GM}{R^2}$

   A) $\dfrac{GM}{g}$ B) $\dfrac{2GM}{g}$

   C) $\sqrt{\dfrac{2GM}{g}}$ D) $\sqrt{\dfrac{4GM}{g}}$

9. $S = \dfrac{\vartheta^2}{2a}$, $\vartheta = ?$

   A) $\dfrac{2S}{a}$ B) $\sqrt{\dfrac{2S}{a}}$ C) $\sqrt{2aS}$ D) $\sqrt{\dfrac{a}{2S}}$

* **The rectangular perimeter formula is $P = 2(w+l)$**

10. Solve for 2w.

    A) $P + 2l$ B) $\dfrac{P - 2l}{2}$ C) $P - 2l$ D) $\dfrac{P + 2l}{2}$

11. Solve for l.

    A) $P - 2w$ B) $P + 2w$

    C) $\dfrac{p + 2w}{2}$ D) $\dfrac{p}{2} - w$

12. The circle area formula is $A = \dfrac{\pi d^2}{4}$. Solve for d.

    A) $\sqrt{\dfrac{\pi A}{2}}$ B) $\sqrt{\dfrac{2A}{\pi}}$

    C) $2\sqrt{\dfrac{A}{\pi}}$ D) $4\sqrt{\dfrac{A}{\pi}}$

TEST – 62

Word Problems – Rate Problems

1. Jack bought 4 dozen packages of pencils for $4.80. What is the unit price per pencil?

   A) $0.80   B) $1.20 C) $0.12 D) $0.10

2. Jack changed 7 tires in 12 minutes. Find how many tires per hour can he change?

   A) 68 tires/1 hour   B) 85 tires/1 hour
   C) 35 tires/1 hour   D) 51 tires/1 hour

3. A machine washes 5 carpets in 50 minutes. Which expression equals the unit rate per hour?

   A) 3   B) 4   C) 5   D) 6

4. Jack bought 7 Algebra books for $35.49. What is the unit price?

   A) $5   B) $5.07
   C) $5.70   D) $4.70

5. Which of the following ration is not equivalent to the other three?

   A) $\dfrac{5}{6}$ B) 5 to 6

   C) 10 to 12   D) 20 to 36

6. Jack bought 7 kilograms of walnuts for $10.50 . What is the unit price per kilogram?

   A) $15/kg   B) $1.50/kg
   C) $3/kg   D) $1.70/kg

7. If 7.2 pounds of apples cost $3.60, what is the unit price?

   A) $0.50   B) $0.60
   C) $0.70   D) $0.80

Use the graph for 8–9

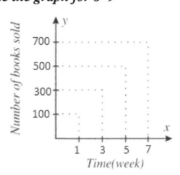

8. How many books sold in 9 weeks?

   A) 800   B) 900   C) 1000   D) 1200

9. Which equation shows this relationship?

   A) y=100x+100   B) y=200x

   C) $y = \dfrac{100}{x}$ D) y=100x

10. If Jack drives 190 miles in 5 hours, how far can he drive in 7 hours?

   A) 370 miles   B) 248 miles
   C) 266 miles   D) 272 miles

Number of cars and washes

Cars (c)	5	7	11
Wash times (w)	60	84	w

The table shows the number of the cars and wash times.

11. Find the w.

   A) 108   B) 132   C) 140   D) 121

12. Which of the following represents the wash times?

   A) c+2   B) c–12   C) c×12   D) c/24

TEST – 63

Word Problems – Age Problems

Jack is now 18 years old and Mario is now 12 years old.

	Jack	Mario	Sum of ages
5 years ago	X	Y	Z
Now	18	12	30
After 6 years	M	N	K

1. Find the N.

    A) 18   B) 23   C) 22   D) 30

2. Find the M.

    A) 26   B) 24   C) 24   D) 20

3. K – N = ?

    A) 24   B) 20   C) 18   D) 12

4. X + Y + Z = ?

    A) 45   B) 38   C) 40   D) 46

5. The ratio of Kevin`s to Linda`s age is 2:3. If the sum of their ages is 30, what is Linda's age?

    A) 6   B) 7   C) 12   D) 18

6. Alvaro is 28 years old and Herby is 19 years old. Calculate the ratio of Alvaro`s age to Herby`s age 6 years ago.

    A) $\dfrac{22}{13}$ B) $\dfrac{13}{22}$ C) $\dfrac{16}{13}$ D) $\dfrac{13}{16}$

7. The sum of the ages of 6 siblings is 84. Find the sum of their ages 4 years ago.

    A) 60   B) 66   C) 70   D) 80

8. A father is 36 years old, and his son is 8 years old. In how many years will the ratio of their ages be 3:1?

    A) 4   B) 5   C) 6   D) 8

9. A 67 year old father has three children whose ages add to 14. In how many years will the father's age be 4 times the sum of his children's ages?

    A) 1   B) 2   C) 3   D) 4

10. Three brothers have ages in ratio 2:3:4. If the sum of the brothers' ages is 45, find the eldest brother`s age.

    A) 10   B) 15   C) 20   D) 25

11. The sum of the ages of 5 siblings is 48. What was the sum of their ages 4 years ago?

    A) 28   B) 30   C) 40   D) 44

12. Malik is 25 years old and his brother is 15 years old. In how many years will the ratio of their ages be $\dfrac{3}{2}$?

    A) 6   B) 7   C) 5   D) 8

TEST – 64
Word Problem – Consecutive Integer Problems

1. The sum of two consecutive integers is 29. Find the product of these integers.

   A) 195   B) 200   C) 205   D) 210

2. The sum of three consecutive integers is 48. Find the smallest number.

   A) 14   B) 15   C) 16   D) 17

3. The sum of three even consecutive integers is 9n. Find the biggest number.

   A) 3n   B) 3n-2   C) 3n+2   D) 3n+4

4. The sum of two odd consecutive integers is 60. Find the product of these numbers.

   A) 899   B) 783   C) 1023   D) 1024

5. The sum of two numbers is 56 and their difference is 12. What is the value of the smaller number?

   A) 18   B) 22   C) 34   D) 36

6. The positive difference between the squares of two consecutive odd integers is 40. Find the small number.

   A) 9   B) 3   C) 12   D) 13

7. The sum of the squares of two integers is 676 and these numbers' ratio is 5:12. Find the biggest number.

   A) 12   B) 10   C) 17   D) 24

8. A and B are positive integers. A·B is 54. Their ratio is 2:3. Find the small number.

   A) 2   B) 6   C) 8   D) 9

9. The sum of the squares of two positive consecutive odd integers is 394. Find the ratio of the numbers.

   A) $\dfrac{13}{15}$ B) $\dfrac{16}{15}$ C) $\dfrac{15}{17}$ D) $\dfrac{17}{19}$

10. The sum of two consecutive integers is 19. Find the product of these integers.

    A) 70   B) 80   C) 90   D) 96

11. How many odd integers are between 36 and 96?

    A) 29   B) 30   C) 31   D) 32

12. The product of two numbers is 156, difference is one. Find the average of the numbers?

    A) 12   B) 12.5   C) 13   D) 13.3

TEST – 65
Laws of Exponents

1. $18^4 \cdot 5^4 \cdot 10^4 = ?$
   A) 90^4 B) 9^4 C) 10^4 D) 900^4

2. $\left(\dfrac{2}{5}\right)^{-3} - \left(\dfrac{2}{3}\right)^{-3} = ?$
   A) $\dfrac{98}{2}$ B) $\dfrac{49}{2}$ C) $\dfrac{49}{4}$ D) $\dfrac{2}{98}$

3. $\left(\dfrac{a^3 b^3 c^3}{a^{-5} b^{-5} c^{-5}}\right)^{-2}$
   A) $(abc)^6$ B) $(abc)^8$
   C) $(abc)^{-16}$ D) $(abc)^{16}$

4. Simplify: $\dfrac{a^7 b^8 c^3}{a^{-5} b^3 c^{12}}$
   A) $a^2 b^{11} c^{15}$ B) $a^{12} b^8 c^9$
   C) $a^{12} b^5 c^{-9}$ D) $a^{12} b^8 c^{15}$

5. $\left((16)^5\right)^{\frac{3}{4}}$
   A) 2^{10} B) 2^{15} C) 2^{20} D) 2^{12}

6. $\left(\dfrac{3}{2}\right)^{-3} = ?$
   A) $\dfrac{8}{9}$ B) $\dfrac{8}{27}$ C) $\dfrac{27}{8}$ D) $\dfrac{9}{8}$

7. Simplify: $\dfrac{\left(5 \cdot 10^{-5}\right) \cdot \left(30 \cdot 10^{-8}\right)}{15 \cdot 10^{-15}}$
   A) 10 B) 10^1 C) 10^2 D) 10^3

8. $2^6 \cdot 3^6 \cdot 5^6 \cdot 6^6 = ?$
   A) 220^6 B) 120^6 C) 240^6 D) 180^6

9. Simplify: $\left(\dfrac{a^{-7} b^{-3}}{a^{-5} b^7}\right)^{-2}$
   A) $a^{-4} b^{-20}$ B) $a^4 b^{20}$
   C) $a^{-24} b^{-20}$ D) $a^{24} b^{20}$

10. $\left(-\dfrac{1}{3}\right)^{-3} + \left(-\dfrac{1}{3}\right)^{-2} + \left(-\dfrac{1}{3}\right)^{-1}$
    A) -39 B) -21 C) 21 D) 39

11. Simplify: $(3x^{-5}) \cdot (7x^{-3})$
    A) $21x^8$ B) $21x^{-8}$ C) $\dfrac{3x^{-2}}{7}$ D) $42x^{-2}$

12. $\dfrac{-15^2 \cdot 15^3 \cdot 15^4}{5^2 \cdot 5^3 \cdot 5^4}$
    A) -15^{15} B) 9^9 C) -3^9 D) 3^9

77

TEST – 66
Distributive Property

1. $-\dfrac{1}{7}(28m - 14n - 56) = ?$

   A) –4m–2n-8   B) –4m+2n+8
   C) –4m–2n+8   D) –4n–2m–8

2. Simplify: –5(x+3) + 4(–4+x)
   A) 9x–13   B) –x–13
   C) –x–31   D) –x–1

3. Simplify: $2^4(8 - 8 \div 4)^2$
   A) 1   B) 576   C) 564   D) 582

4. Simplify: $\dfrac{1}{3}(9a - 12b + 15)$

   A) 3a+4b   B) 5–4b+3a
   C) 5+4a+3b   D) 4a+4+3b

5. Simplify: 9+3x–2(2x–4)
   A) –x+5   B) 17+7x
   C) 6x–6   D) –x+17

6. Simplify: $3(5 - 3)^2 + 4(6 - 4)^2$
   A) 28   B) 24   C) 30   D) 20

7. $\dfrac{7a - 4b}{a - b} + \dfrac{b - 4a}{a - b} = ?$

   A) 3a-3b   B) 3b-3a
   C) 3   D) 4(a+b)

8. $9\left(\dfrac{5n}{3} - \dfrac{4}{3}\right) - 6\left(\dfrac{7n}{3}\right) = ?$

   A) 29n–12   B) n–12
   C) 36n–6   D) 18n+6

9. $\dfrac{5}{6}(n + 1) + \dfrac{7}{6}(n + 2) - 2(n + 3) = ?$

   A) $24n - \dfrac{17}{6}$ B) $\dfrac{17}{6}$

   C) $\dfrac{17n}{6}$ D) $-\dfrac{17}{6}$

10. $2(y^2+3)+2(y^2–3) - 4(y^2+3)=?$
    A) 6   B) 8y²+6
    C) –12   D) 8y²–12

11. $\dfrac{3}{5}(2n + 1) + \dfrac{1}{5}(2n - 2) = ?$

    A) $\dfrac{8n}{5}$ B) 8n   C) $\dfrac{1}{5}$ D) $\dfrac{8n + 1}{5}$

12. $\dfrac{2}{5}(3n + 4) + 0.6(3n - 1)=?$

    A) 3n+1   B) 3n   C) 3n+5   D) 1

TEST – 67
Fractions

1. $\sqrt{27}$ is $\frac{3}{8}$ of what number?

   A) $3\sqrt{3}$ B) $6\sqrt{3}$
   C) $8\sqrt{3}$ D) $9\sqrt{3}$

2. Simplify the expression: $\left(-\frac{3}{12}\right)\cdot\left(\frac{36}{5}\right)$

   A) $-\frac{3}{5}$ B) $\frac{3}{5}$ C) $-\frac{6}{5}$ D) $-\frac{9}{5}$

3. 32 is $\frac{4}{7}$ of what number?

   A) 32   B) 40   C) 48   D) 56

4. If a Mathcounts club consists of 8 girls and 15 boys, what part of the club is boys?

   A) $\frac{8}{23}$ B) $\frac{15}{23}$ C) $\frac{8}{15}$ D) $\frac{15}{8}$

5. Find the ratio of $\frac{2}{7}$ to $\frac{4}{7}$.

   A) $\frac{1}{2}$ B) $\frac{1}{4}$ C) $\frac{8}{49}$ D) $\frac{49}{8}$

6. If $\frac{7}{13}$ of a number is 105, what is the number?

   A) 196   B) 156   C) 175   D) 195

7. Jack paid $84.63 for 7 books. How much did he pay per book?
   A) $12.09   B) $11.90
   C) $12.9   D) $8.24

8. The four sides of a garden measure $1\frac{1}{4}$ meters, $13\frac{3}{4}$ meters, $17\frac{3}{4}$ meters and $9\frac{1}{4}$ meters. Find the length of fence needed to enclose the garden.

   A) 40   B) 42   C) $40\frac{1}{4}$ D) $40\frac{3}{4}$

9. Ryan's workbook has 280 questions. Ryan solved $\frac{1}{7}$ of questions on Monday and $\frac{1}{4}$ of questions on Tuesday. How many questions did Ryan solve?

   A) 100   B) 110   C) 115   D) 120

10. The new geometry book was on sale for $\frac{4}{9}$ of the original price. If the original price was $72 what was the sale price?

    A) $32   B) $28   C) $40   D) $36

11. Which is a rational number but not an integer?

    A) -8 B) 3   C) $\frac{\sqrt{20}}{\sqrt{5}}$ D) $\frac{\sqrt{5}}{\sqrt{20}}$

12. Last week Jack walked $5\frac{3}{8}$ miles. Oskar walked 8 times as far. How many miles did Oskar walk?

    A) 40   B) 43   C) 48   D) 52

TEST – 68

Percent Convert to Fraction and Decimal

1. Convert to fraction in the simplest form: 0.28

   A) $\frac{7}{25}$ B) $\frac{14}{25}$ C) $\frac{7}{50}$ D) $\frac{18}{25}$

2. Convert 33% to a decimal?
   A) 33   B) 3.33   C) 0.3   D) 0.33

3. Find 40% of 60.
   A) 240   B) 120   C) 24   D) 12

4. Find 80% of 4.
   A) 32   B) 3.6   C) 36   D) 3.2

5. Find 70% of 800
   A) 700   B) 560   C) 490   D) 330

6. Convert to fraction in the simplest form: 0.45

   A) $\frac{9}{25}$ B) $\frac{9}{20}$ C) $\frac{8}{25}$ D) $\frac{7}{20}$

7. Convert 47% to a decimal.
   A) 4.7   B) 47   C) 0.477   D) 0.47

8. Find 60% of 60.
   A) 160   B) 60   C) 36   D) 30

9. Convert $\frac{1}{5}$ to percent.

   A) 4%   B) 10%   C) 20%   D) 25%

10. Convert $\frac{9}{25}$ to a percent.

    A) 18%   B) 27%   C) 21%   D) 36%

11. Convert $\frac{7}{50}$ to a percent.

    A) 7%   B) 14%   C) 21%   D) 28%

12. Convert $\frac{8}{20}$ to a percent.

    A) 20%   B) 32%   C) 40%   D) 36%

TEST – 69

Proportion

1. If, $\dfrac{x}{7} = \dfrac{5}{21}$, x = ?

   A) $\dfrac{5}{4}$ B) $\dfrac{5}{3}$ C) $\dfrac{1}{3}$ D) $\dfrac{5}{21}$

2. $\dfrac{x+5}{5} = \dfrac{10}{11}$, x = ?

   A) $-\dfrac{5}{11}$ B) $\dfrac{17}{11}$ C) $-\dfrac{11}{17}$ D) $\dfrac{12}{17}$

3. $\dfrac{x+7}{6} = \dfrac{x+9}{7}$, x = ?

   A) 7   B) 5   C) 5.5   D) 2.5

4. In Mr Roberts' class the ratio of girls to boys is 5:9 . What is the ratio of girls to the all class?

   A) $\dfrac{5}{10}$ B) $\dfrac{5}{14}$ C) $\dfrac{14}{5}$ D) $\dfrac{9}{14}$

5. A square's side is 3 cm. Find the ratio of perimeter to area.

   A) 4   B) $\dfrac{9}{12}$ C) $\dfrac{11}{9}$ D) $\dfrac{4}{3}$

6.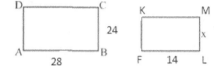

   If AB = 22 and CD = 26 Find the ratio of area of circle I to II.

   A) $\dfrac{121}{169}$ B) $\dfrac{169}{121}$ C) $\dfrac{11}{13}$ D) $\dfrac{13}{11}$

7.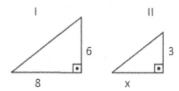

   Triangle I is similar to triangle II. Find the x value.

   A) 2   B) 3   C) 4   D) 5

8. ABCD rectangle is similar to FLMK. Find the x.

   A) 12   B) 18   C) 7   D) 20

9. ABC is right triangle.

   $\dfrac{\angle A}{\angle C} = \dfrac{2}{7}$ if $\angle C$=?

   A) 10°   B) 60°   C) 30°   D) 70°

10. 30 workers can complete a home construction in 9 days. How many workers will be required to complete this home construction in 6 days?

    A) 45   B) 40   C) 54   D) 20

11. 8 books cost $32. How many books can be bought with $48?

    A) 12   B) 10   C) 6   D) 8

12. The currency in Mexico is the Pesos. If I exchange $250 at the exchange office, how many Pesos will I get in return? $1=19.90 Pesos

    A) 4975 Pesos   B) 1256 Pesos
    C) 5660 Pesos   D) 5000 Pesos

TEST – 70
Algebra Fractions

1. What is the value of $\dfrac{a^3 + b^3}{a + b}$ when a=5, and b=4?

   A) 20   B) 21   C) 22   D) 25

2. If $\left(\dfrac{1}{2x} + x\right) = 4$ what is the value of $\dfrac{1}{4x^2} + x^2$ to the nearest whole number?

   A) 15   B) 17   C) 16   D) 14

3. $\dfrac{x^2 + 4x - 21}{x^2 + 3x - 28} = ?$

   A) $\dfrac{x-3}{x+7}$ B) $\dfrac{x-3}{x-7}$ C) $\dfrac{x-3}{x+4}$ D) $\dfrac{x-3}{x-4}$

4. $\dfrac{4}{x^2 - 16} - \dfrac{x}{x^2 - 16} = ?$

   A) $-\dfrac{1}{x+4}$ B) $\dfrac{1}{x+4}$ C) $\dfrac{4-x}{x+4}$ D) $\dfrac{1}{4-x}$

5. $\dfrac{x^2 + 10x + 25}{x + 5} + \dfrac{x^2 + 16x + 64}{x + 8} = ?$

   A) 3x+13   B) 2x+13
   C) 2x -13   D) 2x+8

6. $\dfrac{x^2 - 4x - 21}{x^2 - 5x - 14} = ?$

   A) $\dfrac{x-2}{x+3}$ B) $\dfrac{x-7}{x+2}$ C) $\dfrac{x+2}{x+3}$ D) $\dfrac{x+3}{x+2}$

7. (a + b) = 10 if $a^2 + b^2 = ?$

   A) 100   B) 10 - 2ab
   C) 100–2ab   D) 100 + 2ab

8. What is the value of $\dfrac{x^2 - 6x + 9}{x - 3}$ when x=7.5?

   A) 4.5   B) 10.5   C) 7.5   D) 5.5

9. What is the value of $\dfrac{x^2 + 2xy + y^2}{x - y}$ when x=3.7 and y=2.3?

   A) $\dfrac{36}{14}$ B) $\dfrac{180}{7}$ C) $\dfrac{14}{36}$ D) $\dfrac{14}{360}$

10. Solve for x: $\dfrac{7}{x} = \dfrac{3}{a} + \dfrac{2}{b}$

    A) $\dfrac{7ab}{3b + 2a}$ B) $\dfrac{7ab}{3b - 2a}$
    C) $\dfrac{7ab}{2a - 3b}$ D) $\dfrac{6ab}{3b + 2b}$

11. $\dfrac{x^2 + 9x + 20}{x^2 + 6x + 5} = ?$

    A) $\dfrac{x+5}{x+1}$ B) $\dfrac{x+4}{x+5}$ C) $\dfrac{x+4}{x+1}$ D) $\dfrac{x+5}{x+4}$

12. Solve for x: $\dfrac{3}{x} = \dfrac{2}{a} - \dfrac{5}{b}$

    A) $\dfrac{3ab}{2b + 5a}$ B) $\dfrac{3ab}{5a - 2b}$
    C) $\dfrac{3ab}{5b - 2a}$ D) $\dfrac{3ab}{2b - 5a}$

TEST – 71
Linear Equations

1. For what value of x is
$11(x + 3) + 2 = x + 95$?

   A) 6   B) $\frac{1}{6}$ C) 13   D) -6

2. Solve: $\frac{8x + 4}{4} = 16x - 13$

   A) 2   B) -1   C) 1   D) $\frac{6}{7}$

3. Solve for x: $\frac{9m}{3} = 4x + 2\pi x$

   A) $\frac{12x - 2\pi}{9m}$ B) $\frac{12x + 6\pi}{9m}$

   C) $\frac{9m}{12 - 6\pi}$ D) $\frac{3m}{4 + 2\pi}$

4. Solve: $\frac{a}{b} = \frac{2}{5}$, $\frac{b + 3a}{b - a} = ?$

   A) $\frac{3}{11}$ B) $\frac{11}{3}$ C) $\frac{17}{3}$ D) $\frac{3}{17}$

5. $\frac{11a}{3} - 17 = 10 + a$, a = ?

   A) $\frac{8}{81}$ B) $-\frac{21}{8}$ C) $\frac{81}{8}$ D) $\frac{81}{14}$

6. Solve for x: $ax + 3bx + 6 = 8 - bx$

   A) $\frac{2}{a - 4b}$ B) $\frac{a + 4b}{2}$

   C) $\frac{2}{a + 4b}$ D) $\frac{14}{a + 4b}$

7. Solve for x: $15x + 7y = 2(x + y)$

   A) $\frac{5y}{13}$ B) $\frac{-5y}{13}$ C) $\frac{13}{-5y}$ D) $\frac{13}{5y}$

8. Solve for x: $\frac{3}{7} = \frac{12}{5x + 8}$

   A) 1   B) 3   C) 4   D) 5

9. Solve for x: $\frac{x + 3}{7} = \frac{x + 4}{9}$

   A) $\frac{1}{2}$ B) $\frac{1}{3}$ C) $\frac{1}{16}$ D) $\frac{1}{28}$

10. $2x + 6 = 2^2 + 2^0 - 2^2 + 2^3$, x = ?

    A) 1.5   B) 3   C) 1   D) 5

11. $\frac{3^3 + 3^2}{2^2 + 2^3} = x - 7$

    A) 4   B) 11   C) 10   D) 9

12. $\frac{5x - y}{y + 5} = 14$, if x = ?

    A) 3y + 14   B) 3y - 14

    C) 15y + 70   D) $\frac{13y + 70}{5}$

TEST – 72
Inequalities

1. Solve for x: $4x + 7 < 2x + 21$
   A) $x > 7$ B) $x < 7$
   C) $x > 14$ D) $x < 14$

2. $6x + 9 \geq 11x - 6$
   A) $x \geq 3$ B) $x \geq 2$
   C) $x \leq 3$ D) $x \geq \dfrac{1}{2}$

3. $2(3x + 3) \geq 5(x + 3)$
   A) $x \geq 3$ B) $x \leq 3$
   C) $x \geq 9$ D) $x \geq -9$

4. $\dfrac{1}{3}(x + 5) < 2x + 3$
   A) $x > 2$ B) $x < 0.6$
   C) $x > 3$ D) $x > -0.8$

5. $\dfrac{x - 5}{4} \leq \dfrac{5x - 2}{2}$
   A) $x \leq \dfrac{1}{9}$ B) $x \geq \dfrac{1}{9}$
   C) $x \geq -\dfrac{1}{9}$ D) $x \geq 9$

6. $17 < 2t - 3 \leq 25$
   A) $10 < t \leq 14$ B) $10 < t < 10$
   C) $20 < t < 28$ D) $2 < t < 14$

7. Solve for x: $5(2x + 3) \geq 25$
   A) $x \leq -1$ B) $x \geq 1$
   C) $x \leq 2$ D) $x \geq 2$

8. Solve the inequality: $-3 \leq \dfrac{3x + 3}{2} \leq 6$
   A) $-3 < x < 4$ B) $-3 \leq x \leq 3$
   C) $-6 \leq x \leq 13$ D) $-3 \leq x < 6$

9. Solve the inequality: $6 < x - 7 < 11$
   A) $13 < x < 18$ B) $13 < x < 4$
   C) $1 < x < 4$ D) $-13 < x < 4$

10. Solve the inequality: $\dfrac{9x + 4}{3} \leq 2x + 3$
    A) $x \geq \dfrac{5}{3}$ B) $x > \dfrac{3}{5}$
    D) $x > \dfrac{5}{6}$ D) $x < \dfrac{5}{3}$

11. $-5 \leq \dfrac{x + 3}{2} < 2$
    A) $-11 \leq x \leq 2$ B) $-13 \leq x < 1$
    C) $-11 \leq x \leq 13$ D) $5 \leq x \leq 9$

12. $\dfrac{x - 3}{2} > \dfrac{x + 5}{6}$
    A) $x > 6$ B) $x > 7$
    C) $x < 7$ D) $x < 6$

TEST – 73
Fractional Equations

1. Solve for x $\dfrac{5}{3} - \dfrac{x+1}{3} = \dfrac{x}{7}$.

   A) $\dfrac{5}{14}$ B) $\dfrac{14}{5}$ C) $\dfrac{3}{5}$ D) $\dfrac{7}{5}$

2. Solve equation: $\dfrac{a+2}{5} + 7 = 8$

   A) 5   B) 4   C) 2   D) 3

3. Solve equation: $\dfrac{2x-2}{6} = 3$

   A) 12   B) 11   C) 10   D) 9

4. Solve equation: $\dfrac{5x}{6} + \dfrac{5}{3} = 4 + \dfrac{8}{3}$

   A) 6   B) $\dfrac{4}{5}$ C) 5   D) 7

5. Solve equation: $\dfrac{8-8x}{2} = \dfrac{4}{5}$

   A) $\dfrac{5}{4}$ B) $\dfrac{4}{5}$ C) $\dfrac{2}{3}$ D) $\dfrac{3}{2}$

6. Solve equation: $\dfrac{5x-3}{3} = \dfrac{4x-3}{5}$

   A) $\dfrac{13}{6}$ B) $\dfrac{6}{13}$ C) $-\dfrac{12}{13}$ D) $\dfrac{1}{6}$

7. $\dfrac{5(a-4)}{3} = a+2$, $a = ?$

   A) 11   B) 12   C) 13   D) 15

8. Solve equation: $\dfrac{6}{b-4} = \dfrac{7}{b+7}$

   A) 60   B) 70   C) 80   D) 67

9. Solve for x: $\dfrac{3}{x} = \dfrac{5}{m} + \dfrac{4}{n}$

   A) $\dfrac{3mn}{5m+4n}$ B) $\dfrac{4mn}{5m+3n}$

   C) $\dfrac{5mn}{4m+3n}$ D) $\dfrac{15mn}{4m+3n}$

10. Solve equation: $\dfrac{4}{2x-6} = \dfrac{3}{x-2}$

    A) 3   B) 4   C) 5   D) 6

11. If $\dfrac{x-y}{y} = \dfrac{7}{5}$, which of the following must also be true?

    A) $\dfrac{y}{x} = \dfrac{5}{12}$ B) $\dfrac{x}{y} = \dfrac{5}{13}$

    C) $\dfrac{2x}{y} = \dfrac{10}{13}$ D) $\dfrac{x+y}{y} = \dfrac{5}{13}$

12. Solve for x: $\dfrac{x}{3} = \dfrac{15}{6} - \dfrac{x}{2}$

    A) $\dfrac{15}{4}$ B) $\dfrac{4}{15}$ C) 3   D) 4

TEST – 74
Exponential Equations

1. Solve for x, $4^{\frac{x}{2}-1} = 64$?

   A) 5   B) 6   C) 7   D) 8

2. If $7^{\frac{2}{x}} = 49^{\frac{1}{y}}$, what is the ratio of y to x?

   A) 1   B) 2   C) $\frac{1}{2}$ D) $\frac{1}{4}$

3. Solve for x, $5^{x^2-2x} = 125$?

   A) {-3, 1}   B) {-1, 3}
   C) {1, 3}   D) {1, 2}

4. Solve for x, $3^{3x+1} = 9^{2x-1}$?

   A) 3   B) 2   C) 1   D) 5

5. Solve equation: $6^{2x+5} = \frac{1}{216}$

   A) –4   B) –3   C) $\frac{4}{5}$ D) $\frac{3}{4}$

6. Solve for x: $81^{2x-10} = 9^{2x+2}$

   A) 11   B) 12   C) 13   D) 14

7. Solve for x: $4^x \cdot 4^3 = 256$

   A) $\frac{1}{2}$ B) $\frac{3}{2}$ C) 1   D) -2

8. $15^x = 5^x \cdot B$, B = ?

   A) 8^x B) 3   C) 3^x D) 3^{-x}

9. $15^x = \left(\frac{1}{2}\right)^x \cdot A$, A = ?

   A) 15^x B) 30   C) 40^x D) 30^x

10. Find 20% of 10^6.

   A) $2 \cdot 10^5$ B) $2 \cdot 10^6$ C) $2 \cdot 10^4$ D) 10^5

11. $7^{\frac{1}{x}} = 343^{\frac{1}{2y}}$. What is the ratio of x to y?

   A) 2   B) 1/2   C) $\frac{2}{3}$ D) $\frac{3}{2}$

12. $11^x \cdot 11^y = 121^y$. What is the ratio of y to x?

   A) $\frac{1}{2}$ B) 2   C) 3   D) 1

TEST – 75
Factoring

1. $x^2 - y^2 = 17$ if $x^2 + y^2 = ?$
   A) 146   B) 145   C) 147   D) 150

2. $64x^2 + mxy + 16y^2$ represents the perfect square of x . What is the value of m?
   A) 62   B) 66   C) 64   D) 70

3. If $x = \sqrt{5} - 7$, what is the value of $x^2 + 14x + 49$?
   A) $\sqrt{5}$ B) $\sqrt{3}$ C) 25   D) 5

4. Evaluate: $7001 \cdot 7004 - 7002 \cdot 7003$
   A) 5   B) 6   C) –2   D) –6

5. If $x - \dfrac{2}{x} = 8$, then $x^2 + \dfrac{4}{x^2} = ?$
   A) 36   B) 60   C) 64   D) 68

6. If $x^2 \cdot y = 100$ and $y^2 \cdot x = 25$, find the ratio of x to y.
   A) 2   B) 3   C) 4   D) 5

7. Which polynomial is a perfect square trinomial?
   A) x^2+3x+9 B) $x^2+14x+49$
   C) $4x^2+12xy+3y^2$ D) $x^2-6xy+17y^2$

8. Which shows $x^2 - 8x + 15$ in factored form?
   A) (x - 3)(x - 5)   B) (x + 3)(x + 5)
   C) (x - 1)(x - 5)   D) (x - 5)(x + 1)

9. Which expression shows $(7x - 2)^2$ written in simplest form?
   A) $7x^2 - 14x + 4$ B) $49x^2 - 14x + 4$
   C) $49x^2 - 28x + 4$ D) $7x^2 - 28x + 4$

10. $\dfrac{y^2 + 7y + 12}{y^2 + 9y + 18} = ?$

    A) $\dfrac{y+4}{y+6}$ B) $\dfrac{y+3}{y+4}$ C) $\dfrac{y+6}{y+3}$ D) $\dfrac{y-4}{y+3}$

11. Which shows $2x^2+x-15$ in factored form?
    A) $(x+3)\cdot(x+5)$ B) $(2x+1)\cdot(x+5)$
    C) $(x + 3)\cdot(2x-5)$ D) $(x+3)\cdot(2x + 5)$

12. $\dfrac{y^2 - 7y + 12}{y^2 - 10y + 21} = ?$

    A) $\dfrac{y-4}{y-7}$ B) $\dfrac{y+4}{y-7}$ C) $\dfrac{y-7}{y-4}$ D) $\dfrac{y+7}{y-4}$

TEST – 76
Linear Equations

1. $7x + 5y = 13$, find the slope.

   A) $\frac{5}{7}$ B) $-\frac{5}{7}$ C) $\frac{7}{5}$ D) $-\frac{7}{5}$

2. Find the slope of the line passing through the points A(-5, 5) and B(2, 3)

   A) $\frac{2}{7}$ B) $-\frac{2}{7}$ C) $\frac{7}{2}$ D) $-\frac{7}{2}$

3. Find the equation of the line with a slope of 5 that passes through the point (5, 7).

   A) y= 5x - 18   B) y= 5x + 18
   C) y= 5x + 32   D) y= 5x – 10

4. Find the equation of the line passing through the points (0, 8) and (4, 0)

   A) 6x + 3y =42   B) 6x - 3y = –24
   C) 6x + 4y = 24   D) 6x + 3y = 24

5. Which linear equation models the function shown in the table?

x	Y
0	–7
-6	–11
9	-1
-9	-13
12	1

   A) $y = \frac{2}{3}x - 6$ B) $y = \frac{2}{3}x + 6$

   C) $y = \frac{2}{3}x - 7$ D) $y = \frac{2}{3}x + 7$

6. Which line is parallel to $y = \frac{5}{7}x + \frac{1}{7}$?

   A) $y = \frac{5}{7}x + 7$ B) $y = -\frac{5}{7}x + \frac{1}{7}$

   C) $y = \frac{7}{5}x + \frac{7}{4}$ D) $y = -\frac{7}{5}x - 5$

7. Which line is perpendicular to 2x+5y=14?

   A) $y = \frac{2}{5}x - \frac{14}{5}$ B) $y = \frac{2}{5}x + \frac{14}{5}$

   C) $y = \frac{10}{7}x + 6$ D) $y = \frac{5}{2}x - 1$

8. Which line is perpendicular to the line y=x - 7?

   A) $y = \frac{1}{2}x - 7$ B) y= - x + 7

   C) $y = \frac{1}{2}x + 5$ D) $y = -\frac{1}{2}x + 5$

9. If ax+3y+10=0 and the slope is –3, find the a.

   A) 9   B) –9   C) 6   D) –6

10. Find the equation of the line.
    A) 5x + 2y = 10
    B) 5x + 2y = –10
    C) 2x + 5y = 10
    D) 5y + 6x = -10

11. Which line is parallel to 6x+5y=17?

    A) y = -6x + 17   B) $y = -\frac{6}{5}x + 5$

    C) $y = \frac{6}{5}x + 7$ D) $y = \frac{6}{5}x + 5$

12. If ax+by+c=0 and the slope is –5, find the ratio $\frac{b}{a}$.

    A) –5   B) 6   C) $\frac{1}{5}$ D) $\frac{1}{6}$

TEST – 77
Radical Equations

1. Solve for x: $\sqrt{x+3} = 7$
   A) 46   B) 43   C) 42   D) 44

2. Solve for x: $\sqrt{3x-5} = 4$
   A) 5   B) 6   C) 7   D) 4

3. Solve for x: $\sqrt{2x+5} + 7 = 12$
   A) 25   B) 10   C) 11   D) 12

4. Solve for x: $\sqrt{x^2 + 7} = x + 7$
   A) 3   B) -3   C) 4   D) –4

5. Solve for x: $\sqrt{x^2 + 8} - 4 = x$
   A) 1   B) –1   C) 2   D) 3

6. Solve for *x*: $\sqrt[3]{2x-5} = 3$
   A) 14   B) 16   C) 27   D) 9

7. Solve for x: $\sqrt[5]{3x-4} = 2$
   A) 11   B) 10   C) 9   D) 12

8. Solve for x: $\sqrt{2x+14} = x+3$
   A) 1   B) 2   C) 4   D) 5

9. Solve for x: $\sqrt{2x+7} = x-4$
   A) 1   B) 9   C) 8   D) 10

10. Solve for x: $\sqrt[3]{7x+1} = 3$
    A) $\dfrac{26}{7}$ B) $\dfrac{7}{26}$ C) 8   D) 7

11. $\sqrt{7x-10} = \sqrt{2x+5}$. What is x?
    A) 5   B) 9   C) 3   D) 2

12. $\sqrt{6x-5} + 5 = 10$. What is *x*?
    A) 5   B) 6   C) 25   D) 3

TEST – 78
Quadratic Equations

1. Find the solution of $x^2 - 7x + 12 = 0$.
   - A) 2 and 6
   - B) 1 and 12
   - C) 3 and 4
   - D) –3 and –4

2. Given the function $y = x^2 + 9x + 14$, what is the best estimate of the solution?
   - A) –2 and +7
   - B) –3 and –4
   - C) –1 and –14
   - D) –2 and –7

3. The function $y = x^2 - 16$ is graphed. What is the best estimate of the solution of $x^2 - 16$?
   - A) $x = -4$ and $x = +4$
   - B) $x = -3$ and $x = 3$
   - C) $x = -1$ and $x = +1$
   - D) $x = -2$ and $x = +2$

4. Solve the equation: $(x - 4)^2 - 2 = 7$
   - A) 7 and -1
   - B) - 7 and 1
   - C) 7 and 1
   - D) -7 and -1

5. Solve the equation: $x^2 + 26x + 169 = 0$
   - A) $x = 13$
   - B) $x = -13$
   - C) $x = -11$
   - D) $x = -11$ and 13

6. $\frac{6}{5} x^2 = 30$. Solve for x
   - A) ± 6
   - B) ± 5
   - C) ± 4
   - D) ± 7

7. Solve the equation: $(x - 7)^2 = 5$
   - A) $7 \pm \sqrt{5}$
   - B) $7 \pm \sqrt{3}$
   - C) $5 \pm \sqrt{7}$
   - D) $\pm \sqrt{7}$

8. Solve the equation: $x^2 - 8x + 8 = 0$
   - A) $4 \pm \sqrt{2}$
   - B) $3 \pm \sqrt{15}$
   - C) $5 \pm \sqrt{15}$
   - D) $3 \pm \sqrt{5}$

9. Find the equation that has the solutions $x = 1$ and $x = \frac{3}{2}$.
   - A) $2x^2 + 5x + 3 = 0$
   - B) $3x^2 - 5x + 3 = 0$
   - C) $2x^2 - 5x + 3 = 0$
   - D) $5x^2 + 2x - 3 = 0$

10. $x^2 + 8x + 15 = 0$, $(x_1 \cdot x_2) \div (x_1 + x_2) = ?$
    - A) $\frac{8}{15}$
    - B) $-\frac{8}{15}$
    - C) $\frac{15}{8}$
    - D) $-\frac{15}{8}$

11. Find the solution of $x^2 + 9x + 20 = 0$
    - A) $\{-4, -2\}$
    - B) $\{-5, -4\}$
    - C) $\{-5, 4\}$
    - D) $\{-5, -3\}$

12. $25x^3 = 675$. Solve for x.
    - A) 1
    - B) 2
    - C) 3
    - D) 4

TEST – 79
Increase and Decrease

1. Geometry book cost $12 .It is reduced to $8 in a sale . How much is the percentage reducation?

   A) 33%   B) 36%   C) 40%   D) 42%

2. Anew math book costs $40 . It is reduced to $25 in the sale . By what percentage was the price reduced?

   A) 22%   B) 37.5%
   C) 32%   D) 35.5%

3. Jack works in university library for $12 per hour. If his pay increased to $14, then what is the percent's increase in pay?

   A) 16%   B) 19%   C) 20%   D) 17%

4. If the cost of a dress is $75 and Ayse gets on sale for $60 . What is the percent of discount?

   A) 18%   B) 23%   C) 25%   D) 20%

5. What is the percent of change in the cost of Algebra book sold for $30 and is the now a sale for $24?

   A) 10%   B) 15%   C) 18%   D)20%

6. A geometry book cost $45 . It is sold for $20 in sale. Find the sale percent?

   A) 40% Increase   B) 32% decrease
   C) 44 % decrease   D) 44% increase

7. Find the percent's change. From 60 inches to 75 inches?

   A) 28% increase   B) 25% decrease
   C) 21% increase   D) 25%increase

8. Find the percent change from 36 grams to 24 grams.

   A) 33% decrease   B) 30% decrease
   C) 20% increase   D) 31% decrease

9. What is the percent decrease of a $300 item on sale for $250?

   A) 15%   B)18%   C) 17%   D) 25%

10. Find the percent decrease from 240 to 200?

    A) 17%   B) 16%   C)15%   D) 14%

11. What is the percent increase of a $50 item on sale for $75?

    A) 30%   B) 20%   C) 50%   D) 40%

12. Find the percent decrease from 160 to 120?

    A) 20%   B) 22%   C) 25%   D) 30%

TEST – 80

Probability

1. Find the probability of getting a number less than 6 in a single throw of a die.

   A) $\dfrac{5}{6}$ B) $\dfrac{3}{6}$ C) $\dfrac{4}{6}$ D) $\dfrac{1}{6}$

2. A standard dice is rolled. What is the probability that a 1,3 or 6 will be rolled?

   A) $\dfrac{1}{4}$ B) $\dfrac{1}{5}$ C) $\dfrac{1}{6}$ D) $\dfrac{1}{2}$

3. A die is rolled. Find the probability that a odd number is obtained.

   A) $\dfrac{1}{6}$ B) $\dfrac{1}{7}$ C) $\dfrac{1}{4}$ D) $\dfrac{1}{2}$

4. A jar contains 4 blue and 6 yellow. If marbles is dawn from the jar at random. What is the probability that this marble is yellow.

   A) $\dfrac{3}{5}$ B) $\dfrac{1}{5}$ C) $\dfrac{2}{3}$ D) $\dfrac{1}{6}$

5. A die is rolled find the probability that the number obtained is greater than 5.?

   A) $\dfrac{1}{2}$ B) $\dfrac{1}{3}$ C) $\dfrac{1}{4}$ C) $\dfrac{1}{6}$

6. A die is rolled once. What is the probability of getting a composite number?

   A) $\dfrac{1}{4}$ B) $\dfrac{1}{2}$ C) $\dfrac{1}{6}$ D) $\dfrac{1}{3}$

7. A die is rolled once. What is the probability of getting a prime number less than 4?

   A) $\dfrac{1}{6}$ B) $\dfrac{1}{5}$ C) $\dfrac{1}{3}$ D) $\dfrac{1}{2}$

8. Ticket numbered 1 to 16 are mixed up and then a ticket is drawn at random. What is the probability that the ticket drawn has a number which's a multiply of 3.?

   A) $\dfrac{9}{16}$ B) $\dfrac{7}{16}$ C) $\dfrac{6}{16}$ D) $\dfrac{5}{16}$

9. What is the probability of getting a sum 8 from two throws of the dice?

   A) $\dfrac{1}{5}$ B) $\dfrac{1}{6}$ C) $\dfrac{1}{9}$ D) $\dfrac{1}{12}$

10. Which of the following cannot be the probability of an A event?

    A) $\dfrac{1}{2}$ B) $\dfrac{1}{3}$ C) $\dfrac{2}{3}$ D) $\dfrac{3}{2}$

11. There are 7 black and 3 green balls in bag. What is the probability of randomly selected ball not coming green?

    A) $\dfrac{3}{10}$ B) $\dfrac{6}{10}$ C) $\dfrac{7}{10}$ D) $\dfrac{1}{2}$

12. There are 6 blue and 8 yellow balls in a bag. What is theoretically the probability of a randomly selected ball coming yellow.?

    A) $\dfrac{3}{7}$ B) $\dfrac{4}{7}$ C) $\dfrac{5}{7}$ D) $\dfrac{6}{7}$

TEST – 81

Graphing Linear Graphs

1. Find the slope of the line from the graph.

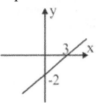

A) $\dfrac{4}{3}$ B) $-\dfrac{4}{3}$ C) $\dfrac{2}{3}$ D) $-\dfrac{2}{3}$

2. Find the y if the line through (–2,–10) and (2, y) has a slope of 4.

A) 1   B) 2   C) 4   D) 6

3. Find the slope of the line through (–7, 5) and (3, 4)

A) $\dfrac{1}{10}$ B) -10   C) $-\dfrac{1}{10}$ D) $\dfrac{1}{6}$

4. Graph the inverse variation statement $y = -\dfrac{5}{x}$.

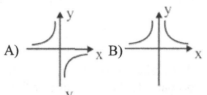

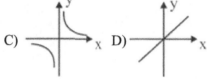

5. Find the graph of 3x - 2y=12

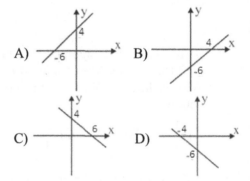

6. Find the graph of 2x + 7y = 14

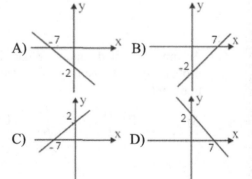

7. Graph the lines x = 7 and y = –3.

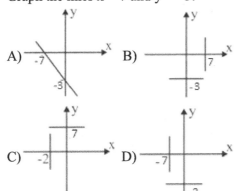

A)   B)

C)   D)

10. Find the graph of x - 3y = 6

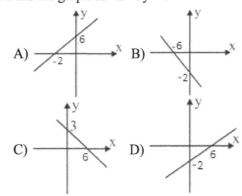

A)   B)

C)   D)

8. Find the graph of x - y = -7.

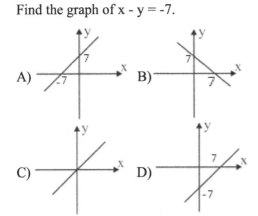

A)   B)

C)   D)

11. Find the graph of $\dfrac{x}{2} + \dfrac{3y}{2} = \dfrac{6}{4}$

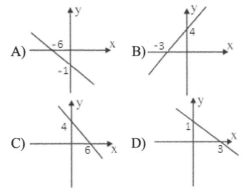

A)   B)

C)   D)

9. Find the slope of the line from graph.

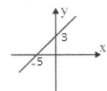

A) $\dfrac{5}{3}$ B) $-\dfrac{5}{3}$ C) $\dfrac{3}{5}$ D) $-\dfrac{3}{5}$

12. Find the slope of the line from graph.

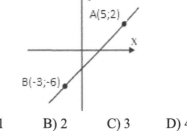

A) 1   B) 2   C) 3   D) 4

TEST – 82

Graphing Inequalities

1. $y \leq 3x+9$. Which graph is correct?

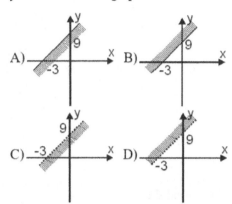

2. $x - y < -1$

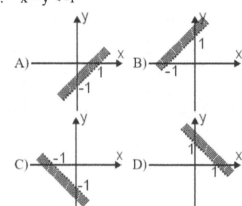

3. $y \leq -2x$

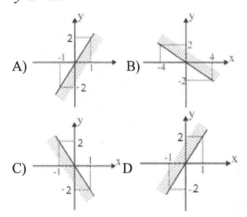

4. $x > 1$

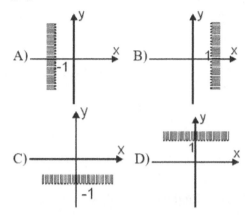

5. Graph the inequality: $x + 2y \leq 8$

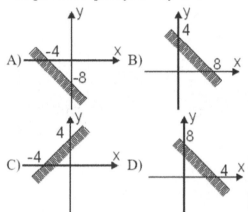

6. $2x - y \geq 8$

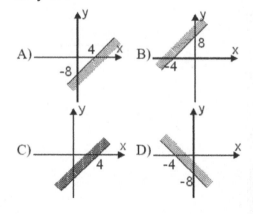

7. 2x<−3y+6

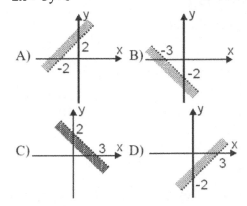

8. y ≥ 2x + 10

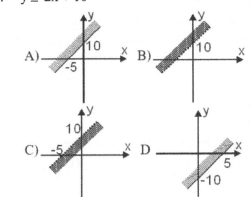

9. y ≥ x

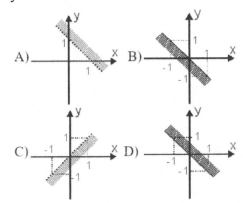

10. y ≥ -2

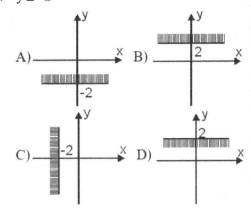

11. x≥−4

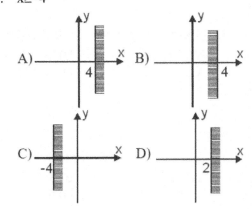

12. x ≤ 3

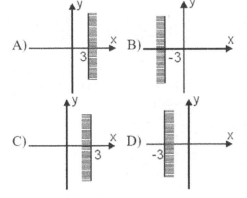

TEST – 83
Algebraic Functions

1. $f(x)=2x^2 + 1$, $g(x)=3x+2$. $f(1)+g(2)=?$
   A) 10 B) 11 C) 13 D) 15

2. $f(x)=7x^2+5$, $g(x)=3x^2+5$. $f(x)-g(x)=?$
   A) $4x^2$ B) $5x^2$
   C) $4x^2+3$ D) $4x^2+10$

3. $f(x)=2x+1$, $g(x)=x^2+2x$. $f(x)\cdot g(x)=?$
   A) $2x^3+5x^2+2$ B) $2x^3+5x^2+2x$
   C) $2x^3+5x^2-2$ D) $x(x^2+2x+3)$

4. $f(x)=x^2+1$, $g(x)=3x$. $f(g(x))=?$
   A) $9x^2+1$ B) $9x^2 - 1$
   C) $9x^2+x$ D) $9x^2$

5. $f(x)=x^2+10x+7$, $g(x)=(x+5)^2$. Which is correct?
   A) $g(x)=f(x)$ B) $f(x)=g(x)+2$
   C) $g(x)=f(x)+18$ D) $g(x)=f(x)+1$

6. $f(x)=(x+3)^2$, $g(x)=x+3$. Which is correct?
   A) $f(x)=g(x)^2$
   B) $f(x)=g(x) - 9$
   C) $f(x)=g(x) + 9$
   D) $f(x)=g(x+3)-9$

7. $f(x)=x^2+6$ if $f(x-3)=?$
   A) $x^2-6x+15$ B) x^2-6x+9
   C) $x^2-6x-15$ D) x^2-6x

8. $f(x)=7x-2$, $g(x)=3x+1$. $f(g(2))=?$
   A) 44 B) 46 C) 47 D) 48

9. $f(x)=x^3+1$, $g(x)=3x+2$. $g(f(1))=?$
   A) 20 B) 18 C) 16 D) 8

10. $f(x)=2x^2+3x+2$, $g(x)=4x^2+4$, $h(x)=2x^2+5x$. $\dfrac{f(2) + g(1)}{h(2)} = ?$

    A) $\dfrac{3}{4}$ B) $\dfrac{4}{3}$ C) $\dfrac{4}{5}$ D) $\dfrac{5}{4}$

11. $f(x) = x^{\frac{1}{2}}$, $g(x) = x^{\frac{1}{3}}$. $g(27)-f(16)=?$
    A) -1 B) 1 C) 2 D) –2

12. $f(x)=x^2+3x$, $g(x)=x+2$. $f(x)\cdot g(x)=ax^3+bx^2+cx$, $a+b+c=?$
    A) 11 B) 12 C) 13 D) 14

TEST – 84
Probability

1. Find the probability of getting a number less than 6 in a single throw of a die.

   A) $\dfrac{5}{6}$ B) $\dfrac{3}{6}$ C) $\dfrac{4}{6}$ D) $\dfrac{1}{6}$

2. A standard dice is rolled. What is the probability that a 1, 3 or 6 will be rolled?

   A) $\dfrac{1}{4}$ B) $\dfrac{1}{5}$ C) $\dfrac{1}{6}$ D) $\dfrac{1}{2}$

3. A die is rolled. Find the probability that a odd number is obtained.

   A) $\dfrac{1}{2}$ B) $\dfrac{1}{7}$ C) $\dfrac{1}{4}$ D) $\dfrac{1}{6}$

4. A jar contains 4 blue and 6 yellow. If marbles is dawn from the jar at random. What is the probability that this marble is yellow.

   A) $\dfrac{3}{5}$ B) $\dfrac{1}{5}$ C) $\dfrac{2}{3}$ D) $\dfrac{1}{6}$

5. A die is rolled find the probability that the number obtained is greater than 5?

   A) $\dfrac{1}{2}$ B) $\dfrac{1}{3}$ C) $\dfrac{1}{4}$ C) $\dfrac{1}{6}$

6. A die is rolled once. What is the probability of getting a composite number?

   A) $\dfrac{1}{4}$ B) $\dfrac{1}{2}$ C) $\dfrac{1}{6}$ D) $\dfrac{1}{3}$

7. A die is rolled once. What is the probability of getting a prime number less than 4?

   A) $\dfrac{1}{6}$ B) $\dfrac{1}{5}$ C) $\dfrac{1}{3}$ D) $\dfrac{1}{2}$

8. Ticket numbered 1 to 16 are mixed up and then a ticket is drawn at random. What is the probability that the ticket drawn has a number which's a multiply of 3?

   A) $\dfrac{7}{16}$ B) $\dfrac{9}{16}$ C) $\dfrac{6}{16}$ D) $\dfrac{5}{16}$

9. What is the probability of getting a sum 8 from two throws of the dice?

   A) $\dfrac{1}{5}$ B) $\dfrac{1}{6}$ C) $\dfrac{1}{9}$ D) $\dfrac{1}{12}$

10. Which of the following cannot be the probability of an A event?

   A) $\dfrac{1}{2}$ B) $\dfrac{1}{3}$ C) $\dfrac{3}{2}$ D) $\dfrac{3}{4}$

11. There are 7 black and 3 green balls in bag. What is the probability of randomly selected ball not coming green?

   A) $\dfrac{3}{10}$ B) $\dfrac{6}{10}$ C) $\dfrac{7}{10}$ D) $\dfrac{1}{2}$

12. There are 6 blue and 8 yellow balls in a bag. What is theoretically the probability of a randomly selected ball coming yellow?

   A) $\dfrac{3}{7}$ B) $\dfrac{4}{7}$ C) $\dfrac{5}{7}$ D) $\dfrac{6}{7}$

TEST – 85

Direct and Inverse Variation

1. If y varies directly as x and y=21 when x=7, what is y when x=18?

   A) 54   B) 52   C) 32   D) 34

2. If y varies inversely as x and y=12 when x=3, what is y when x=6?

   A) 6   B) 12   C) 16   D) 18

3. If y varies inversely as x and y=15 when x=4, what is y when x=5?

   A) 10   B) 12   C) 14   D) 30

4. Which is the inversely proportional graph?

   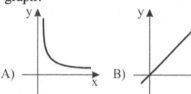

5. Which is the directly proportional graph?

   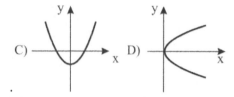

6. The arithmetic mean of 9, 10, 5a, 4a is 25. Find $a^{\frac{1}{2}}$.

   A) 3   B) 9   C) 81   D) 100

7.

x	1	2	3
y	8	16	24

   Find the constant of proportionality.

   A) 3   B) 4   C) 5   D) 8

8.

x	2	4	16
y	16	8	2

   y varies inversely as x. Find the constant of proportionality.

   A) 32   B) 14   C) 16   D) 38

9. If y varies inversely as x and y=22 when x=4, what is y when x=8?

   A) 10   B) 11   C) 12   D) 20

10. If y varies inversely as x and y=30 when x=3, what is y when x=18?

    A) 5   B) 6   C) 5.5   D) 7

11. If $\dfrac{a+b}{a} = 7$, $\dfrac{b}{a-b} = ?$

    A) $\dfrac{5}{6}$ B) $-\dfrac{5}{6}$ C) $-\dfrac{6}{5}$ D) $\dfrac{6}{5}$

12. If $\dfrac{a+b}{b} = \dfrac{3}{2}$, $\left(\dfrac{a}{b-a}\right)^2 = ?$

    A) $\dfrac{1}{4}$ B) $\dfrac{9}{4}$ C) 2   D) 1

TEST – 86

Statistics (Mean, Median and Range)

1. Find the mean, median and range for: 7, 5, 4, 6, 3, 9 and 1.
   A) 5, 7, 9   B) 5, 5, 8
   C) 7, 9, 5   D) 5, 5, 6

2. Find the mean, median and range for: 1, 2, 8, 11, 6, 5 and 13.
   A) $\frac{43}{7}$, 8, 13   B) 9, 6, 11
   C) $\frac{46}{7}$, 6, 12   D) $\frac{46}{7}$, 8, 12

3. Find the mode for: 7, 3, 5, 4, 9, 4, 2 and 11.
   A) 3   B) 7   C) 2   D) 4

4. Find the range for:-9, 11, -12, 3 and -2.
   A) 19   B) 23   C) 6   D) 5

5. Find the median of: 2, 5, 9, 13, 21, 6.
   A) 19   B) 13   C) 7.5   D) 5

6. Find the mode of 11, 5, 7, 9, 7, 3, 2, 7, 16, 11.
   A) 11   B) 9   C) 7   D) 16

7. Find the range of the numbers: 0, 7, 11, 13, -17, 19.
   A) 36   B) 19   C) 12   D) 19

8. Which of the following groups of data has two modes?
   A) 3, 3, 1, 1, 6, 7, 9, 4
   B) 2, 2, 2, 4, 4, 5, 7, 10
   C) 3, 5, 7, 9, 9, 11
   D) 1, 5, 7, 10, 7, 13

9. Find the range of 3, -6, 2, 11, 13, 27.
   A) 33   B) 25   C) 24   D) 16

10. Find the mean of the numbers: -5, 6, 3, 11, 4, 8.
    A) $\frac{27}{7}$ B) $\frac{13}{4}$ C) $\frac{9}{2}$ D) $\frac{25}{6}$

11. Find the median of the numbers: 5, 7, 13, 4, 2, 8.
    A) 5   B) 7   C) 4   D) 6

12. Find the range of: 11, 8, 9, -6, 40, 35, 67.
    A) 73   B) 56   C) 58   D) 37

TEST – 87

Fractions and Decimals
(Verbal Problems Involving Fractions)

1. The math association has 11 boys and 33 girls. What is the ratio of girls to boys in the math association?

   A) $\dfrac{1}{3}$ B) $\dfrac{1}{2}$ C) 3   D) 2

2. $A = \dfrac{1}{3}$, $B = \dfrac{2}{3}$, $C = 2$. Find the average.

   A) $\dfrac{5}{3}$ B) $\dfrac{3}{5}$ C) 1   D) 3

3. If $\dfrac{5}{9}$ of a number is 40, what is $\dfrac{11}{8}$ of that number?

   A) 64   B) 88   C) 99   D) 72

4. Which fraction is equivalent to $\dfrac{16}{32}$?

   A) $\dfrac{6}{5}$ B) $\dfrac{44}{110}$ C) $\dfrac{55}{110}$ D) $\dfrac{6}{18}$

5. Which of the following is more than $\dfrac{3}{5}$?

   A) $\dfrac{2}{5}$ B) $\dfrac{6}{10}$ C) $\dfrac{6}{9}$ D) $\dfrac{5}{9}$

6. Which of the following is not correct?

   A) $\dfrac{1}{2} < \dfrac{1}{3}$ B) $\dfrac{2}{3} < \dfrac{3}{4}$

   C) $\dfrac{4}{12} = \dfrac{1}{3}$ D) $\dfrac{2}{5} < \dfrac{4}{6}$

7. Which of the following is not equivalent to $\dfrac{33}{21}$?

   A) $\dfrac{11}{7}$ B) $\dfrac{22}{14}$ C) $\dfrac{55}{28}$ D) $\dfrac{44}{28}$

8. If $\dfrac{x}{2} + \dfrac{2x}{3} + \dfrac{4x}{5} = 6a + 2b$, $\dfrac{x}{4} + \dfrac{x}{3} + \dfrac{2x}{5} = ?$

   A) 3a+b   B) a+b
   C) 6a+b   D) 6a+3b

9. $a = \dfrac{x}{\sqrt{2}}, b = \dfrac{x^2}{2}, c = \dfrac{(2x)^2}{4}$

   Which is correct?

   A) b>a   B) b>c   C) b=a   D) a>b

10. Jan ate 1/3 of a pizza and Susan ate 1/4 of it. What fraction of the pizza was not eaten?

    A) $\dfrac{7}{12}$ B) $\dfrac{5}{12}$ C) $\dfrac{6}{12}$ D) $\dfrac{3}{12}$

11. $\dfrac{2}{a} + \dfrac{1}{2a} + \dfrac{1}{3a} = ?$

    A) $\dfrac{4}{6a}$ B) $\dfrac{14}{6a}$ C) $\dfrac{17}{6a}$ D) $\dfrac{17}{6a^2}$

12. $a = 1, b = 4\left(\dfrac{1}{\sqrt{2}}\right)^2, c = \dfrac{\sqrt[3]{27}}{\sqrt{9}}$.

    Which is correct?

    A) a>b>c   B) a<b<c
    C) a=c<b   D) a>b=c

TEST – 88
Statistics (Mean, Median and Range)

1. Find the mean, median and range for: 8, 9, 11, 13, 16, 16 and 18.
   A) 13, 13, 11   B) 13, 13, 10
   C) 13, 11, 14   D) 9, 10, 13

2. Find the mean, median and range for: 4, 3, 9, 8, 12, 6 and 10.
   A) $\dfrac{52}{7}$, 8, 9   B) $\dfrac{42}{9}$, 8, 9
   C) $\dfrac{53}{8}$, 8, 9   D) $\dfrac{49}{6}$, 9, 8

3. Find the mode for: 6, 2, 8, 9, 6, 6, 3 and 12.
   A) 3   B) 6   C) 2   D) 9

4. Find the range for: 12, 19, 13, 4, 3 and 15.
   A) 10   B) 16   C) 12   D) 13

5. Find the median of: –5, 13, –7, $\dfrac{3}{2}$, 14.
   A) –5   B) –7   C) 14   D) $\dfrac{3}{2}$

6. Find the mode of 13, 5, 3, 12, 12, –4, –3, 12, 13, 15.
   A) 13   B) 3   C) 5   D) 12

7. Find the range of the numbers: 12, 19, 28, 11, –6, 0, 12.
   A) 30   B) 31   C) 32   D) 34

8. Which of the following groups of data has two modes?
   A) 3, 3, 1, 1, 6, 9, 9, 7, 4
   B) 3, 4, 5, 6, 7, 8, 9, 11, 12
   C) 6, 7, 8, 9, 10, 11, 12, 13, 17
   D) 1, 8, 9, 6, 4, 3, 2, 14, 18

9. Find the mean of –4, 6, 10, 3, –5, 12.
   A) $\dfrac{11}{3}$ B) $\dfrac{11}{4}$ C) $\dfrac{12}{7}$ D) $\dfrac{3}{11}$

10. Find the range of the numbers: –4, 6, –1, 12, 24, 3, 5.
    A) 28   B) 24   C) 20   D) 18

11. Find the median of the numbers: 12, 8, 4, 9, 5.
    A) 5   B) 4   C) 8   D) 9

12. Find the range of: 14,12,8,20,5,42,63, 21,36.
    A) 58   B) 52   C) 53   D) 54

TEST – 89
Equations of Lines

1. Find the equation of the line through the point (3, 5) that has a slope of 2.
   A) y=2x+1   B) y=2x–1
   C) y=3x-5   D) y=3x+5

2. Find the equation of the line through the point (11, 9) that has a slope of 5.
   A) y=5x–46   B) y=5x+46
   C) y=5x+55   D) y=5x–55

3. Find the equation of the line through the point (9,–3) that has a slope of –2.
   A) y=2x+15   B) y=–2x–15
   C) y=–2x+15   D) y=–15x+2

4. Find the equation of the line through the point (–3,–2) that has a slope of –1.
   A) y= –x–5   B) y= –x+2
   C) y= –x+1   D) y= x+1

5. Find the equation of the line passing through (–3,2) and (5, 3).
   A) $y = \dfrac{x+19}{8}$ B) $y = \dfrac{x-19}{8}$
   C) $y = \dfrac{x-16}{8}$ D) $y = \dfrac{x+16}{8}$

6. Find the equation of the line passing through (6, 3) and (–5, –3).
   A) $y = \dfrac{6x-3}{11}$ B) $y = \dfrac{5x-46}{11}$
   C) $y = \dfrac{6x-20}{11}$ D) $y = \dfrac{20-8x}{11}$

7. Find the equation of the line passing through (–7, 5) and (4, 1).
   A) $y = \dfrac{4x}{11}$ B) $y = \dfrac{27-4x}{11}$
   C) $y = \dfrac{4x+27}{11}$ D) $y = \dfrac{4x-27}{11}$

8. x+5y=15. Find the slope.
   A) $\dfrac{1}{5}$ B) $-\dfrac{1}{5}$ C) $\dfrac{3}{5}$ D) $-\dfrac{3}{5}$

9. Line m_1 has the equation y= $-\dfrac{1}{3}$x+5.
   Line m_2 is parallel to m_1 and passes through the point (3, 8). Find the equation of m_2.
   A) y= –3x+24   B) y= –3x–24
   C) y= $-\dfrac{1}{3}$x+9   D) y= $\dfrac{1}{3}$x+12

10. Line m has equation y= -3x+6. Find the equation of a line parallel to line m
    A) y= –3x+4   B) y= 3x+5
    C) y=3x+10   D) y= $\dfrac{1}{3}$x+6

11. m_1 line: 5x - 2y + 4=0
    m_2 line: 5x + my + 12=0
    $m_1 \| m_2$ if m=?
    A) 3   B) –3   C) 2   D) –2

12. Find the equation of the line.
    A) $\dfrac{x}{3}+\dfrac{y}{6}=2$
    B) $\dfrac{x}{3}+\dfrac{y}{6}=1$
    C) $\dfrac{x}{6}+\dfrac{y}{3}=1$ D) $\dfrac{x}{3}-\dfrac{y}{6}=1$

TEST – 90
Algebraic Functions

1. If $f(x)= -2x+5$, $f(-2)=$?
   A) 0   B) 9   C) 10   D) 12

2. What is the domain of $y = 3 - \sqrt{x-1}$
   A) $x \geq 2$ B) $x \leq 2$ C) $x \leq 1$ D) $x \geq 1$

3. $f(x)=3x^2+2x$ and $g(x)=x+2$, $(f\text{-}g)(x)=$?
   A) $3x^2+3x+2$ B) $3x^2+x-2$
   C) x^2+x-2 D) $2x^2+x+2$

4. Given $f(x)= -x+3$ and $g(x)=2x^2-5$, $(f+g)(3)=$?
   A) 11   B) 12   C) 13   D) -13

5. $(f+g)3=$?
   A) 8
   B) 10
   C) 11
   D) 12

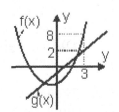

6. Find the inverse of $y = \dfrac{1}{2x} + 3$

   A) $\dfrac{1}{2x-6}$ B) $\dfrac{1}{3x-2}$

   C) $\dfrac{1}{6x-2}$ D) $\dfrac{1}{2x+6}$

7. Which of these graphs represents a function?

   A) 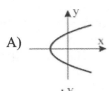   B)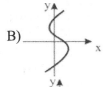

   C)    D)

8. Which of these graphs is not a function?

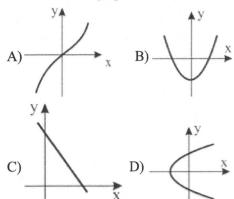

9. $f(x)=2x-t$ and $g(x)= \dfrac{1}{2x+t}$, $\dfrac{f(x)}{g(x)} = $?
   A) $4x^2 + t^2$ B) $4x^2 - t^2$
   C) $2x^2+ t$ D) $4x + t$

10. Find an equation for inverse of $y=2x^2+3$.
    A) $y = \sqrt{\dfrac{x-3}{2}}$ B) $y = \sqrt{\dfrac{x+3}{2}}$

    C) $y = \sqrt{\dfrac{2}{x+3}}$ D) $y=x^2+2$

11. A moving company charges \$45 for monthly truck rental plus \$3.60 per mile. Find the function.
    A) $y=45x+3.6$ B) $y=45x-3.6$
    C) $y=3.6x+45$ D) $y=3.6x-45$

12. A summer soccer club charges a one–time maintenance fee of \$25 plus \$5 for each day. Which function describes the situation?
    A) $y=25x+5$ B) $y=25x-5$
    C) $y=5x-25$ D) $y=5x+25$

TEST – 91
Data Interpretation

1. The pie chart in the figure shows a student's scores in Algebra I, Algebra II and Geometry exams. Which of the following shows the Algebra I : Algebra II : Geometry ratio?

    A) 3:2:4
    B) 4:3:2
    C) 2:3:4
    D) 3:4:4

2. The distance between cities A and B is 900km. Following graph shows the time–distance graph for two vehicles. How many hours does it take for these two vehicles to meet each other?

    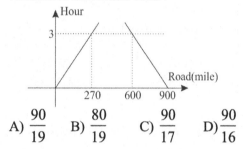

    A) $\dfrac{90}{19}$ B) $\dfrac{80}{19}$ C) $\dfrac{90}{17}$ D) $\dfrac{90}{16}$

3. Given table shows the number of employees of a company who come late to work for a month. Which of the following statements is wrong according to the table?

Late days	Late–coming employee	
	Male	Female
2–4	10	6
5–7	11	8
8–10	13	8
11–13	8	4
14–16	6	10

    A) Number of male employees who have ever come late is 48.
    B) Number of female employees who have ever come late is 36.
    C) Ratio of late–coming females to late–coming males is ¾
    D) The company has 84 employees total.

4. The following graph shows the number of female and male students in four classes in a school. Which of the following information is false according to the graph?

    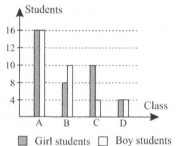

    A) The total number of students is 72.
    B) The ratio of total female students to total male students is 19/17
    C) The ratio of female students to male students in class A is 1.
    D) The highest percentage of female students is in class A.

5. The following table shows the costs and profit ratios of some books. If selling some physics books brings $702 of revenue, how many physics books have been sold?

Book Type	Cost	Income Ratio
Math	$60	25
Physics	$90	30
Chemistry	$40	10
Biology	$80	80

    A) 6   B) 7   C) 8   D) 9

6. The given graph shows the number of visitors to a museum between January and May. What is the average number of visitors in January, March and May?

    A) 1800
    B) 1900
    C) 2000
    D) 2100

7. The given graph shows the number and models of the cars that a car dealer has sold in a week. Which of the following is wrong according to the graph?

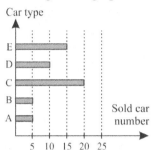

Car type

Sold car number

A) Models A and B are the least sold models
B) Average number of cars sold per model is 11
C) Sum of model A and E cars sold is equal to the model C cars sold.
D) Models B and C are the most popular ones.

8. The given graph shows the number of residents in an apartment building according to their professions. A: doctors, B: teachers, C: engineers, D: faculty members. Which of the following would be the pie chart of this graph?

Number

Job

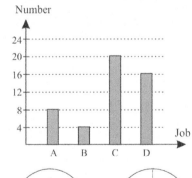

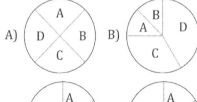

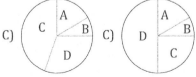

9. The graph given in the figure shows the amount of paper used in five schools. What is the average of least paper – consuming three schools? (y axis: school, x axis: packs of paper consumed)

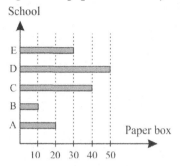

School

Paper box

A) 15   B) 18   C) 20   D) 22

10. Following graph shows the number of people who go shopping to a mall in a week. What is the ratio of weekend shoppers to weekday shoppers?

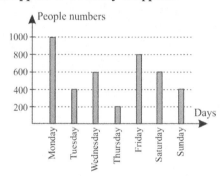

People numbers

Days

A) $\dfrac{5}{13}$ B) $\dfrac{5}{14}$ C) $\dfrac{6}{13}$ D) $\dfrac{1}{3}$

11. Following table shows the number of books and faulty books printed by a publishing company within 3 months. What is the probability of a randomly selected book being a faulty book printed in February?

	Jan.	Feb.	March
Number of published books.	900	1200	1500
Number of faulty books	18	20	30

A) $\dfrac{1}{90}$ B) $\dfrac{11}{180}$ C) $\dfrac{5}{180}$ D) $\dfrac{1}{180}$

12. Following graph shows the number of students who have graduated from four different universities in 2015. Which of the following information is wrong according to the graph?

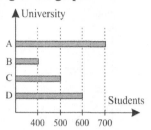

A) The average number of graduated students is 550.

B) The ratio of greatest number of graduates to least number of graduates is 4/7.

C) The university which is closest to the average is C and D

D) The university with the least number of graduates is B.

TEST – 92
Standard Equation of a Line

1. 6x–2y+12=0. Find the slope
   A) 6   B) –2   C) 12   D) 3

2. Given 7x+8y=14 find the x – intercept.
   A) (2,0)   B) (0,–2)
   C) (7,8)   D) $\left(\frac{7}{2}, \frac{8}{2}\right)$

3. 3x+5y=15 find the y - intercept
   A) (0, 3)   B) (3, 0)
   C) (5, 0)   D) (0, 5)

4. Given a line with $m = \frac{1}{2}$ and containing point (6,4) , find the equation of the line in standard form.
   A) 2y–x–1=0   B) 2x+y+1=0
   C) 2y-x-2=0   D) x+2y–1=0

5. Given points (2,4) and (3,5) on a line, find the equation of the line in slope – intercept form.
   A) x–y=4   B) x–y+2=0
   C) 2x+3y=2   D) y=x+2

6. Identify the line with the same slope as the line. $y = \frac{4x}{3} + 14$
   A) 3x+4y=14   B) 4x+3y=16
   C) 3y–4x-12=0   D) x+3y=14

7. Find the equation for the line passing through (2,4) and (-3;2)
   A) 3x+5y=17   B) 5x+3y=14
   C) 5y-2x=16   D) 6x+3y=12

8. 6x+4y=24. Find the slope.
   A) 6
   B) 4
   C) –6
   D) $-\frac{3}{2}$

9. Find the slope for the above graph.
   A) $\frac{5}{4}$ B) $-\frac{5}{4}$ C) $\frac{4}{5}$ D) $\frac{4}{7}$

10. Find the linear equation for the above graph.
    A) 5x+4y=1   B) 4x+5y=1
    C) 5x+4y= -20   D) 5x+4y=20

    Given: 5x+4y–20=0

11. Find the x – intercept.
    A) (0, 5)   B) (4, 0)   C) (4, 5)   D) (5, 4)

12. Find the y – intercept.
    A) (0, 5)   B) (5, 0)
    C) (0, –5)   D) (0, –4)

TEST – 93
Parallel and Perpendicular Lines

1. Identify the an equation of the that line passes through (4,–2) and is parallel to y=3x–2:

   A) $y=-3x+14$ B) $y=3x-14$

   C) $y=2x+3$ D) $y=\dfrac{x}{3}+2$

2. Given that y=6x+14 and y=mx+12 are parallel lines, what is the m?

   A) 6   B) 4   C) 3   D) 2

3. For what value of n are the graphs of 2x+3y=12 and 15y=nx+4 parallel?

   A) 10   B) 5   C) –10   D) –5

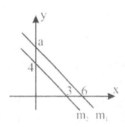

   If m₁, and m₂ are parallel lines.

4. a=?

   A) 5   B) 6   C) 7   D) 8

5. Find the slope of the lines in the above graph .

   A) $\dfrac{3}{4}$ B) $\dfrac{4}{3}$ C) $-\dfrac{3}{4}$ D) $-\dfrac{4}{3}$

6. Find the equation for the line m₂ above.

   A) 4x+3y=12   B) 2x+3y=6
   C) 3x+2y=14   D) 6x+3y+9

7. Which equation is perpendicular to y=4x+3?

   A) $y=\dfrac{1}{4}x+2$ B) $y=-\dfrac{1}{4}x+3$

   C) y=6x+5   D) y=-4x+ 3

8. Which equation is perpendicular to graph 4x+3y=18

   A) $y=-\dfrac{4x}{3}+2$ B) y=3x /4+8

   C) 2x+3y=6   D) 6x+7y=9

9. Which is the equation of a line that passes through (3,7) and is parallel to y=4x–6

   A) y=5x+4   B) y=4x+5
   C) y=4x+3   D) y=4x–5

10. Which equation is perpendicular to $y=\dfrac{x}{3}+4$?

    A) $y = 3x + 2$ B) $y=-\dfrac{x}{3}+4$

    C) $y = -3x + 7$ D) $y=-4x+7$

11. 4x+3y+7=0 and mx+5y+8= 12, are parallel lines. Find m=?

    A) $\dfrac{20}{3}$ B) $-\dfrac{20}{3}$ C) $\dfrac{3}{20}$ D) $-\dfrac{3}{20}$

12. 6x=8y+2 and mx+3y=14 are parallel lines. Find the value m?

    A) $\dfrac{4}{9}$ B) $\dfrac{9}{4}$ C) $-\dfrac{9}{4}$ D) $-\dfrac{4}{9}$

TEST – 94
Radical Equations with Quadratics

1. Solve: $\sqrt{3x+2}=4$

    A) $\dfrac{14}{5}$ B) $\dfrac{14}{3}$ C) $\dfrac{15}{3}$ D) $\dfrac{3}{4}$

2. Solve: $\sqrt{6x+13}=(x+3)$

    A) 1   B) 2   C) 3   D) 4

3. Solve: $\sqrt{x+3}=5$

    A) 20   B) 21   C) 22   D) 23

4. Solve: $\sqrt{x+2}=x$

    A) 1   B) 2   C) 3   D) –2

5. Solve: $\sqrt{x^2+2}+2=x-2$

    A) $\dfrac{7}{4}$ B) $\dfrac{4}{7}$ C) $-\dfrac{7}{4}$ D) $\dfrac{1}{3}$

6. Solve: $\sqrt{x+20}=\sqrt{x-1}+3$

    A) 3   B) 4   C) 5   D) 6

7. Solve: $\sqrt{3x-2}=\sqrt{x+10}$

    A) 6   B) 7   C) 8   D) 9

8. Solve: $\sqrt[3]{2x+1}=2$

    A) $\dfrac{1}{2}$ B) $\dfrac{1}{3}$ C) $\dfrac{1}{5}$ D) $\dfrac{7}{2}$

9. Solve: $\sqrt[3]{3x-1}=3$

    A) 28   B) $\dfrac{28}{3}$ C) $\dfrac{3}{28}$ D) $\dfrac{27}{4}$

10. $\sqrt{3x-3}=\sqrt{2x+2}$, $x=?$

    A) 5   B) 6   C) 7   D) 8

11. $\dfrac{\sqrt{5x+2}}{3}=\dfrac{1}{2}$, $x=?$

    A) $\dfrac{1}{5}$ B) $\dfrac{1}{10}$ C) $\dfrac{1}{15}$ D) $\dfrac{1}{20}$

12. Solve: $\sqrt{x^2+4x}=x+3$

    A) $\dfrac{1}{3}$ B) $\dfrac{2}{3}$ C) $-\dfrac{9}{2}$ D) $-\dfrac{2}{9}$

TEST – 95

Sets

1. A={9,10,11,12}, B={11,12,14}
   $A \cup B = ?$
   A) {9,10,11,12,13}
   B) {9,10,11,12,14}
   C) {11,12}
   D) {11,12,10}

2. A={7,8,9,12}, B={9,12,13,14}, A∩B=?
   A) {7,8,9}   B) {8,9,12}
   C) {9,12}   D) {9,12,13}

3. In a class of 36 students, 20 students register for art club and 12 for math club. How many students do not register for either club?
   A) 4   B) 5   C) 6   D) 8

4. Find the intersection of the sets
   A={2,4,6,8,10}, B={8,10,12,14}
   A) {8,10}   B) {6,8,12}
   C) {12,14}   D) {6,8,14}

5. A={1,3,5,7,9}, B={7,9,11,13,15}.
   Find the union of the sets

   A) {7,11,9}
   B) {5,7,13}
   C) {11,13,15}
   D) {1,3,5,7,9,11,13,15}

6. n(A∩B)=?
   A) 3   B) 4   C) 7   D) 8

7. n(B∩C)=?
   A) 7   B) 4   C) 11   D) 12

8. n (A∩B∩C)=?
   A) 4   B) 7   C) 8   D) 3

9. n(A∩C)=?
   A) 11   B) 10   C) 9   D) 12

10. Let A={n/n is positive integer less than 12.] and let B={n/n is a composite number less than 12.]   Find A∩B=?
    A) {4,6,8,9,10,12}   B) {4,8,10,12}
    C) {4,6,8,10,12}   D) {4,6,8,10,11}

11.

    Use the Venn diagram above to find A∪B=?
    A) {1,3,5,6}   B) {1,3,5,6,8}
    C) {1,2,3}   D) {3}

12.

    n(A)+n(B)=?
    A) 12   B) 16   C) 24   D) 28

TEST – 96

Translating Word Problems

1. Six less than six times a number is 12. What is the number?

    A) 2   B) 3   C) 4   D) 6

2. At school with 240 students, there are 60 more girls than boys. Find the ratio of boys to girls.

    A) $\dfrac{3}{5}$ B) $\dfrac{3}{4}$ C) $\dfrac{2}{5}$ D) $\dfrac{5}{3}$

3. Fifteen more than twice a number is twenty. Find the equation.

    A) 2m+20=15   B) 2m–15=20
    C) 2m+15=20   D) 2m–15=15

4. The difference of a number squared and 5 is 20. Find the number.

    A) 8   B) 7   C) 6   D) 5

5. Six less than seven times a number is equal to twenty one. Find the equation.

    A) 6x+7=21   B) 7x+6=21
    C) 6x–7=21   D) 7x–6=21

6. Seven eighths of a number is –14. Find the half of the number.

    A) –7   B) –8   C) –9   D) –10

7. The quotient of a number and 7 is 2. Find the square of the number.

    A) 196   B) 225   C) 256   D) 400

8. Three sevenths of a number is 9. Find 30% the number.

    A) 5.3   B) 6.3   C) 7.4   D) 8.3

9. When seven is added to six times a number, the result is 43. Find the number cubed?

    A) 146   B) 214   C) 216   D) 316

10. The length of a rectangle is 12 cm. and its perimeter is 40 cm. Find the area.

    A) 64 cm^2 B) 76 cm^2
    C) 86 cm^2 D) 96 cm^2

11. If eight is subtracted from three times a number, the result is sixteen. Find the 40% the number

    A) 2.2   B) 3.2   C) 3.6   D) 4.6

12. The sum of two consecutive integers is 41. Find the square of the larger number?

    A) 420   B) 441   C) 423   D) 436

TEST – 97

Arithmetic Progression

1. What is the common difference of a_n which $a_9 - a_1 = 48$?
   A) 9   B) 8   C) 7   D) 6

2. The first term of an arithmetic progression is 7, the last term is 56. Find the sum of all terms.
   A) 252   B) 242   C) 232   D) 222

3. Find the sum of the following arithmetic progression A. P
   2,4,6,8......98?
   A) 2300   B) 2450
   C) 2400   D) 2500

4. Let a_n be an arithmetic progression. If $a_1 = 13$ and $a_6 = 78$, determine a_{12}?
   A) 151   B) 152   C) 153   D) 156

5. Determine the difference of an arithmetic progression a_n, if $a_2 = 6$ and $a_{10} = 30$.
   A) 2   B) 3   C) 4   D) 6

6. Let a_n be an arithmetic progression if $a_2 + a_4 = 24$, $a_3 = ?$
   A) 12   B) 16   C) 18   D) 20

7. $a_{10} - a_4 = 12$, $a_5 - a_2 = ?$
   A) 10   B) 8   C) 6   D) 4

8. General term: $a_n = 2n + 4$
   Find the common number.
   A) 1   B) 2   C) 3   D) 4

9. $a_2 + a_8 = 40$, $a_5 = ?$
   A) 10   B) 16   C) 18   D) 20

10. $a_4 + a_{12} = 4m$, $a_8 = ?$
    A) 2m   B) 4m   C) 8m   D) 10m

11. $a_n = 7, 14, 21 \ldots \ldots$
    $a_{11} = ?$
    A) 77   B) 78   C) 80   D) 87

12. $a_2 = 12$, $a_4 = 24$
    Find the common difference.
    A) 7   B) 6   C) 5   D) 4

TEST – 98

Translations

1.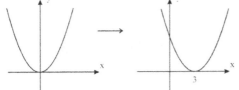

A) The graph moves two units right
B) The graph moves three units right
C) The graph moves two units left
D) The graph moves three units up

4.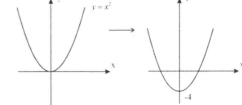

The graph moves
A) 4 units up
B) 4 units left
C) 4 units right
D) 4 units down

2.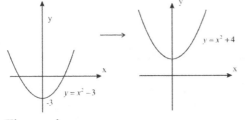

The graph moves
A) 4 units up   B) 6 units up
C) 7 units up   D) 6 units down

5.

The graph moves
A) 2.5 units down   B) 2.5 units up
C) 2.5 units left   D) 25 units up

3.

The graph moves
A) 2 units right   B) 3 units right
C) 5 units right   D) 3 units left

6.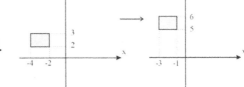

Move the object
A) 1 unit right, 5 unit up
B) 1 unit right, 3 unit up
C) 2 units right, 3 unit up
D) 3 units right, 2 unit up

7.

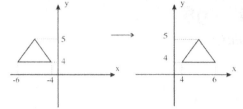

Move the object
A) 2 unit right
B) 4 unit right
C) 6 unit right
D) 10 unit right

8.

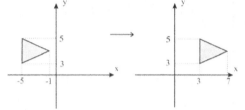

Move the object
A) 6 unit right   B) 7 unit right
C) 8 unit right   D) 9 unit right

9.

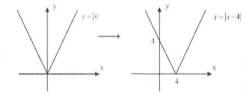

f(x) function moves
A) 4 unit up   B) 4 unit down
C) 4 unit left   D) 4 unit right

10.

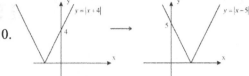

f(x) function moves
A) 4 unit left   B) 4 unit up
C) 9 unit up   D) 9 unit right

11.

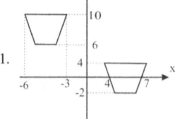

Move the object
A) 10 unit right, 6 unit up
B) 10 unit right, 6 unit down
C) 6 unit up, 10 unit down
D) 4 unit up, 6 unit down

12.

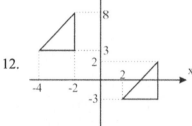

Move the triangle
A) 6 unit right, 6 unit down
B) 6 unit down, 5 unit right
C) 6 unit down, 4 unit up
D) 3 unit right, 5 unit down

TEST – 99
Data Interpretation

1. Figure shows the number of books sold by a publisher in a month. How many more physics – biology books are sold than history – chemistry books?

	History	Math	Physics	Chemistry	Biology
History				300	
Math				360	400
Physics					400
Chemistry	300	360			
Biology			700	440	

   A) 300   B) 350   C) 400   D) 500

The graph shows the number of pizzas ordered in schools A, B, C and D throughout a year.

☐ : PIZZA MARGARITA

▨ : VEGETARIAN PIZZA

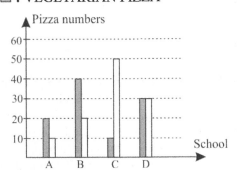

2. Which school has the lowest vegetarian /margarita pizza ratio?

   A) A   B) B   C) C   D) D

3. What is the ratio of margarita pizzas to all pizzas sold?

   A) 3   B) 2   C) 1   D) $\dfrac{11}{21}$

4. Following table shows the number of students and the amount of charities collected by the students in four schools.

School	Number of students	Amount of Charity
A	40	1600$
B	50	1500$
C	60	1800$
D	30	600$

What is the ratio of the charity collected by school B to the entire charity collected?

   A) $\dfrac{3}{11}$ B) $\dfrac{3}{10}$ C) $\dfrac{11}{3}$ D) $\dfrac{4}{11}$

5. The table shows the number of students studying at schools A, B, C and D in years 2014 and 2015. Which school's number of students has increased about 23%?

School	2014 Year	2015 Year
A	300	364
B	400	404
C	420	440
D	325	400

   A) A   B) B   C) C   D) D

6. Table below shows the ratio of salary expenses to the school budget for schools A, B, C, D and E in years 2014 and 2015. Which school's salary expense ratio has increased the least in 2015 with respect to 2014?

School	Ratio of salary expenses to school budget in 2014 (%)	Ratio of salary expenses to school budget in 2015 (%)
A	24	32
B	31	39
C	30	33
D	20	26
E	25	32

   A) A   B) B   C) C   D) E

7. Which of the following could NOT be found by using the data in the table in problem #6?

   A) Average budget of the five schools
   B) Average salary expenses ratio of the five schools
   C) Average increase in salary expenses for the five schools
   D) Increase of salary expenses for each school

8. The table below table shows the sports activities in a summer school and the number of students who attend these activities in years 2014 and 2015. Which sport has attracted the greatest number of new students in 2015?

Sport Activity	Number of students	
	2014	2015
Basketball	300	410
Football	300	370
Tennis	200	290
Swimming	320	500
Volleyball	130	160

   A) Basketball
   B) Football
   C) Tennis
   D) Swimming

9. The given graph shows the number of guests in a hotel according to their professions. If this graph was to be shown as a pie chart, what would the angle of the engineers be? (A: teachers, B: engineers, C: nurses, D: doctors)

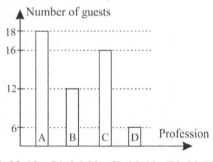

   A) 83.1°   B) 86.2°   C) 89.3°   D) 92.3°

10. Following table shows the number of students who have visited a science museum. By how much percent has the number of visiting students in May 2015 increased with respect to May 2014?

Months	2014	2015
February	240	180
March	290	240
April	390	440
May	440	490

   A) 11.4   B) 12.4   C) 13   D) 16

11. Let A be the sum of all the even numbers between 1 and 11. Let B be the sum of all the odd numbers between 2 and 12. Let C be the sum of all the prime numbers between 4 and 14.

   $$\frac{(A+B)}{(A+B+C)} = ?$$

   A) $\frac{65}{102}$ B) $\frac{65}{101}$ C) $\frac{65}{104}$ D) $\frac{66}{101}$

12. The table below shows the price of books in a bookstore. The books are either sold separately, or in packs of 3, while 3–pack books are sold with 60% discount. How much does a person need to pay if he buys 1 math, 3 physics and 6 chemistry books?

Books	Price
Math	15
Physics	20
Chemistry	30
Biology	40
History	10

   A) 47   B) 48   C) 50   D) 111

TEST – 100
Data Interpretation

The graph shows the four most popular forms of transportation and the daily number of passengers using them in a city.

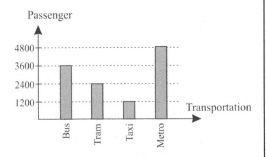

1. Which of the following is wrong according to the graph? (Bus–Tram–Taxi–Metro)

   A) Passengers use metro and tram the most.
   B) There are four times more passengers using metro than taxi.
   C) The number of bus passengers is 3 times the number of taxi passengers.
   D) Tram is the most expensive form of transportation, and buses have the least number of passengers.

2. What is the weekly number of passengers?

   A) 74000
   B) 84000
   C) 840000
   D) 940000

3. What is the average number of passengers for 4 days?

   A) 80000
   B) 90000
   C) 100000
   D) 110000

4. Following graph shows the number of pages that a student reads in 5 days. How many pages does he read daily on average?

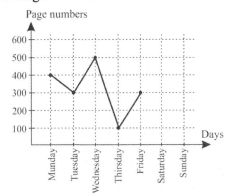

   A) 320   B) 340   C) 360   D) 380

5. Following graph shows the amount of water in a pool with respect to time while it is being emptied. How long does it take to empty this pool?

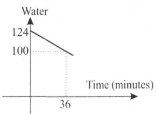

   A) 1 hour and 23 minutes
   B) 1 hour and 30 minutes
   C) 3 hour and 6 minutes
   D) 2 hours and 30 minutes

Please answer the questions 6–7 according to the information below.

Age	Comp. Eng.	Eco–nomy	Medicine	Civil Eng.
18–20	36	32	26	28
20–22	28	30	22	22
22–24	26	24	20	18
24–26	24	22	16	14

6. Which of the following is the major that the students aged between 20 to 24 studies the least?

   A) Civil Engineering
   B) Medicine
   C) Economy
   D) Computer Engineering

7. Which is the major that the students aged around 25 study the most?

   A) Civil Engineering
   B) Medicine
   C) Economy
   D) Computer Engineering

8. Following graph shows the number of questions a student has solved within a week. Find out the total questions that this student has solved in the two days that he/she has solved the most and the least questions.

   A) 380
   B) 390
   C) 400
   D) 420

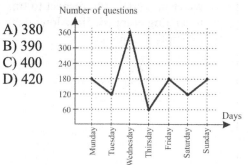

9. Following graph shows the unit price of four of five products and how many of each product has been purchased. If $1600 has been spent to purchase all these five products, what is the unit price of the last product, knowing that 6 of them were bought?

   A) 60
   B) 70
   C) 80
   D) 40

10. Following graph shows the number of books published by a publishing company. Which year has this company published 60 000 books?

    A) 2002
    B) 2004
    C) 2006
    D) 2008

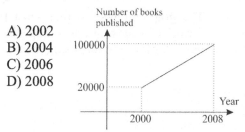

Please answer the questions 11–12 according to the information below.

Below table shows the results of a survey about future professions conducted with 11th graders of a school.

	Doctor	Comp. Eng.	Accountant	Teacher
Girl	20	12	18	18
Boy	10	18	16	10
Total	30	30	32	28

11. What is the probability of a student chosen being male or future computer engineering?

    A) $\dfrac{3}{4}$ B) $\dfrac{4}{5}$ C) $\dfrac{5}{4}$ D) $\dfrac{11}{20}$

12. What is the probability of a student chosen being female or future teacher?

    A) $\dfrac{11}{70}$ B) $\dfrac{37}{60}$ C) $\dfrac{35}{37}$ D) $\dfrac{47}{120}$

TEST – 101

Permutations

1. $\dfrac{6!}{4!} = ?$

   A) 40   B) 30   C) 28   D) 24

2. A password of 6 digits is made of digits 435113. How many possible passwords are there?

   A) 160   B) 170   C) 180   D) 190

3. How many ways can the letters of the word "Book" be arranged?

   A) 12   B) 24   C) 30   D) 36

4. 8 students have participated in a math competition, in which the top three get a prize. How many possible ways are there to get the prize winners?

   A) 330   B) 333   C) 336   D) 340

5. How many ways can you order 3 out of 10 different math books?

   A) 620   B) 640   C) 710   D) 720

6. Six students are to be arranged in a line from left to right. How many ways can they be arranged?

   A) 700   B) 720   C) 760   D) 840

7. How many ways can 5 people sit around a round table?

   A) 14   B) 16   C) 18   D) 24

8. How many ways can the letters of the word "Houston" be arranged?

   A) 30   B) 28   C) 24   D) 21

9. How many ways can the letters of the word "Turkey" be arranged?

   A) 700   B) 720   C) 730   D) 760

10. How many ways can 6 people sit around a round table?

    A) 120   B) 130   C) 140   D) 160

11. Find $_6P_3 = ?$

    A) 100   B) 110   C) 120   D) 140

12. Find $_8P_3 = ?$

    A) 336   B) 338   C) 340   D) 360

TEST – 102

Combination

1. How many ways can 2 teams be selected out of 10 teams?
   A) 45   B) 46   C) 48   D) 50

2. Find $_7C_3$=?
   A) 30   B) 35   C) 40   D) 45

3. How many committees of 4 can be formed from a group of 6 students?
   A) 10   B) 12   C) 14   D) 15

4. How many ways can a coach choose 4 goalkeepers from among 6 goalkeepers?
   A) 30   B) 32   C) 36   D) 15

5. 8 points are in a circle. How many quadrilaterals can be formed over the circle?
   A) 60   B) 65   C) 70   D) 75

6. How many ways can a basketball team of 5 players be chosen from 9 players?
   A) 110   B) 118   C) 121   D) 126

7. How many ways can a GT team of 4 students be chosen from 8 students?
   A) 70   B) 75   C) 80   D) 90

8. How many ways can a coach choose 6 goalkeepers from among 8 goalkeeper?
   A) 60   B) 45   C) 39   D) 28

9. A teacher whose class has 15 students wants to choose 3 for a math competition. How many ways can he choose 3 students?
   A) 325   B) 425   C) 435   D) 525

10. In a group of 8 people two $10 prizes will be given. How many ways can the prizes be distributed?
    A) 24   B) 28   C) 35   D) 56

11. There are 10 teams .A match needs 2 teams. How many ways can teams be selected out of 10 teams.
    A) 32   B) 36   C) 45   D) 38

12. Find $_6C_2$=?
    A) 10   B) 15   C) 30   D) 40

TEST – 103

Translating word problems

1. When seven is added to five times a number, the result is 37. Find the square of the number.

   A) 36   B) 49   C) 25   D) 81

2. The sum of 3 is and by $\frac{3}{11}$ of a number is 9. Find half of the number.

   A) 18   B) 17   C) 16   D) 15

3. The sum of 6 and 8 times a number is 78.

   A) 8+6a=78   B) 6+8a=78
   C) (6+8)a=78   D) 8a–6=78

4. 6 less than 5 times a number is 39. Find the number.

   A) 8   B) 9   C) 10   D) 11

5. What is 40 percent of 40?

   A) 12   B) 16   C) 18   D) 20

6. Six is .... less than eight. Which of the following fills in the blank?

   A) two   B) three   C) four   D) five

7. How much greater than $(m+3)^2$ is $(m–3)^2$?

   A) 6m   B) $2m^2$ C) 9   D) 12m

8. The sum of a number and a number square is 12. Find the number.

   A) 3   B) 4   C) 5   D) 6

9. The sum of half a number and the number is 12. Find the number squared.

   A) 44   B) 64   C) 81   D) 100

10. What is 20 percent of 30?

    A) 10   B) 9   C) 8   D) 6

11. How much greater than (7m–5) is (5–7m)?

    A) 14m   B) 10
    C) 14m–10   D) 14m+10

12. How much greater than (2m+n–5) is (n–2m+5)?

    A) 4m   B) 10
    C) 2n   D) 4m–10

TEST – 104
Geometric reasoning

1. How many triangle are in the figure?
   A) 3   B) 4
   C) 5   D) 6

2. How many rectangle are in the near figure.
   A) 4   B) 5
   C) 6   D) 7

3. Which equation could be used to find the value of a,b, c?

   A) a+b+c=180
   B) a+b+c=90
   C) a+b+c=75
   D) a+b+c=60

4. Which equation could be used to find the value a, b ?

   A) $\angle a = \angle b$
   B) $\angle b - \angle a = 180$
   C) $\angle a = 2\angle b$
   D) $\angle a + \angle b = 180$

5. Which equation could be used to find the value of a,b, x?

   A) $\angle x = \angle a + \angle b$
   B) $\angle x = \angle a - \angle b$
   C) $\angle x = \dfrac{\angle a + \angle b}{2}$
   D) $\angle x = \angle a - 2\angle b$

6. Which equation could be used to find the value of a,b, x?

   A) $\angle x = \angle a - \angle b$
   B) $\angle x = \angle a + \angle b$
   C) $\angle x = \angle b - \angle a$
   D) $\angle x = \angle a + \angle b + 90$

7.
   A) $\angle a + \angle b = \angle y + \angle x$
   B) $\angle a = \angle y$
   C) $\angle x = \angle b$
   D) $\angle a + \angle b + \angle y + \angle x = 180°$

8. Area of ABC=?
   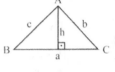
   A) $\dfrac{b \cdot c}{2}$ B) $\dfrac{b \cdot a}{2}$
   C) $\dfrac{a \cdot c}{2}$ D) $\dfrac{a \cdot h}{2}$

9. Area of ABC=?
   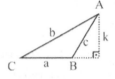
   A) $\dfrac{a \cdot k}{2}$ B) $\dfrac{k \cdot c}{2}$
   C) $\dfrac{b \cdot k}{2}$ D) $\dfrac{a \cdot c}{2}$

10.
    A) $a^2+b^2=4x^2$
    B) $a^2+b^2=2x$
    C) $a^2-b^2=2x$
    D) $\dfrac{a \cdot b}{2} = 2x$

11. ABCD is square. A(ABE)=?
    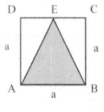
    A) $\dfrac{a}{2}$ B) $\dfrac{a^2}{2}$
    C) $\dfrac{a^2}{4}$ D) $4a$

12.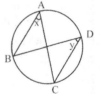
    A) $\angle x = \angle y$
    B) $\angle x = 2\angle y$
    C) $\angle y = 2\angle x$
    D) $\angle x + \angle y = 180°$

TEST – 105
Geometric Progression

1. Find the common ratio of the geometric progression: 7,21,63,189……
   A) 2   B) 3   C) 4   D) 7

2. Find the 8th term in the geometric progression: 6,18,54….
   A) 14383   B) 14482
   C) 14586   D) 13122

3. Find the number of terms in the geometric progression: 3,6,12, …,1536
   A) 7   B) 8   C) 9   D) 10

4. Find the 6th term of geometric progression: $\frac{1}{3}, \frac{1}{9}, \frac{1}{27}, ...$
   A) $\frac{1}{64}$ B) $\frac{1}{243}$ C) $\frac{1}{143}$ D) $\frac{1}{729}$

5. Find the common ratio: 180,90,45,22.5,….
   A) 2   B) 1   C) $\frac{1}{2}$ D) $\frac{1}{3}$

6. Find the common ratio: 5,10,20,40,80,…….
   A) 1.5   B) 2   C) 2.5   D) 3.5

7. $a_1 = \frac{1}{4}$ and the common ratio is 3. Find a_6.
   A) $\frac{243}{4}$ B) $\frac{243}{5}$ C) $\frac{233}{4}$ D) $\frac{143}{4}$

a_n: $\frac{1}{2}, \frac{1}{4}, \frac{1}{8}, ...$

8. Find the common ratio.
   A) $\frac{1}{2}$ B) $\frac{1}{3}$ C) $\frac{1}{4}$ D) $\frac{1}{8}$

9. Find the 10th term.
   A) $\frac{1}{2^8}$ B) $\frac{1}{2^9}$ C) $\frac{1}{2^{10}}$ D) $\frac{1}{2^{12}}$

10. Find the general term for: 4,8,16,32………
    A) 2^n B) 2^{n-1} C) 2^{n+1} D) 2^{2n}

11. Find the 5th term: 200,50,12.5,……..
    A) 0.78   B) 0.88   C) 0.98   D) 0.68

12. $a_1=3$, $a_2=1$ find the 6th term.
    A) $\frac{1}{27}$ B) $\frac{1}{81}$ C) $\frac{1}{243}$ D) $\frac{1}{256}$

TEST – 106
Simplifying Complex Fraction

1. $\dfrac{x^2 + 6x + 8}{(x+2)} = ?$

   A) x+4   B) x+2   C) x+3   D) x+5

2. $(x^2+9x+18) \div (x+6) = ?$

   A) (x+3)   B) (x+6)
   C) (x+8)   D) (x+7)

3. $(x^2+6x+9) \div (x+3) = ?$

   A) (x+3)   B) (x–3)
   C) (x+1)   D) (x²+2)

4. $\dfrac{x^2 + 4x + 4}{x+2} + \dfrac{x^2 + 14x + 49}{x+7} = ?$

   A) (x+2)   B) 2x+9
   C) 2x+6   D) x+6

5. $\dfrac{x^2 - 6x + 9}{x-3} + \dfrac{x^2 + 8x + 16}{x+4} = ?$

   A) 2x–1   B) 2x+1
   C) 3x–1   D) 3x–3

6. $\dfrac{a^2 - 10a + 25}{a-5} + \dfrac{10a}{a-5} = ?$

   A) $\dfrac{a^2 - 24}{a-5}$ B) $\dfrac{a^2 + 24}{a+5}$
   C) $\dfrac{a^2 + 25}{a-5}$ D) $\dfrac{a^2 + 27}{a-3}$

7. $\dfrac{3x^2 + 17x + 10}{3x+2} + \dfrac{x^2 + 10x + 25}{x+5} = ?$

   A) 3x+10   B) 2x+10
   C) 2x+8   D) 3x+11

8. $\dfrac{3x^2 + 13x + 4}{9x^2 - 1} + \dfrac{4}{3x-1} = ?$

   A) $\dfrac{x+8}{3x-1}$ B) $\dfrac{3x+5}{3x+1}$
   C) $\dfrac{4x+5}{3x-1}$ D) $\dfrac{5x+4}{3x-2}$

9. $\dfrac{x^2 - 4}{x+2} + \dfrac{(x+2)^2}{x+2} + \dfrac{x^2 + 6x + 8}{x+2} = ?$

   A) 3x   B) 3x+4
   C) 3x+6   D) 3x+8

10. $\dfrac{(x+5)(x+1)}{x^2 + 6x + 5} + \dfrac{x^2 - 14x + 49}{x-7}$

    A) x – 7   B) x – 6
    C) x – 5   D) x – 4

11. $\dfrac{4x^2 - 4x + 1}{2x-1} + \dfrac{1 - 4x + 4x^2}{1-2x} = ?$

    A) 0   B) 1   C) 4x   D) 2x+2

12. $\dfrac{(x+3)^2}{3x+9} + \dfrac{x^2 + 8x + 16}{4x+16} = ?$

    A) $\dfrac{7x+24}{12}$ B) $\dfrac{7x+20}{12}$
    C) $\dfrac{8x+20}{14}$ D) $\dfrac{9x+26}{12}$

TEST – 107
Word Problems

1. What is the maximum sum of two numbers whose product is equal to 60?

   A) 61   B) 62   C) 66   D) 68

2. If the sum of two consecutive even numbers is equal to 46, what is the smaller number?

   A) 18   B) 19   C) 20   D) 22

3. If two consecutive odd numbers add up to 52, what is the greater number?

   A) 17   B) 19   C) 21   D) 27

4. The sum of three consecutive even numbers is equal to 60. What is the greatest of these numbers?

   A) 19   B) 20   C) 22   D) 24

5. Three consecutive positive numbers add up to 36. What is the smallest of these numbers?

   A) 11   B) 12   C) 13   D) 14

6. The product of two consecutive numbers is equal to 156. What is the sum of these numbers?

   A) 25   B) 26   C) 27   D) 28

7. What is the least three digit number divisible by 3, 5 and 7?

   A) 102   B) 103   C) 104   D) 105

8. 3/5 of the 30 students in a class are females. How many male students are there in this class?

   A) 11   B) 12   C) 14   D) 15

9. 5/7 of the students in a class wear eyeglasses. If there are 14 students who don't wear glasses, what is the size of this class?

   A) 49   B) 50   C) 51   D) 54

10. Ahmet and Jack have $800 together. If the ratio of their money is 3/7 how much money does Jack have?

    A) $160   B) $180   C) $560   D) $480

11. ab and ba are 2 digit numbers. If ab–ba=27, a–b=?

    A) 6   B) 7   C) 8   D) 3

12. When the hundreds digit of a three digit number is increased by 3 and the tens and units digits are decreased by 5 each, how would this number change?

    A) increases by 145
    B) decreases by 245
    C) increases by 245
    D) increases by 154

TEST – 108
Word Problems

1. a and b being positive integers, if a:b=7/9, which of the following could be (a+b)?

   A) 11   B) 12   C) 13   D) 16

2. There are 25 students in a class. The ratio of male students to female students is 1/4. How many female students are there in this class?

   A) 20   B) 21   C) 22   D) 23

3. The passengers of a bus consist of males, females and children, whose numbers are proportional with 3, 4 and 2 respectively. If there are 36 passengers in this bus, how many of them are children?

   A) 12   B) 10   C) 9   D) 8

4. Positive integers x and y are directly proportional. If x=15 when y=20, which of the following is the value of y for x=12?

   A) 12   B) 16   C) 18   D) 20

5. Five workers with equal capabilities can prepare 60 fruit packs in a day. How many fruit packs can three workers prepare in a day?

   A) 32   B) 33   C) 34   D) 36

6. Positive integers x and y are inversely proportional. If x=14 for y=15, what is the value of y for x=21 ?

   A) 5   B) 7   C) 9   D) 10

7. Nine workers with equal capabilities paint a building in 24 days. How many days would it take for 6 workers?

   A) 30   B) 32   C) 36   D) 39

8. What is the product of two numbers, whose ratio is 9/10 and sum is 38?

   A) 300   B) 360   C) 370   D) 380

9. The ratio of two numbers is 5/7. If the smaller number is 25, find the greater number.

   A) 25   B) 28   C) 30   D) 35

10. How much does a customer who buys 400 g of honey at \$12.24 per kg need to pay?

    A) \$3.87   B) \$4.14
    C) \$3.88   D) \$4.90

11. What is 2/5 of a number, if 7/10 of the number is equal to 140?

    A) 80   B) 100   C) 120   D) 140

12. A student first reads 3/14, then reads another 9/14 of a book. What is the ratio of unread pages to the entire book?

    A) $\dfrac{5}{14}$ B) $\dfrac{6}{14}$ C) $\dfrac{7}{14}$ D) $\dfrac{1}{7}$

TEST – 109
Word Problems

1. A worker who gets paid $3600 yearly gets an increase of 1/20 of his salary. How much is his new salary?
   A) $4500   B) $4244
   C) $3780   D) $4487

2. What is 30% of 200?
   A) 40   B) 60   C) 70   D) 80

3. What is 60% of 40?
   A) 20   B) 24   C) 28   D) 12

4. A student solved 1/6 of the questions on a test and then solved 1/4 of the remaining questions. If he has solved 72 questions, how many questions are there on the test?
   A) 192   B) 194   C) 196   D) 198

5. Find the equation to represent 6 more than 1/5 of a number is equal to 8 less than itself?

   A) $\dfrac{x}{4} - 5 = x - 6$ B) $\dfrac{x}{5} + 6 = x - 8$

   C) $\dfrac{x}{2} + 5 = x + 6$ D) $4x - 5 = x - 6$

6. The ratio of Ahmet's pens to Jack's pens is 3/19. How many more pens does Jack have than Ahmet?
   A) 11   B) 16   C) 117   D) 22

7. Ahmet has $120 and Jack has $80. If Ahmet gives 3/4 of his money to Jack, how many times more money does Jack have than Ahmet?
   A) 5   B) 17/3   C) 17/4   D) 6

8. The weight difference between two cats with a weight ratio of 5/9 is 4.8 pounds. How much does the big cat weight?
   A) 12.9 pounds   B) 10.8pounds
   C) 16.5 pounds   D) 15.4 pounds

9. A car travels 5/12 of a trip, with 280 miles remaining. What is the total mileage of the trip?
   A) 210   B) 270   C) 480   D) 600

10. Three siblings with ages 1, 3 and 5 share their allowance of $270 proportional to their ages. How many dollars would the oldest sibling get?
    A) $140   B) $146   C) $148   D) $150

11. There are 75 students total in art, music and algebra clubs of a school. If the number of club participants is proportional to 3, 5 and 7 respectively, how many students have chosen music club?
    A) 15   B) 35   C) 45   D) 55

12. 16 workers with equal capabilities finish a job in 28 days. How many days would it take for 4 workers to finish the same job?
    A) 112   B) 116   C) 124   D) 128

TEST – 110
Word Problems

1. Positive integers a and b are inversely proportional. If a=16 for b=20, what is the value of b for a=5?

   A) 44   B) 48   C) 54   D) 64

2. How much does a person who buys 1200 g of walnuts sold for $8.24 per kg need to pay?

   A) $13.72   B) $14.24
   C) $9.88   D) $ 9.78

3. How much does a person who buys 1700 g of figs sold for $3.09 per kg need to pay to the nearest cent?

   A) $6.32   B) $2.25
   C) $5.253   D) $8.78

4. The edges of a triangle are proportional to 2, 4 and 6. If the perimeter of the triangle is 48 cm, how many cm is the shortest edge?

   A) 12   B) 10   C) 9   D) 8

5. The dimensions of a rectangle are proportional to 4 and 7. What is the minimum possible perimeter of this rectangle?

   A) 19   B) 22   C) 21   D) 23

6. The dimensions of a rectangle are proportional to 7 and 9. If the perimeter of this rectangle is 64cm, which of the following could be the area?

   A) 252   B) 250   C) 248   D) 160

7. Which expressions show the difference between 4 more than 5 times a number x and 3 less than 4 times itself?

   A) x+7   B) 2x+5
   C) 3x+10   D) 5x+10

8. Which expressions show the difference between the square of 4 less than a number x and 4 less than the square of x?

   A) 20–8 x   B) 10–8x
   C) 12–8x   D) 20–6x

9. Six more than twice a number is 28. What is the number?

   A) 10   B) 11   C) 12   D) 15

10. Six times a number a is equal to 60 more than two times itself. What is the square of a?

    A) 223   B) 238   C) 259   D) 225

11. One of the two numbers whose sum is equal to 65 is 4 times the other one. What is the product of these two numbers?

    A) 400   B) 500   C) 600   D) 676

12. One of the two numbers whose product is equal to 147 is 3 times the other one. What is the greater number equal to?

    A) 11   B) 16   C) 21   D) 24

TEST – 111
Word Problems

1. Ten less than 3/7 of a number is 8. What is the number?

   A) 42   B) 44   C) 46   D) 49

2. The sum of 10% of a number and 30% of the same number is 24. Find the number.

   A) 60   B) 55   C) 50   D) 40

3. After reading ¼ of a book, Jack realizes that there are 126 more pages to read. How many pages are there in this book?

   A) 168   B) 250   C) 400   D) 500

4. Jack has $35 left after buying a book with 2/9 of his money. How much is his initial amount

   A) $43   B) $44   C) $45   D) $48

5. The sum of ¼ of a number and 3/5 of the same number is 68. Find the number.

   A) 66   B) 77   C) 80   D) 96

6. Eight -ninths of a number is 64. What is 6 more than 1/3 of the number?

   A) 21   B) 22   C) 23   D) 30

7. AB being the greatest two-digit composite number, what is $\dfrac{A+B}{B}$ equal to?

   A) 2   B) 3   C) 4   D) 5

8. What is the ratio of the smallest two-digit prime number to the greatest two-digit composite number?

   A) 11/96   B) 1/9
   C) 11/95   D) 11/94

9. There are only double and triple rooms in a 28-room hotel. If the total capacity of the hotel is 66, how many rooms are double?

   A) 18   B) 13   C) 14   D) 16

10. A farm has both chickens and rabbits, totaling 20 animals .if there are 64 legs. How many rabbits are there?

    A) 16   B) 15   C) 13   D) 12

11. 6 kg of apples and 4kg of pears cost $13, while 3kg of apples and 5kg of pears cost $14. How much would 1kg of apples and 1kg of pears cost?

    A) $2   B) $3   C) $4   D) $2.80

12. The total number of teachers at a school is 4 times the number of male teachers. What is the ratio of male teachers to female teachers?

    A) 1/3   B) 1/2   C) 1/4   D) 1/5

TEST – 112
Word Problems

1. Jack's age is x and Mehmet is y years old. What will the sum of their ages be in 2t years?

   A) x+y+2t   B) x+y+4t
   C) x+y+2   D) x+y+3

2. The sum of Jack's and Mehmet's ages is 3x. Which of the following gives the sum of their ages t years ago?

   A) 2x+2t   B) 2x+t
   C) 3x–2t   D) 2x–2

3. The ratio of Jack's age 6 years ago to his age in 4 years is 3/8. How old is Jack now?

   A) 10   B) 11   C) 12   D) 14

4. A 25-year old mother has a 5-year old daughter. After how many years will the mother's age be 3 times that of her daughter?

   A) 4   B) 5   C) 6   D) 7

5. A 36-year old father has a 4-year old son. After how many years will the father's age be 5 times of his son's age?

   A) 8   B) 7   C) 6   D) 4

6. A 25-year old father has a 5-year old son. After how many years will the ratio of their ages be 3:1?

   A) 3   B) 4   C) 5   D) 6

7. A mother is 40 years old, while the total of her two children's ages is 16. Find the sum of the mother and the children's ages in 5 years.

   A) 42   B) 52   C) 54   D) 71

8. A father is 32 years old, while his son is 8 years old. What will the ratio of their ages be in another 8 years?

   A) 5/3   B) 5/2   C) 5/4   D) 5/6

9. The sum of a father's and his four children's ages is equal to 74. What was the sum of their ages 4 years ago?

   A) 30   B) 32   C) 33   D) 54

10. The sum of a mother's and her four children's ages will be equal to 98 in 5 years. What is the sum of their current ages?

    A) 73   B) 68   C) 58   D) 48

11. A mother is 42 years old while the sum of her two children's ages is 8. What will the ratio of the sum of the children's ages to the mother's age be in 6 years?

    A) 7/20   B) 5/12
    C) 9/20   D) 11/20

12. A father is 48 years old, while the sum of his three children's ages is 24. In how many years will the age of the father be equal to the sum of his children's ages?

    A) 6   B) 12   C) 8   D) 9

TEST – 113
Word Problems

1. What is the arithmetic mean of 30, 32 and 46

   A) 39   B) 36   C) 42   D) 44

2. What is the arithmetic mean of 10, 16 and –8?

   A) 15/4   B) 16/3   C) 16/5   D) 6

3. The arithmetic mean of A and B is 16, while the arithmetic mean of C and D is 24. What is the arithmetic mean of A, B, C and D?

   A) 12   B) 11   C) 10   D) 20

4. The arithmetic mean of three consecutive even numbers is 14. If the greatest one is 16, find the arithmetic mean of the other two numbers.

   A) 10   B) 13   C) 12   D) 14

5. If the arithmetic mean of 16 numbers is equal to 24, what is the sum of these numbers?

   A) 350   B) 360   C) 370   D) 384

6. The arithmetic mean of 16 numbers is 28. Twelve more numbers with a sum of 280 are added to this set. Which of the following is closest to the arithmetic mean of the new set?

   A) 16   B) 17   C) 18   D) 26

7. The sum of the ages of students in an art club is 368, while the average age is 16. How many students are there in this club?

   A) 23   B) 21   C) 21   D) 20

8. Jack can finish in job alone in 20 days, while Mario can finish in 15 days. How many days does it take for them to finish this job if they work together?

   A) 45/6   B) 45/7   C) 45/8   D) 60/7

9. Jack can paint a wall in 14 hours, while his brother can paint it in 16 hours. How many hours does it take to finish it if they paint together?

   A) 60/23   B) 50/22
   C) 60/11   D) 112/15

10. Together six equivalent workers complete a job in 15 days. How many days does it take for 8 workers to complete this job?

    A) 27   B) 45/4   C) 20   D) 18

11. A father is 33 years old, while his son is 3 years old. What will the ratio of their ages be in another 7 years?

    A) 6   B) 5   C) 4   D) 3

12. Two students remain ungrouped when the students of a class are grouped by 5, and 4 students remain ungrouped when they are grouped by 7. What is the size of this classroom?

    A) 32   B) 24   C) 27   D) 28

TEST – 114
Word Problems

1. There are 12 table in a physics lab, each one being designed for either 4 or 6 students. If the total seating capacity is 64, how many of the tables are for four?

   A) 9   B) 8   C) 6   D) 4

2. The average age is 32 in a 7-member art club. When m more members with an average age of 10 joins this club the new age average becomes 24. Find m.

   A) 3   B) 4   C) 5   D) 6

3. 10 liters of 24% sugar solution are mixed with 15 liters of 10% sugar solution. Find the new sugar percentage.

   A) 14%   B) 15.6%
   C) 17%   D) 17.3%

4. A 100cm×20cm paper is to be cut into square pieces. What is the minimum number that can be obtained?

   A) 6   B) 7   C) 8   D) 5

5. If the sum of 4 consecutive odd numbers is 56, what is the smallest of these numbers?

   A) 7   B) 9   C) 11   D) 13

6. Ahmet finishes a test book in 6 days by solving 20 more questions in a day than the previous day. If the book has 450 questions, how many questions has he solved the first day?

   A) 70   B) 60   C) 25   D) 30

7. If the sum of three consecutive even numbers is 78, what is the greatest of these numbers?

   A) 20   B) 22   C) 28   D) 30

8. How much would a book now cost with a price tag of $80 sold with a 30% discount?

   A) $40   B) $44   C) $48   D) $56

9. A bookstore profits $140 by selling a math book for $5 a copy, and loses $42 by selling each copy for $4. How many books does the store have in stock?

   A) 182   B) 162   C) 168   D) 160

10. There are two windows in some of the 20 classrooms in a school, while the rest have 3 windows. If there are 48 windows in total, how many classrooms are there with 3 windows?

    A) 10   B) 9   C) 8   D) 7

11. Which of the following numbers add to an integer when added to 6.25?

    A) 2.25   B) 3.74   C) 6.95   D) 6.75

12. A cat finishes a pack of food in 60 days, while its kitten finishes it in 80 days. How many days does it take to finish this pack if they eat together?

    A) 24.6   B) 26.8   C) 28   D) 34.3

TEST – 115
Word Problems

1. What is the percentage increase of an item sold for $280 which is originally priced at $200?

   A) 10%   B) 23%   C) 40%   D) 20%

2. What is the arithmetic mean of 3.24, 4.76 and 5.79?

   A) 4.26   B) 2.94   C) 2.96   D) 4.6

3. How many composite numbers are there between 3 and 21?

   A) 11   B) 10   C) 9   D) 8

4. What is the percentage increase from 160 to 180?

   A) 29%   B) 28%
   C) 12.5%   D) 16%

5. What is the simple interest on $3000 at an annual rate of 6% over 4 years?

   A) $720   B) $300   C) $350   D) $400

6. What is the simple interest on $9000 at an annual rate of 5% over 8 years?

   A) $3600   B) $3690
   C) $4200   D) $4800

7. If 16 pounds of watermelon costs $21, how much would a 48 pound watermelon cost?

   A) 48   B) 50   C) 63   D) 64

8. If the sum of five consecutive integers is 50, what is the smallest of these integers?

   A) 7   B) 8   C) 9   D) 10

9. The sum of two integers is 22. If the greater one is 8 more than the smaller one, what is the square of the greater one?

   A) 121   B) 144   C) 225   D) 256

10. Chickens in a farm finish a pack of feed in 40 days, while pigeons finish in 160 days. How many days does it take to finish a pack if chickens and pigeons are fed together?

    A) 22   B) 32   C) 25   D) 30

11. How many positive divisors does 28 have?

    A) 8   B) 9   C) 10   D) 6

12. Find the percentage increase in a squares area when each of the edges is increased by 25%.

    A) 156.25%   B) 51%
    C) 56.25%   D) 5.6%

TEST – 116
Word Problems

1. What is the least possible sum of four prime numbers between 12 and 24?

   A) 60   B) 64   C) 72   D) 76

2. Find the percentage increase in the area of a square when each of the edges is increased by 40%.

   A) 64%   B) 96%   C) 76%   D) 86%

3. The ratio of female students to male students at a school is 9:11. Which of the following could be the number of students attending this school?

   A) 84   B) 60   C) 127   D) 256

4. If the first day of a year is Friday, what day is the 196th day?

   A) Saturday   B) Friday
   C) Monday   D) Tuesday

5. For A being the greatest two-digit prime number, which of the following is the square of A?

   A) 9409   B) 9600
   C) 9877   D) 9742

6. Find the sum of all composite numbers between 3 and 13.

   A) 49   B) 37   C) 38   D) 59

7. If the first day of a year is Wednesday, what day is the 226th day?

   A) Monday   B) Friday
   C) Thursday   D) Sunday

8. Find the arithmetic mean of the numbers 10, 12, 14 and –16.

   A) 5   B) 6   C) 7   D) 8

9. Mehmet can finish a job alone in 9 days, while Jack can finish in 12 days. In how many days can they complete this job if they work together?

   A) 40/9   B) 40/7   C) 36/7   D) 7

10. Ahmet and Jack can finish a job in 20 hours when they work together, while Jack can finish it alone in 30 hours. How many hours does it take for Ahmet to finish this job alone?

    A) 70   B) 65   C) 60   D) 40

11. Mehmet can finish a job in 2m days and Jack can finish it in 3n days when they work alone. If it takes 10 days to finish this job when they work together, which of the following is the expression of n in terms of m?

    A) $\dfrac{7m}{3m+2}$ B) $\dfrac{6m}{2m-5}$

    C) $\dfrac{10m}{3m-15}$ D) $\dfrac{10m}{3m+5}$

12. Mehmet can work twice fast as Jack can. How many days would it take for Jack to complete a job alone, which they finish together in 16 days?

    A) 12   B) 24   C) 30   D) 48

TEST – 117
Word Problems

1. If eight equivalent workers can finish a job in 24 days, how many days would it take for 6 of them to complete it?

    A) 19   B) 24   C) 32   D) 35

2. A pipe can fill an empty pool in 14 hours, while another one can fill it in 16 hours. How many hours would it take to fill this pool if both pipes are opened simultaneously?

    A) 112/15   B) 60/13
    C) 50/11   D) 55/15

3. Mehmet and Jack can finish a job in 10 hours working together. If Jack can finish it alone in 14 hours. How many hours it will take for Mehmet to finish this job alone?

    A) 24   B) 26   C) 30   D) 35

4. Mehmet can finish a job in 3m days while Jack can finish it in 4m/5 days. If they can finish it in 14 days working together, what is m equal to?

    A) 12   B) 14   C) 19   D) 22

5. Jack and Mehmet are carpenters. Jack can finish 10 tables in 7 days, while Mehmet can finish 16 tables in 14 days. How many tables can they finish in 21 days if they work together?

    A) 90   B) 94   C) 96   D) 54

6. Mehmet can work three times as fast as Jack can. If they can finish a job in 15 days when they work together, how many days would it take for Jack to finish it alone?

    A) 62   B) 52   C) 60   D) 20

7. A pipe can fill an empty pool in 14 hours, while another one can fill it in 21 hours. How many hours would it take to fill this pool when both pipes are opened?

    A) 6   B) 6.8   C) 8.4   D) 7.4

8. A car is driven from city A to B with a constant velocity of 35 mph. If the distance between the two cities is 210 miles, how many hours does this trip take?

    A) 7   B) 6   C) 5   D) 4

9. How many hours would it take for a car with constant velocity of 75mp/h to travel the distance which could be taken in 8 hours with a constant velocity of 100 mp/h?

    A) 10.6   B) 11   C) 12.4   D) 13

10. A car travels from city A to B with a constant velocity of 60 mph and returns back with a constant velocity of 40 mph. What is the average velocity?

    A) 48   B) 55   C) 56   D) 59

11. Ten percent of twenty percent of a number is 32. What is the number?

    A) 1600   B) 1700   C) 1800   D) 1900

12. 60% of a class consists of male students and 30% of the male students are in football club. What is the percentage of male students who are not in football club to the entire class?

    A) 40%   B) 42%   C) 44%   D) 48%

TEST – 118
Word Problems

1. A book store buys some algebra books for $20 and sell them for $25. What is the profit percentage?

   A) 20%   B) 25%   C) 30%   D) 33%

2. A table costing $240 is sold with a loss of 20%. What is the sale price of this table?

   A) $200   B) $204   C) $208   D) $192

3. $3000 is deposited in a bank with a simple annual interest rate of 6%. How much money will be in the account in four years?

   A) $3200   B) $3000
   C) $2800   D) $3720

4. The sum of 15% of a number and 12% of the same number is 27. What is the number?

   A) 100   B) 150   C) 200   D) 220

5. Sonya solved 30% of questions in an algebra book. She solved 40% of the remaining questions. There are still 84 unsolved questions. How many total questions are in the book?

   A) 500   B) 400   C) 200   D) 220

6. A math book's price is increased by 30% to $39. What is the original price of the book?

   A) $50   B) $48   C) $40   D) $30

7. A bookstore loses $60 when new books are sold for $3 and profits $180 when they are sold for $4. How much did the bookstore pay for the books?

   A) $100   B) $200   C) $300   D) $400

8. What is the salt percentage of the mixture prepared with 28g of salt and 156g of water?

   A) 15%   B) 25%   C) 33%   D) 44%

9. 30kg of sugar is mixed with 90 liters of water. What is the sugar ratio of the mixture?

   A) 10%   B) 15%   C) 20%   D) 25%

10. A chicken can be fed for 20 days with a pack of feed, while the same pack is enough for a parrot for 30 days. How many days would this pack last if both of them are fed together?

    A) 18   B) 12   C) 11   D) 10

11. Find the sum of squares of all prime numbers between 4 and 12.

    A) 187   B) 184   C) 192   D) 195

12. Find the sum of all prime numbers between 1 and 30.

    A) 140   B) 136   C) 132   D) 129

TEST – 119
Word Problems

1. A rectangle's sides are in the ratio 9:11. If the perimeters is 80cm, what is the area?

    A) 130cm^2 B) 140cm^2
    C) 150cm^2 D) 396cm^2

2. Jack can paint a home wall in 12 hours. It takes 10 hours for Mario to paint the same wall alone. If they work together how long should it take to paint the wall?

    A) 24/7   B) 24/5   C) 60/11   D) 15/7

3. Jack is 14 years older than Mario. If the sum of their ages is 58 today, how old will Mario be in two years?

    A) 16   B) 15   C) 19   D) 24

4. In Angelina's rectangular garden the, ratio of the sides is 2 to 17. Find the minimum garden perimeter.

    A) 30   B) 32   C) 36   D) 38

5. Mario is 15, Jack is 16 and Xuis an 19 years old. Find their average age.

    A) 16.3   B) 16.6   C) 16.7   D) 16.8

6. Three student heights are 148cm, 172cm and 178cm. Find the average height.

    A) 160cm   B) 162cm
    C) 166cm   D) 164cm

7. There are 300 apples in a bag. 120 apples are green. What percentage of apple are not green?

    A) 78%   B) 60%   C) 80%   D) 81%

8. There are 30 students in a class. 12 student wear glasses. What percentage of students does not wear glasses?

    A) 60%   B) 66%   C) 67%   D) 68%

9. Jack's book has 1600 pages. He read 30% of the book. How many pages has he read?

    A) 490   B) 480   C) 460   D) 430

10. There are 24 students in a class. 25% of them registered for Geometry Club. How many students did not register for Geometry Club?

    A) 11   B) 12   C) 13   D) 18

11. Jack has $4000 in his saving account. The bank pays 3.5% interest per year. How much interest will Jack earn after four years?

    A) $200   B) $210   C) $560   D) $570

12. Find the sum of 7% of $70 and 60% of $60.

    A) $40.9   B) $42   C) $45   D) $46

TEST – 120
Word Problems

1. Mario saved $300. His brother saved 40% more than Mario. Find the difference of their savings.

   A) $60   B) $70   C) $80   D) $120

2. Seven times a number minus 6 is 22. What is the number squared?

   A) 16   B) 25   C) 81   D) 100

3. Six times a number squared is 54. What is the cube of the number?

   A) 8   B) 27   C) 125   D) 64

4. The sum of two numbers is 3. Their product is –28. What is the ratio of the numbers?

   A) -7/4   B) 3/4   C) -3/4   D) 4/7

5. The sum of two odd numbers is 2. Their product is –35. What is the sum of each number's square?

   A) 101   B) 103   C) 105   D) 74

6. How many composite numbers are between 3 to 31?

   A) 16   B) 17   C) 18   D) 19

7. How many prime numbers are between 6 to 36?

   A) 8   B) 10   C) 11   D) 12

8. Mario's room measures a by b feet, where a is the smallest two-digit prime number and b is the largest two-digit prime number. Find the room's perimeter in feet.

   A) 212   B) 214   C) 216   D) 226

9. The ratio of teachers to students in a school is 7:13. If there are 28 teachers, how many students are in the school?

   A) 100   B) 121   C) 132   D) 52

10. Seven math books sell for $28.14. How much do 6 books cost?

    A) $31.60   B) $24.12
    C) $33   D) $34.60

11. The lake water level decreased from 8.24m to 6.12 m. Find the percent of decrease?

    A) 20%   B) 26%   C) 30%   D) 36%

12. What is the total cost of a $40 pair of books, if the sales tax is 6%?

    A) $35   B) $36
    C) $33.50   D) $42.4

TEST – 121
Word Problems

1. A new book store marked up their stock 20%. What will be the new price of a $60 book?

    A) $91   B) $90   C) $88   D) $72

2. Ahmet bought a $22 geometry book at 20% off. How much did he pay for the book?

    A) $18.12   B) $19.62
    C) $17.60   D) $17.42

3. Jack invested $4000 at 4% for 6 years. How much money did he have at the end of 6 years?

    A) $6800   B) $7100
    C) $4960   D) $7800

4. Find the number that is divisible by 11 and 13.

    A) 572   B) 255   C) 372   D) 125

5. The members of a soccer team have heights of 1.65 meter, 1.67 meter and 1.77 meter. Find the mean of their heights.

    A) 1.697   B) 1.720
    C) 1.730   D) 1.740

6. Jack is one-fourth as old as his father. If Jack is 9 years old, how old is Jack's father?

    A) 32   B) 36   C) 42   D) 48

7. Jack has $142.72, which is $16.21 less than what Mario has. How much money does Mario have?

    A) $197.5   B) $196.5
    C) $195   D) $158.93

8. $\angle B$ and $\angle C$ are complementary angles. $\angle B : \angle C = 1:3$. Find $\angle B$ angle measure.

    A) 32   B) 22.5   C) 27   D) 30

9. The difference of complementary measures is 8 degrees. What is the measures of the larger angle?

    A) 60° B) 48° C) 44° D) 49

10. A 30° angle is supplementary to an angle that measures $4x^\circ$. Which of the following equations represents this situation?

    A) $0+2x=90$ B) $20-2x=90$
    C) $30+4x=180$ D) $20-2x=180$

11. Find the algebraic expression for the phrase 5 less than 6 times the square of a number m.

    A) $3m+3$ B) $3m-3$
    C) $3m^2+4$ D) $6m^2-5$

12. Find the number that is divisible by 17 and 15.

    A) 165   B) 175   C) 255   D) 275

TEST – 122
Combination

1. How many subsets of a 6-element set have 2 elements?
   A) 15　　B) 18　　C) 20　　D) 30

2. How many different ways can 4 pens be selected among 9 pens?
   A) 120　B) 126　C) 128　D) 160

3. C (5, 2) =?
   A) 5　　B) 10　　C) 15　　D) 20

4. C (5,3) + C (6,3) =?
   A) 30　B) 36　C) 40　D) 60

5. According to 8 girls and 6 boys apply to the school football team, how many different ways 2 girls and 2 boys can be selected?
   A) 55　B) 60　C) 64　D) 420

6. How many different ways can a group of 5 people be formed between 6 girls and 7 boys?
   A) 1200　B) 1277　C) 1280　D) 1300

7. How many different ways can 3 students be selected for the quiz among 10 students?
   A) 80　B) 90　C) 100　D) 120

8. In a group of 8 people, everyone is shaking hands with each other. What is the number of handshakes in this group?
   A) 56　B) 28　C) 20　D) 14

9. How many triangles can be drawn that accept 6 different points on a Circle?
   A) 20　B) 15　C) 14　D) 12

10. In a 10-question exam, students are asked to answer 8 questions. How many different choices can a student make in the exam?
    A) 90　B) 45　C) 42　D) 40

11. There are 6 different algebra books in the school library. How many different choices can a student get from two of these books?
    A) 15　B) 20　C) 30　D) 45

12. 8 lines in the same plane, how many points can they intersect with each other?
    A) 56　B) 28　C) 20　D) 16

TEST – 123

Counting Principle - 1

1. How many different ways can 1 teacher and 1 administrator be chosen between 4 teachers and 3 administrators?

   A) 7   B) 8   C) 10   D) 12

2. There are 4 different highways and 2 different railways from A to B. How many different ways you can go from city A to city B?

   A) 4   B) 5   C) 6   D) 8

3. There are 10 female and 12 male students in a classroom. Accordingly, how many different ways can one female student or one male student be selected in this class?

   A) 120   B) 60   C) 30   D) 22

4. There are 4 algebra and 6 geometry books in a bookshelf. Accordingly, how many different ways can 1 algebra and 1 geometry books be selected?

   A) 10   B) 24   C) 30   D) 2

5. How many different ways can a president and a vice-president be chosen from a group of 12 people?

   A) 144   B) 121   C) 132   D) 142

6. Set A={2,4,6,8,10}. Three-digit natural numbers are written with the elements of set A. How many numbers can be written with different numbers?

   A) 60   B) 40   C) 25   D) 20

7. How many different ways can 1 blue or 1 red ball be selected among 7 blue, 8 red balls in a box?

   A) 56   B) 54   C) 28   D) 15

8. How many different natural numbers can be written with the elements of set A = {7,8,9} .

   A) 3   B) 9   C) 18   D) 27

9. A={0,2,4,5}. How many different natural numbers greater than 200 can be written with the elements of set A?

   A) 50   B) 48   C) 44   D) 24

10. In a restaurant there are 5 different soups and 4 different pizzas. How many different ways can one choose 1 soup and 1 pizza at this restaurant?

    A) 10   B) 9   C) 20   D) 14

11. Ahmet has 5 different trousers and 3 different shirts. How many different ways can Ahmet wear 1 trouser or 1 shirt?

    A) 15   B) 8   C) 2   D) 16

12. There are 5 kinds of meat dishes and 4 kinds of soup in a 2 desert kinds restaurant. How many different ways can a person choose if he wants to eat only 1 meat dish or 1 soup at this restaurant?

    A) 40   B) 20   C) 11   D) 16

TEST – 124
Counting Principle - 2

1. Ahmet has 4 different t-shirts and 7 socks. Accordingly, how many different ways can Ahmet chose 1 t-shirt or 1 socks?

   A) 11   B) 12   C) 28   D) 30

2. How many different ways can 1 Biology or 1 Physic or 1 Geometry book be selected among 5 Biology, 3 Physic, 4 Geometry books?

   A) 60   B) 30   C) 12   D) 24

3. In a group of 14 ladies and 12 men, how many different ways can a leader be selected?

   A) 26   B) 20   C) 18   D) 4

4. Ahmet has 6 blue and 4 red pens. Accordingly, how many different ways can Ahmet chose 1 blue pen or 1 red pen?

   A) 24   B) 20   C) 18   D) 10

5. How many different ways can a chairman and a vice-chairman be elected in an 11-member board?

   A) 121   B) 110   C) 44   D) 88

6. How many different ways can a person with 5 trousers and 4 jackets choose a trouser or a jacket?

   A) 20   B) 12   C) 9   D) 8

7. How many different 3-digit natural numbers can be written with the elements of set A = {2,4,6}?

   A) 9   B) 12   C) 15   D) 27

8. There are 6 books of physics and 8 books of algebra on the shelf of a bookstore. How many different ways can a person choose 1 physics or 1 algebra book?

   A) 16   B) 15   C) 14   D) 12

9. There are 4 kinds of vegetable dishes and 5 kinds of pizzas in a restaurant. How many different ways can a meal and a pizza be chosen?

   A) 9   B) 10   C) 20   D) 24

10. 4 different Physics, 5 different Algebra and 6 Geometry books will be placed on a shelf. How many different ways can be placed?

    A) 120   B) 60   C) 30   D) 15

11. Houston-3 way - Dallas-5 way- Oklahoma city. How many different ways can go from Houston to Oklahoma city?

    A) 15   B) 12   C) 9   D) 8

12. There are 8 kinds of phone and 6 kinds of phone cases in a phone store. How many different ways can a person choose 1 phone and 1 phone case?

    A) 14   B) 24   C) 34   D) 48

TEST – 125
Measures of Central Tendency - 1

1. What is the arithmetic mean of 2, 12, 42 and 84?
   A) 20   B) 24   C) 25   D) 25.5

2. What is the arithmetic mean of 4, 4, 8, 10 and 24?
   A) 9   B) 9.5   C) 10   D) 12

3. What is the arithmetic mean of 6.4, 7.2, 9.4?
   A) 7   B) 7.2   C) 7.6   D) 7.8

4. What is the arithmetic mean of 24 and - 8?
   A) 8   B) 9   C) 10   D) 12

5. Find the median of 6, 7, 8, 10 and 4.
   A) 6   B) 7   C) 8   D) 4

6. Find the median of 6, 7, 8, 14.
   A) 7   B) 7.5   C) 8   D) 8.5

7. Find the median of 4, 8, 6, 102, 14.
   A) 4   B) 6   C) 8   D) 7

8. Find the mode of 4, 5, 6, 7, 7, 8, 9, 10.
   A) 6   B) 7   C) 8   D) 9

9. Find the mode of 4, 8, 9, 12, 12, 12, 19, 20.
   A) 9   B) 12   C) 19   D) 9

10. Find the range of the following numbers. 4, 9, 2, 14, 3
    A) 10   B) 11   C) 12   D) 13

11. Find the range of the following numbers. 21, 10, 84, 100, 94
    A) 90   B) 80   C) 70   D) 60

12. Find the range of the following numbers. 4, 27, 16, 97, 83
    A) 90   B) 92   C) 93   D) 94

TEST – 126

Measures of Central Tendency – 2
Mean Mode Median and Range

1. 4, 2, 8, 10, 10, 10, 6, 14, 32, 21 are given, accordingly answer the questions 1 to 4 below. Find the mean.
   A) 8   B) 11.7   C) 6   D) 14

2. Find the median.
   A) 10   B) 6   C) 8   D) 14

3. Find the mode.
   A) 4   B) 2   C) 6   D) 10

4. Find the range of numbers.
   A) 30   B) 28   C) 26   D) 21

5. 6, -4, 8, 2, -8, 14, 20, 9, 32, 6 are given, accordingly answer the questions 5 to 8 below. Find the mean.
   A) 8   B) 8.3   C) 8.7   D) 8.5

6. Find the median.
   A) 6   B) 7   C) 8   D) 9

7. Find the mode.
   A) 2   B) 4   C) 6   D) 8

8. Find the range of numbers.
   A) 40   B) 32   C) 30   D) 27

9. What is the median score on 8 math quizzes? 64, 72, 84, 76, 90, 82, 70, 66
   A) 70   B) 71   C) 72   D) 73

10. The mean of four numbers is 72. If three of the numbers are 44, 48, 68, what is the value of the fourth number?
    A) 84   B) 88   C) 88   D) 89

11. What is the mean of the following numbers? 14, 20, -12, 27, 44
    A) 18   B) 18.6   C) 20   D) 21

12. Find the mode of the following numbers? 4, 8, 12, 4, 9, 21, 6, 4, 7, 3, 3
    A) 6   B) 4   C) 8   D) 7

TEST – 127

Permutation

1. A = {2,3,4,5,6,7}. How many 3-digit natural numbers can be written using elements of set A?

    A) 70   B) 80   C) 128   D) 216

2. A = {4,5,6,7,8,9}. How many 3-digit natural odd numbers can be written using elements of set A?

    A) 108   B) 120   C) 160   D) 216

3. How many different ways can 6 different books be placed on a book shelf?

    A) 620   B) 680   C) 720   D) 820

4. How many different ways can they sit in a chair, provided that 2 out of 6 people are next to each other?

    A) 30   B) 32   C) 60   D) 64

5. At the end of a meeting attended by 20 people, everyone shook hands with each other. How many handshakes has been total?

    A) 160   B) 170   C) 180   D) 190

6. How many different 7-letters meaningful or meaningless words can be written using the letters of the word ALABAMA?

    A) 210   B) 220   C) 240   D) 280

7. How many different ways can 4 different books be placed on a book shelf?

    A) 40   B) 30   C) 24   D) 16

8. How many different ways can 8 people sit around a table?

    A) 4040   B) 4080
    C) 5020   D) 5040

9. How many different ways can one sit in a group of 6 people, provided that 2 people are always together?

    A) 120   B) 180   C) 240   D) 280

10. 4 boys and 3 female students are in a queue, how many different ways can they be placed?

    A) 7!   B) 6!   C) 5!   D) 4!

11. 5 different algebra books and geometry books will be placed on a shelf. Accordingly, how many different layouts can be made with the geometry books on the right and left head sides?

    A) 210   B) 220   C) 240   D) 280

12. How many 2-digits positive integer numbers are there?

    A) 70   B) 80   C) 84   D) 90

TEST – 128
Probability - 1

1. There are 6 blue and 5 yellow balls in a bag. What is theoretically the probability of a randomly selected ball coming blue?

   A) 5/11   B) 6/11   C) 1/6   D) 1/5

2. There are 4 blue, 6 yellow and 7 red balls in a bag. What is theoretically the probability of a randomly selected ball coming red?

   A) 17/7   B) 7/15   C) 7/17   D) 7/11

3. 12 people play basketball and 8 people play football in a class of 30 students. 4 people play both games. Accordingly, what is the probability that a randomly selected person from this group is playing basketball or football?

   A) 1/3   B) 9/15   C) 8/15   D) 8/17

4. In a group consisting of 6 geometry teachers and 4 chemistry teachers, 4 people will be selected. Accordingly, how many elements of events of this group have 2 geometry and 2 chemistry teachers selected?

   A) 60   B) 70   C) 80   D) 90

5. A file contains 12 green, 8 black, 7 blue paper. What is the probability that a randomly selected paper is green or blue?

   A) 19/27   B) 18/27
   C) 7/17   D) 7/27

6. Which of the following cannot be the probability of an A event?

   A) 1/3   B) 1/2   C) 0.25   D) 2.5

7. There are 7 yellow, 4 green, 8 blue balls in a bag. What is the probability of a randomly selected ball coming blue?

   A) 7/11   B) 19/8   C) 8/19   D) 8/17

8. There are 8 black and 4 green balls in a bag. What is the probability of a randomly selected ball <u>not</u> coming green?

   A) 1/3   B) 2/3   C) 1/4   D) 3/4

9. There are 12 balls numbered from 1 to 12 in a bag. If we take two balls in succession without being thrown back from the bag, what are the probability of the balls being even?

   A) 5/33   B) 4/33   C) 7/22   D) 8/19

10. There are 5 yellow, 7 green balls in one bag. What is the probability that both of them will be green if 2 consecutive balls are taken, provided that they are not thrown back into the bag?

    A) 22/7   B) 8/25   C) 7/20   D) 7/22

11. There are 4 boys and 3 female students in a group. What is the probability of that two of the people in this group will be girls?

    A) 6/35   B) 7/32   C) 9/35   D) 8/21

12. There are 8 boys and 7 female students in a group. what is the probability that one of the 2 representatives to be selected in this group will be a girl and the other one will be a boy?

    A) 8/17   B) 8/15   C) 9/15   D) 7/15

TEST – 129
Probability - 2

1. There are 10 cards numbered 4 to 14 in one box. What is the probability that a randomly selected card is a 6 or 12 card?

    A) 1/2   B) 1/3   C) 1/4   D) 1/5

2. What is the probability that the numbers on the top surface of a thrown dice are less than or equal to 3?

    A) 1/6   B) 1/3   C) 2/3   D) 5/6

3. What is the probability that a dice being thrown is 5?

    A) 5/6   B) 1/3   C) 1/6   D) 1/5

4. There are 14 eggs in a box. What is the probability that these eggs will be damaged in 2 randomly selected eggs?

    A) 10/91   B) 10/81   C) 5/91   D) 7/91

5. What is the probability that each of the 3 balls randomly selected from a bag containing 3 green, 3 blue, 3 black balls will each have a different color?

    A) 3/52   B) 3/56   C) 4/57   D) 3/29

6. What is the probability of having a prime number on the upper surface of a dice that is thrown to the air?

    A) 1/2   B) 1/3   C) 1/4   D) 1/5

7. What is the probability of an even number on the top surface of a thrown dice?

    A) 1/6   B) 1/5   C) 1/4   D) 1/2

8. What is the probability of 8 on the top surface of a thrown dice?

    A) 0   B) 1/3   C) 1/4   D) 1/8

9. There are 14 female students in a class of 20 students. What is the probability that a randomly selected student is male?

    A) 12/20   B) 6/10   C) 3/10   D) 3/8

10. 12 Americans, 16 Turks and 8 German students participate in a math competition. What is the probability that the first and second students will be German?

    A) 7/45   B) 4/45   C) 3/17   D) 2/45

11. What is the probability of having a prime number on the upper surface of a dice that is thrown two times?

    A) 1/2   B) 1/3   C) 1/4   D) 1/5

12. What is the probability of 3 on the upper surface of a dice that is thrown two times?

    A) 1/36   B) 1/18   C) 1/9   D) 1/3

TEST – 130

Sets - 1

1. Which of the following expressions specifies a set?

   A) Students of the school's math club
   B) Some teachers
   C) 2-digit prime numbers greater than 10
   D) easy questions in the exam

2. Which of the following expressions specifies a set?

   A) Some months
   B) Green vegetables
   C) Girls of the class
   D) Some regions in Houston

3. Which of the following expressions specifies a set?

   A) Deep seas
   B) Long rivers
   C) Warm countries
   D) Buildings with a height of more than 30 floors in Houston

4. Which of the following expressions specifies a set?

   A) Thin magazines
   B) Thin books
   C) Trees on the street
   D) Girl students in our class

5. Which of the following expressions do not specifies a set?

   A) Students getting high marks from physics
   B) Students getting 4 from biology in a class
   C) Students who get 1200 points from SAT in a classroom
   D) Students who get full mark from ACT in a classroom

6. Which of the following expressions do not specifies a set?

   A) One-digit prime numbers
   B) Two digits prime numbers
   C) Positive prime numbers less than 10
   D) Some odd numbers greater than 40

7. Which of the following expressions do not specifies a set?

   A) Prime numbers 1 to 12
   B) Odd numbers from 2 to 26
   C) Big houses
   D) Numbers with 25 squares

8. Which of the following defines the "A" set of prime numbers 6 to 16?

   A) A = {3, 5, 7, 11, 13}
   B) A = {7, 11, 13}
   C) A = {3, 5, 11}
   D) A = {3, 5, 7, 11, 13, 15}

9. Which of the following defines the "B" set of natural numbers less than 20, divisible by 4?

   A) B = {4, 8, 12, 16}
   B) B = {4, 8, 12, 16, 18}
   C) B = {8, 12, 16, 20}
   D) B = {8, 12, 16}

10. A = {m, n, k, L, m, n}. What is the number of elements of set A?

    A) 5   B) 6   C) 7   D) 8

11. Find the number of elements of the set consisting of the letters of the word "ALGEBRA ".

    A) 8   B) 7   C) 6   D) 5

12. Find the number of elements of the set consisting of the letters of the word "ALABAMA ".

    A) 4   B) 5   C) 6   D) 7

TEST – 131
Sets - 2

1. Which of the following sets consists of members of the word KANSAS.

    A) {KANSAS}
    B) {K,A,N,S,A,S}
    C) {K,A,N,S}
    D) {A,N,S}

2. Which of the following sets consists of members of the word ALASKA.

    A) {ALASKA}
    B) {A,L,S,K}
    C) {ALSKA}
    D) {A,S,K,A}

3. Which of the following sets consists of members of the number 4455678899.

    A) 9   B) 8   C) 7   D) 6

4. Specify the VENN diagram below, which are consists of prime numbers between 4 and 14?

    A) 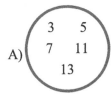   B)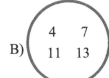

    C) 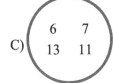   D)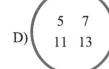

5. Which of the following sets becomes from prime numbers, which are less than 10 and divisible by 10?

    A)   B)

    C)   D)

6. Given sets A={10, 11, 12, 13, 14}, B={10, 11, 13, 14} ,then in order to B⊃A. Which of the following number must be added to set B?

    A) 11   B) 12   C) 13   D) 14

7. A={11, 13, 15, 17, 19} is a subset of which of the following sets?

    A) {11, 13, 15, 17, 21}
    B) { 11, 13, 17,19,21}
    C) {13, 15, 17, 19, 21}
    D) { 11, 13, 15, 17, 19, 23}

8. If given set B={3, 5, 7} then, which of the following set is a subset of set B?

    A) M={5, 9}   B) M={7, 9}
    C) M={5, 7}   D) M={5, 11}

9. If given sets M={3, 7, 9, 11, 13} and N={9, 11} then, show the correct set following A and B on the same VENN diagram.

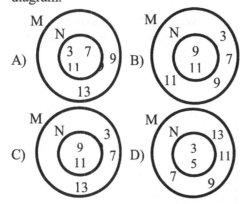

11. Find the number of elements of the set B, which consists of the letters of the word Oklahoma.

A) 9   B) 8   C) 7   D) 6

10. If given sets M={3, 5, 7, 9, 11, 13}, N={7, 9, 11}, K={11,9} then, show the correct set A and B on the same VENN diagram.

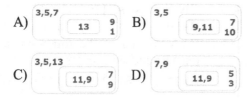

12. Find the number of elements of the set B which consists of the letters of the word Arizona.

A) 5   B) 4   C) 7   D) 6

TEST – 132

Sets - 3

1. Write N in the list format according to the given Venn scheme.

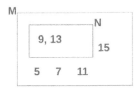

   A) N = {5, 7, 9, 11, 13, 15}
   B) N = {5, 7, 11, 15}
   C) N = {9, 13}
   D) N = {7, 11, 9, 13, 15}

2. Write L in the list format according to the given Venn scheme.

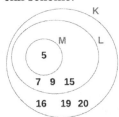

   A) L = {5, 7, 9, 11, 13, 15}
   B) L = {5, 7, 11, 15}
   C) L = {5, 7, 9, 15}
   D) L = {7, 11, 9, 13, 15}

3. Since M = {3, 5, 7} and N = {5, 7} which one of the below represents correctly?

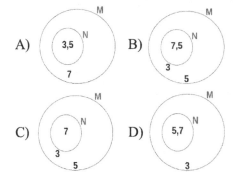

4. 4. A = {a, b, c, d} , B= {a, b, c, d} and C={c}. So, which demonstrates A, B, C sets correct?

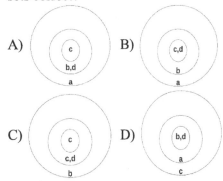

5. Which of the following is the proper list format expression for K, L, M sets?

   A) K={5,7,9,11,17} B) K={3,5,7,9,11,17}
      L={7,9,11,17}   L={7,9,11,17}
      M={11,7}   M={11,7}
   C) K= {5,7,9,17}   D) K={3,5,7,9,11}
      L= {7,9,11,17}   L={7,9,11,17}
      M= {11}   M={11,9,17}

6. Which one defines a set?

   A) smart students at school
   B) some students
   C) some administrators
   D) two-digit prime numbers

7. A= {7,9,11,13} so, What is the number of subsets of set A?

   A) 8   B) 16   C) 32   D) 64

8. A= {3,5,7,11,13} and B ={7,11,13,17} Find AUB ?

   A) {5,7,11,13,17}
   B) {3,5,7,11,13,17}
   C) {11,13}
   D) {5,7,11,13,17,21}

9. According to Venn diagram below find AUB?

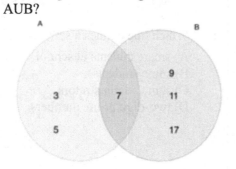

   A) {3,7,9,11,17}
   B) {3,5,7,9,11,17}
   C) {3,5,9,11,17}
   D) {7,5,9,11,9,17}

10. A= {7,9,11,17,21} and B= {17,22}. Find AUB set.

   A) {7,9,11,17,21,22}
   B) {7,9,11,17,22}
   C) {7,9,21,22,17}
   D) {7,9,21,22}

11. According to Venn diagram below find AUB?

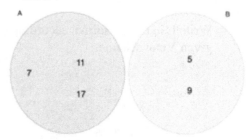

   A) {7,11,17}
   B) {5,9}
   C) {7,11,17,5,9}
   D) {7,5,9,11,9,17}

12. A={7,11,15,17}, B={11,19} and C={21,23}. Find (AUB)UC=?

   A) {7,11,15,17,19,21}
   B) {7,11,15,17,19,21,23}
   C) {7,11,17,19,21,23}
   D) {7,11,21,23}

TEST – 133

Sets - 4

1. According to the Venn Diagram given below, which is the AUB?

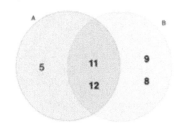

A) {5,8,9,11}   B) {5,8,9,11,12}
C) {11,12}   D) {11,12,15}

2. According to AUB = {11,13,14,17,19} and B= {14,17}. What is the number of elements of set A?

A) 2   B) 3   C) 4   D) 5

3. According to A={7,9,13,17} and B={11,13,19}. Which of the following is A∩B?

A) {11,13}   B) {11,13,19}
C) {13}   D) {13,19}

4. According to A = {5,7,9,13} , B= {7,9,13,15} and C = {13,15,17}. Which of the following is A∩B∩C=?

A) {13}   B) {17}
C) {13,15}   D) {13,15,17}

5. According to given Venn Sheme, which one is M∩N?

A) {11,12,13,14}   B) {11,14,15,16}
C) {13,14}   D) {11,12,15,16}

6. According to given Venn Scheme, which one is A∩B∩C=?

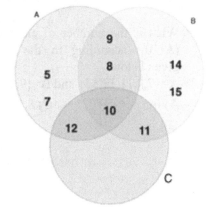

A) {9,8}   B) {11,12,10}
C) {9,8,10}   D) {10}

7. According to given Venn Scheme, which one is M ∩ N =?

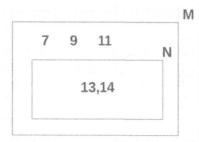

A) {11,7,9}   B) {13,14}
C) {7,9,13,14}   D) {7,9,13,11}

8. According to A = {7,9,11,13,15} and B= {11,13} and C= {11,13,15}. Which one is A ∩ B∩ C set ?

A) {13,15}   B) {13}
C) {11,15}   D) {11,13}

9. What is the number of elements of set (AUB,) according to the information given below.
A={7,9,11,13,15} and B={9,11,17}

A) 6   B) 7   C) 8   D) 9

10. s(AUB) = 14, s(A) =9 and s(A∩B) =5 What is the number of the s(B), according to given information above ?

A) 12   B) 11   C) 10   D) 9

11. According to given Venn Scheme below s(A U B) =?

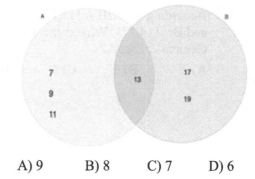

A) 9   B) 8   C) 7   D) 6

12. s(A) = 17, s(B) = 12 and s(A∩B) = 8 find s(AUB) =?

A) 18   B) 19   C) 20   D) 21

TEST – 134
Sets - 5

1. s(A∪B)=18, s(A)=10 and s(B) = 10. Find s(A∩B)=?

   A) 3   B) 4   C) 5   D) 6

2. s(M∪N)=18, s(N)=10 and s(M∩N)=8. Find s(M) =?

   A) 16   B) 18   C) 20   D) 22

3. M and N are two sets. s(M)=9 and s(N)=10. According to given information above, find maximum value of s(M∪N) =?

   A) 19   B) 18   C) 17   D) 16

4. A and B are two sets. s(A)=10 and s(B)=13. According to given information above, find maximum value of s(A∩B)=?

   A) 20   B) 21   C) 22   D) 23

5. M and N are two sets. s(M)=8 and s(M∪N)=17. According to given information above, find minimum value of s(N)= ?

   A) 10   B) 9   C) 8   D) 7

6. Since A={3,5,7,9,12} and B ={3,5,7,13}, find A – B set.

   A) {9,12}   B) {7,9,11}
   C) {3,5,9,7}   D) {9,7,13}

7. Since M = {5,7,8,11} and N = {8,11,13}, find M – N set.

   A) {5,7,8}   B) {7,8,11}
   C) {5,7}   D) {7,8,11,13}

8. A={2,4,6,8,10,12} and B={6,8,10,12,14}, find A – B set.

   A) {2,4,6,8}   B) {4,6,8,10,12}
   C) {10,12,14}   D) {2,4}

9. Which of the following refers to the shaded region, according to Venn Scheme given above?

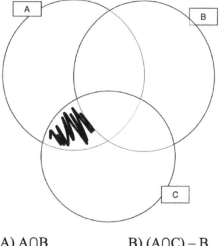

A) A∩B

B) (A∩C) – B

C) (B∩C) – A

D) (A∪C) – B

10. The number of students who are members of the Algebra and Geometry clubs is given in the Venn Chart above. How many students are members of Algebra Club?

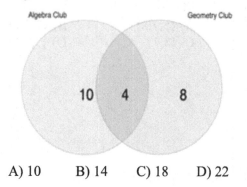

A) 10   B) 14   C) 18   D) 22

11. Turkish and Spanish speaking students are shown in the Venn Diagram above. According to this, How many students speak Turkish?

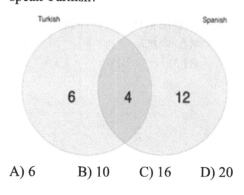

A) 6   B) 10   C) 16   D) 20

12. 75% of the students in a class speak Spanish and 30% speak Turkish. 25% of this class does not speak both languages. Accordingly, what percentage of students speak both languages?

A) 5%   B) 10%   C) 15%   D) 20%

TEST – 135

Angles

1. BD bisects ∠ABC. Find the value of x.

   A) 20
   B) 15
   C) 25
   D) 10

2. ∠EBC=?

   A) 75
   B) 65
   C) 80
   D) 70

   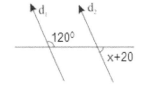

3. ∠B=90º, ∠DBC=54º, ∠ABD=?

   A) 26
   B) 36
   C) 46
   D) 50

4. ∠B=90º, ∠ABD=x+20º, ∠DBC=x, x=?

   A) 45
   B) 35
   C) 40
   D) 55

5. ∠ABC=90º, $\dfrac{\angle ABD}{\angle DBC}=\dfrac{4}{5}$, ∠DBC=?

   A) 40º
   B) 60º
   C) 80º
   D) 50º

   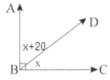

6. d₁∥d₂, x=?

   A) 16
   B) 30
   C) 15
   D) 25

7. d₁∥d₂, x=?

   A) 11
   B) 12
   C) 13
   D) 15

8. d₁∥d₂, x=?

   A) 10
   B) 40
   C) 30
   D) 50

9. d₁∥d₂, x=?

   A) 15
   B) 20
   C) 30
   D) 40

10. x=?

    A) 15
    B) 25
    C) 16
    D) 2

11. If ∠ABD–∠DBC=50º, ∠ABD=?

    A) 115
    B) 105
    C) 125
    D) 120

    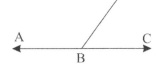

12. If $\dfrac{\angle ABD}{\angle DBC}=\dfrac{5}{1}$, ∠DBC=?

    A) 40
    B) 35
    C) 30
    D) 50

    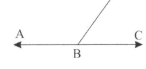

TEST – 136

Angles

1. $d_1\|d_2$, x=?

   A) 10
   B) 8
   C) 9
   D) 18

2. x=?

   A) 15
   B) 25
   C) 17
   D) 21.4

   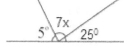

3. $d_1\|d_2$, x=?

   A) 15
   B) 25
   C) 28
   D) 30

   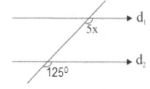

4. $\angle B=90°$, $\angle BAC$=?

   A) 10
   B) 90
   C) 50
   D) 40

   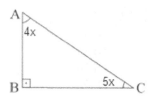

5. $\angle B=90°$, $\angle C=67°$, $\angle A$=?

   A) 13
   B) 23
   C) 63
   D) 35

   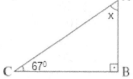

6. $\angle B=90°$, $\angle ABD - \angle DBC=18°$, $\angle DBC$=?

   A) 72
   B) 32
   C) 46
   D) 36

   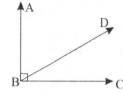

7. $\angle B=90°$, $\dfrac{\angle ABD}{\angle DBC}=\dfrac{5}{1}$, $\angle ABD$=?

   A) 15
   B) 45
   C) 65
   D) 75

   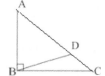

8. $\angle ABD - \angle DBC=50°$, $\angle ABD$=?

   A) 65
   B) 70
   C) 105
   D) 115

   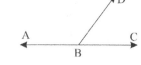

9. $\angle DBC$=?

   A) 15
   B) 30
   C) 150
   D) 75

   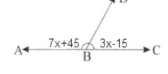

10. $d_1\|d_2$, x=?

    A) 15
    B) 25
    C) 55
    D) 30

    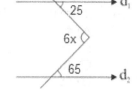

11. 5x=?

    A) 125–7y
    B) 120- 7y
    C) 120+7y
    D) 110–7y

12. $\angle B=90°$, $\dfrac{5x}{2}$ = ?

    A) 90–4y
    B) 110+4y
    C) 100–4y
    D) 45–2y

    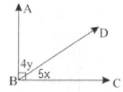

TEST – 137

Slope – Parallel Lines – Perpendicular Lines

1. Find the slope of the line that passes through the points (3, 5) and (7, 10).

   A) $\dfrac{5}{4}$ B) $\dfrac{4}{5}$ C) $-\dfrac{4}{5}$ D) 2

2. Find the slope of the line that passes through the points (6, 8) and (–5, 3).

   A) $-\dfrac{5}{11}$ B) $\dfrac{11}{5}$ C) $\dfrac{5}{11}$ D) $-\dfrac{5}{2}$

3. $y = \dfrac{x}{7} + 3$ Find the slope.

   A) 3   B) $\dfrac{1}{7}$ C) $\dfrac{1}{3}$ D) 4

4. Find the slope of the line that passes through the points (12, 16) and (13, 13).

   A) 1   B) $\dfrac{3}{2}$ C) $\dfrac{3}{5}$ D) –3

5. Find the equation of the line through the point (5, 7) that has a slope of 10.
   A) y = 10x – 43
   B) y=10x+43
   C) y = 5x + 22
   D) y= 5x + 40

6. Find the equation of the line through the point (6, 10) that has a slope of 6.
   A) y = 6x + 16
   B) y = 6x – 16
   C) y = 6x – 26
   D) y=6x–12

7. Line m_1 has the equation y= – 2x+5. Line m_2 is parallel to m_1 and passes through the point (4, 5). Find an equation of m_2.
   A) y = –2x+6
   B) y= –2x+13
   C) y=2x+12
   D) y=2x+12

8. $y = \dfrac{x}{5} + 5$ Find the slope.

   A) 5   B) –6   C) $\dfrac{1}{5}$ D) $-\dfrac{1}{5}$

9. y = 11 - 12x. Find the equation slope.
   A) –12   B) 11   C) 12   D) –11

10. 7x + 21y + 16= 0. Find the slope.

    A) $\dfrac{1}{5}$ B) $\dfrac{1}{3}$ C) 9   D) $-\dfrac{1}{3}$

11. 5x-10y+25=0. Find the slope.

    A) $-\dfrac{1}{2}$ B) $\dfrac{1}{2}$ C) $-\dfrac{1}{10}$ D) $\dfrac{1}{10}$

12. Line m_1 has equation y = -5x + 7. Find the equation of line m_2 that passes through B(3, 3) and is perpendicular to m_1.

    A) $y = \dfrac{x}{5} + \dfrac{12}{5}$ B) $y = \dfrac{x}{5} - \dfrac{13}{5}$

    C) $y = \dfrac{x}{5} + \dfrac{1}{5}$ D) $y = \dfrac{x}{5} - 5$

TEST – 138
Slope

1. $y = \dfrac{1}{3}x + 5$, find the slope.

   A) $-\dfrac{1}{3}$ B) $\dfrac{1}{3}$ C) $\dfrac{1}{2}$ D) $\dfrac{2}{3}$

2. $3x + 7y + 15 = 0$, find the equation's slope.

   A) $-\dfrac{1}{6}$ B) $-\dfrac{3}{7}$ C) $-\dfrac{15}{7}$ D) $\dfrac{3}{7}$

3. $y = \sqrt{3} \cdot x + 6\sqrt{3}$, find the equation's slope.

   A) $\sqrt{2}$ B) $-\sqrt{3}$ C) $\sqrt{5}$ D) $\sqrt{3}$

4. $y = \sqrt{5} \cdot x + 80$, find the equation's slope.

   A) $\dfrac{\sqrt{5}}{10}$ B) $\sqrt{5}$ C) $\dfrac{\sqrt{5}}{\sqrt{3}}$ D) $\dfrac{\sqrt{5}}{80}$

5. Line m has equation $y = 11x + 13$, Which equation is parallel to line m?
  A) $y = 13x + 11$ B) $y = -11x + 13$
  C) $y = 11x$ D) $y = -11x - 13$

6. m_1 line: $9x + 5y + 10 = 0$;
  m_2 line: $ax + 6y + 6 = 0$;
  $m_1 \parallel m_2$ if a = ?

   A) $\dfrac{54}{5}$ B) $\dfrac{55}{4}$ C) $\dfrac{5}{6}$ D) $\dfrac{10}{9}$

7. m_1 line: $3x + 7y = 28$;
  m_2 line: $ax + 5y = 10$;
  m_1 is perpendicular to m_2, find the a = ?

   A) $-\dfrac{35}{3}$ B) $\dfrac{3}{35}$ C) $\dfrac{35}{3}$ D) $\dfrac{7}{11}$

8. Find the d_1 line equation.

   A) $\dfrac{y}{2} + \dfrac{3x}{4} = 2$

   B) $\dfrac{y}{4} + \dfrac{x}{2} = 5$

   C) $\dfrac{y}{2} + \dfrac{x}{5} = 4$ D) $3x + 2y = 6$

9. Find the d_1 line equation.

   A) $\dfrac{x}{8} - \dfrac{y}{5} = 1$

   B) $\dfrac{y}{8} + \dfrac{x}{8} = 16$

   C) $\dfrac{y}{2} + \dfrac{x}{5} = 4$ D) $x + y = 8$

10. $A(3, 5)$, $B(10, 13)$. Find the slope of $\overrightarrow{AB}$?

   A) $\dfrac{7}{8}$ B) $\dfrac{8}{7}$ C) $-\dfrac{7}{8}$ D) $\dfrac{6}{7}$

11. $A(8, 6)$, $B(4, 3)$. Find the slope of $\overrightarrow{AB}$.

   A) $\dfrac{4}{3}$ B) $-\dfrac{4}{3}$ C) $\dfrac{3}{4}$ D) $-\dfrac{3}{4}$

12. $A\left(\dfrac{1}{2}, \dfrac{1}{5}\right), B\left(\dfrac{1}{4}, \dfrac{1}{6}\right)$
  find the slope of $\overrightarrow{AB}$.

   A) $\dfrac{3}{15}$ B) $\dfrac{2}{15}$ C) $\dfrac{15}{2}$ D) $\dfrac{13}{15}$

TEST – 139
Triangles and Angles

1. AB=AC, ∠A=76°, ∠B=?
   A) 52
   B) 54
   C) 62
   D) 65

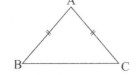

2. ∠A=86°,
   ∠ACD=126°,
   ∠B=x=?

   A) 60   B) 40   C) 50   D) 20

3. ∠A=60°, ∠B=90°,
   ∠ACD=5x, x=?

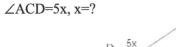

   A) 100   B) 150   C) 30   D) 20

4. ∠A=8x, ∠C=x,
   ∠B=90°, 3x=?

   A) 10   B) 40
   C) 30   D) 50

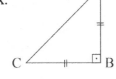

5. ∠B=90°, ∠A=∠C=2x,
   Find the value of 8x.
   A) 80
   B) 100
   C) 180
   D) 90

6. ∠A=124°, AB=AC,
   ∠B=?
   A) 28
   B) 30
   C) 26
   D) 40

7. ∠A=56°, ∠B=48°, ∠C=76°.

   A) AB > AC > BC
   B) |BC|>|AC|> AB
   C) AC > AB > BC
   D) BA > BC > AC

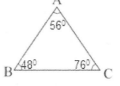

8. x=?
   A) 112
   B) 118
   C) 108
   D) 101

9. x+y=?
   A) 96
   B) 78
   C) 64
   D) 84

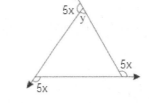

10. α=?

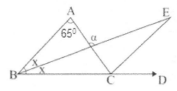

    A) 65+x   B) 2x
    C) 65+2x   D) 65-x

11. BD=DC=AD, ∠C=3x, ∠B=y, 2y+6x=?
    A) 120
    B) 150
    C) 180
    D) 190

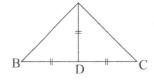

12. AB=AC, AD=DC, 2x=?
    A) 180–2α
    B) 90–2α
    C) 180–3α
    D) 360–6α

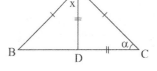

TEST – 140
Congruence and Triangles

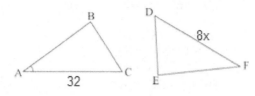

* ∠A=35°, ∠F=(5y–5)°, △ABC ≅ FED

1. Find the value of x.
   A) 4   B) 5   C) 3   D) 1

2. Find the value of y.
   A) 5   B) 8   C) 9   D) 10

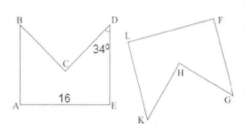

*   AE=16, ∠D=34°,
    FL=2x+4, ∠K=(7y–13)°,
    ABCDE ≅ FGHKL

3. Find the value of x.
   A) 8   B) 5   C) 6   D) 3

4. Find the value of 7y.
   A) 47   B) 48   C) 57   D) 50

5. ∠A=∠E,
   x=?
   A) 134
   B) 66
   C) 46
   D) 24

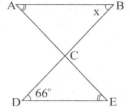

6. ∠F=83°, ∠C=(6x+11)°,
   Find the value of x.

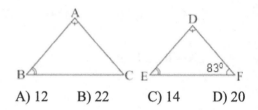

   A) 12   B) 22   C) 14   D) 20

7. ∠B=∠D=98°, ∠E=(3x-5),
   ∠C=∠F=60°, Find the value of x.

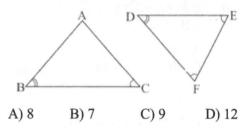

   A) 8   B) 7   C) 9   D) 12

8. ∠ABC ≅ EDF, ∠B=114°, ∠A=32°,
   ∠F=3x+4, Find the value of 3x.

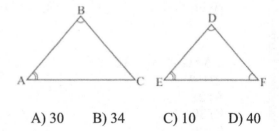

   A) 30   B) 34   C) 10   D) 40

9. Given ∠A=∠E, and ∠D=∠C, ∠B=m+14, Find the value of m.

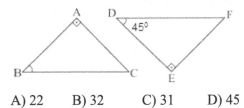

   A) 22   B) 32   C) 31   D) 45

10. Given △ABC ≅ △DEF, ∠A=75°, ∠B=25°, ∠E=(5m-5)°, Find the value of 2m.

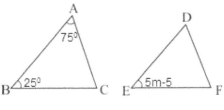

   A) 14   B) 16   C) 18   D) 12

11. DE∥BA, x=?

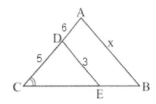

   A) $\dfrac{32}{5}$ B) $\dfrac{33}{5}$ C) $\dfrac{5}{33}$ D) $\dfrac{7}{30}$

12. DE∥BC, AE=12, EC=12, DE=16, x=?

   A) $\dfrac{88}{3}$ B) $\dfrac{80}{3}$

   C) $\dfrac{16}{3}$ D) $\dfrac{7}{3}$

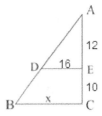

TEST – 141

Isosceles, Equilateral Right Triangles

1. AB=AC, ∠A=78°,
   ∠B=?
   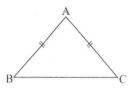
   A) 42
   B) 51
   C) 56
   D) 64

2. AB=AC, ∠A=3x,
   ∠B=x, ∠C=?
   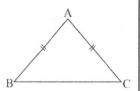
   A) 38
   B) 36
   C) 48
   D) 46

3. AB=AC, ∠ACD=110°, ∠A=?
   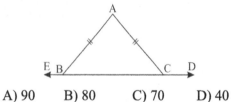
   A) 90   B) 80   C) 70   D) 40

4. AB=AC, ∠A=5y, ∠B=5x, $\dfrac{y}{3}$ = ?
   A) 180–2x
   B) 36–2x
   C) 90–5x
   D) 12-2x/3
   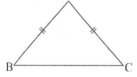

5. AB=AC, AB=30, AC=3x - 3, x=?
   A) 9
   B) 10
   C) 11
   D) 12
   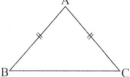

6. AB=AC, ∠A=44°, ∠C – ∠A=?
   A) 12
   B) 14
   C) 24
   D) 26
   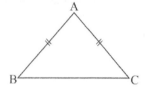

7. AB=AC, ABC is an isosceles triangle,
   DEF is an equilateral triangle. Find the
   sum of the two triangle perimeters.
   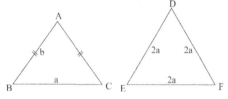
   A) 6a+b   B) 6a+4b
   C) 6a+2b   D) 7a+2b

8. ABC is an isosceles triangle, ∠A=56°,
   DEF is an equilateral triangle.
   (∠B)+(∠D)=?
   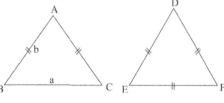
   A) 110   B) 116   C) 118   D) 122

9. ABC is an equilateral triangle. 2x–y=?

A) 90
B) 120
C) 160
D) 180

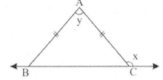

11. ABC is an isosceles triangle, ∠A=x, ∠B=2x+30°, x=?

A) 24
B) 48
C) $\frac{140}{5}$
D) $\frac{50}{3}$

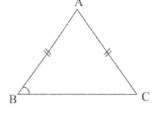

10. ABC is an isosceles triangle, AB=2, BC=6x, DEF is an equilateral triangle, DF=6x+2. Find the sum of the perimeters P(DEF) + P(ABC) =?

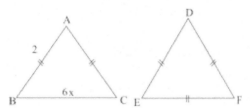

A) 24x–12
B) 24x+10
C) 24x+16
D) 10x+24

12. Find the sum of all triangle perimeters.

A) 50
B) 24
C) 20
D) 32

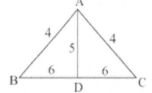

TEST – 142

Bisectors, Median of a Triangle

1. Find the perimeter of triangle.

   A) 4x+4
   B) 6x+6
   C) 6+4x
   D) 12x

   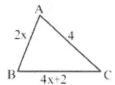

2. How many triangles are in the figure?

   A) 3
   B) 2
   C) 4
   D) 5

   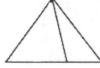

3. Find the sum of triangle perimeters.

   A) 38
   B) 36
   C) 35
   D) 34

   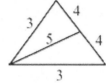

4. How many triangles are in the figure?

   A) 5
   B) 6
   C) 7
   D) 8

* A(ABD)=40cm^2,
  BD=5cm,
  DC=6cm.

   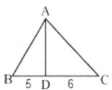

5. Find the area of ΔADC.
   A) 36   B) 40   C) 48   D) 50

6. Find the area of ABC.
   A) 48   B) 68   C) 88   D) 90

   * ∠A=60°,
     AB=AC.

   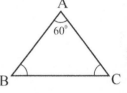

7. Find the ∠C?
   A) 40   B) 50   C) 55   D) 60

8. Find the relationship between the above triangle sides.

   A) ∠A=∠B=∠C
   B) ∠A>∠C>∠B
   C) ∠A<∠B<∠C
   D) ∠A=∠C>∠B

   * AC=CD, ∠B=35°,
     ∠BAC=25°.

   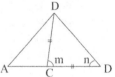

9. n=?
   A) 50   B) 40   C) 60   D) 75

10. m=?
    A) 50   B) 55   C) 60   D) 90

11. Which of the following could not be the x?

    A) 10   B) 9
    C) 13   D) 15

12. Perimeter ABC is 41cm. x=?
    A) 6
    B) 7
    C) 8
    D) 9

TEST – 143
Midsegment Theorem, Midpoint Foremula

1. EF∥BC, BC=42cm, EF=?
   A) 21
   B) 24
   C) 26
   D) 16

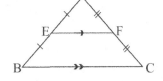

2. DE∥BC, DE=13cm, BC=?
   A) 13
   B) 26
   C) 33
   D) 36

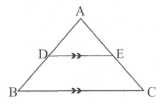

3. DE∥BC, AD=DB, DE=5k, BC=8k+6, BC - DE=?
   A) 45
   B) 15
   C) 30
   D) 24

4. DE∥BC, AD=DB, DE=37, BC=6x+8, x=?
   A) 8
   B) 9
   C) 11
   D) 11.5

5. KE=15, KD=11, DK∥BC, EK∥AC, AC+BC=?
   A) 50
   B) 52
   C) 54
   D) 58

6. BC=2DE, DE∥BC AD=4, AB =?
   A) 4
   B) 8
   C) 12
   D) 16

7. Point A is at (–10, –8) and point B is at (–4, 8). What is the midpoint of line segment AB?
   A) (–7, –2)   B) (–7, 0)
   C) (–9, –2)   D) (–2, 7)

8. A(–5, 13), B(9, 19). Find the midpoint of line segment $\overline{AB}$.
   A)(2,16)   B) (2, 8)
   C) (7, –1)   D) (–1, 8)

9. K is the midpoint of AB. The coordinates K(–3, 7) and A(5, 2) are given. Find the coordinates of point B.
   A) (–11,12)   B) (–16, –9)
   C) (10, 4)   D) (–8, 4)

10. What is the midpoint of the straight line segment joining the points (–3, 7) and (–9, 13)?
    A) (–6, –8)   B) (–6, 10)
    C) (10, –5)   D) (–5, 10)

11. DE∥BC, AD=DB, DE=0.5x+1, BC=?
    A) 2x+6
    B) x +2
    C) 3x+2
    D) 4x+4

12. DE∥AC, BD=DC, DE=3x- 6, AC=?
    A) 4x-5
    B) 5x-4
    C) 6x-12
    D) 4x-6

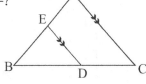

TEST – 144
Parallelograms

1. $\angle C=64°$, $\angle D-\angle A=?$
   A) 52
   B) 53
   C) 54
   D) 55

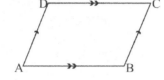

2. $\angle B=130°$, $\angle A=2x$, $x=?$
   A) 50
   B) 30
   C) 25
   D) 15

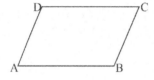

3. How many parallelograms are in the figure?
   A) 1
   B) 2
   C) 3
   D) 4

4. ABCD is a parallelogram. $\angle B=108°$, $\angle D+\angle B=3x$, $2x=?$
   A) 72
   B) 62
   C) 144
   D) 124

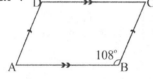

5. $\angle C=48°$, $\angle A=m$, $\angle B=n$, $2n-3m=?$
   A) 120
   B) 90
   C) 110
   D) 86

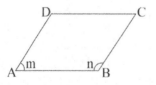

6. ABCD is a parallelogram. $\angle CBE=58°$, $\angle B-\angle C=?$
   A) 122
   B) 112
   C) 64
   D) 52

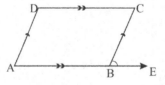

7. ABCD is a parallelogram. AB=27, BC=$\sqrt{28}$, $3x+y^2=?$
   A) 34
   B) $27+\sqrt{7}$
   C) $4+\sqrt{3}$
   D) $9+\sqrt{7}$

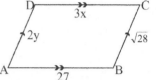

8. ABCD is a parallelogram. AB=5x, BC=3y, $2m+5n=?$
   A) 25
   B) 30
   C) 33
   D) 34

9. $\angle A=120°$, $2x?$
   A) 160
   B) 150
   C) 130
   D) 120

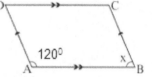

10. ABCD is a parallelogram. $\angle A=5x$, $\angle B=3y$, $10x+6y=?$
    A) 90
    B) 180
    C) 220
    D) 360

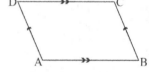

11. Find the perimeter ABCD. AB=x+8, BC=5+x
    A) 26+4x
    B) 4x+16
    C) 30+6x
    D) 4x+18

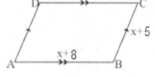

12. DC+AD=?
    A) 4
    B) 2
    C) 2x+8
    D) x – 2

TEST – 145
Rhombuses, Rectangles and Squares

1. ABCD is a rhombus. AB=4x, BC=24, x=?

    A) 8   B) 6
    C) 16   D) 12

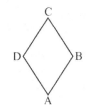

2. ABCD is a square. AL=LB=BE=EC. How many square in the figure?

    A) 3   B) 5
    C) 7   D) 8

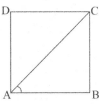

3. ABCD is a square. ∠BAC=3x, ∠ABC=3y, y+x=?

    A) 30
    B) 7.5
    C) 45
    D) 12.5

4. ABCD is a rhombus. ∠A=39°, ∠C=2x, x=?

    A) 16
    B) 24
    C) 19.5
    D) 34

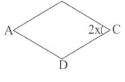

5. ABCD is a parallelogram. AC=48, 2AE–BE=33, BD=?

    A) 15
    B) 30
    C) 36
    D) 48

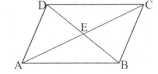

6. ABCD is a rectangle. AB=2x+13, DC=43, BC=3y+3, 2x-2y=10, AD=?

    A) 30
    B) 33
    C) 26
    D) 27

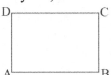

7. ABCD is a rectangle. KLMN is a square. AB=8, BC=6, KL=5, P(KLMN):P(ABCD)=?

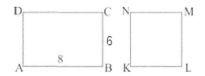

    A) $\frac{2}{3}$ B) $\frac{3\sqrt{7}}{2}$ C) $\frac{3}{2}$ D) $\frac{5}{7}$

8. ABCD is a rectangle. KLMN is a square. If 3a+b=34, P(ABCD)+P(KLMN)=?

    A) 34   B) 41   C) 60   D) 68

9. ABCD is a square. AE=21cm, BD=?

    A) 21   B) 16
    C) 18   D) 42

10. ABCD is a rhombus. AC=24cm, AB =13cm, BD =?

    A) 25   B) 24
    C) 23   D) 10

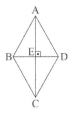

11. Find the perimeter of ABCD.

    A) 6x+16
    B) 5x+10
    C) 6x+ 6
    D) 2x+6

12. Find the area of ABCD.
    A) 6x   B) 6x+9
    C) 9x+15   D) 12x+6

TEST – 146

Areas of Triangles and Quadrilaterals

1. ABC is a triangle. AB=10, DC=3, Find the area of △ABC.

    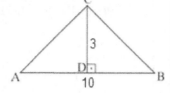

    A) 42
    B) 30
    C) 25
    D) 15

2. ABC is a triangle. AB=12, BC=5, Find the area of △ABC.

    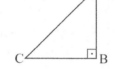

    A) 30
    B) 72
    C) 46
    D) 48

3. AB=x+3, BC=6, A(ABC)=24 cm², x=?

    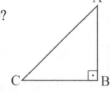

    A) 2
    B) 3
    C) 4
    D) 5

4. A(ABC)=24, AD=8, BC=?

    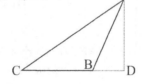

    A) 3
    B) 4
    C) 5
    D) 6

5. A(ABC)=12 sq unit, x=?

    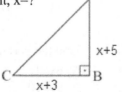

    A) 1
    B) 2
    C) 3
    D) 4

6. AB=AC=BC=10 cm, A(ABC)=?

    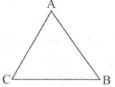

    A) 144
    B) $25\sqrt{3}$
    C) $15\sqrt{3}$
    D) $36\sqrt{3}$

7. ABC is a triangle. ∠A=∠C=45°, A(ABC)=16 cm², BC=?

    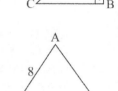

    A) $4\sqrt{2}$ B) $2\sqrt{3}$
    C) $2\sqrt{5}$ D) $2\sqrt{6}$

8. ∠B=α=30°, AB=8, BC=10, A(ABC)=?

    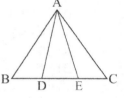

    A) 12
    B) 16
    C) 20
    D) 28

9. ABC is a triangle. BD=DE=EC, A(ABD)=7cm², A(ABC)=?

    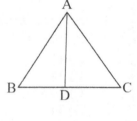

    A) 12   B) 16
    C) 21   D) 24

10. $\dfrac{BD}{DC}=\dfrac{4}{7}$, A(ABD)=16cm², A(ABC)=?

    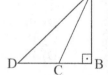

    A) 44cm²
    B) 38cm²
    C) 55cm²
    D) 65cm²

11. ABC is a triangle. AB=16, A(ADC)=48, DC=?

    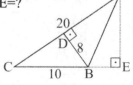

    A) 10   B) 9
    C) 8   D) 6

12. ABC is a triangle. AC=20, BD=8, BC=10, AE=?

    A) 6.6
    B) 8.8
    C) 11
    D) 16

TEST – 147
Area of the Square

1. ABCD is a square. AC=20cm. Find the area of □ABCD.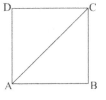

   A) 200   B) 80
   C) 100   D) 400

2. ABCD is a square. Perimeter ABCD is 64cm. Find the area of □ABCD.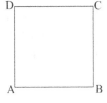

   A) 256   B) 225
   C) 128   D) 64

3. ABCD is a square. AE=7cm. Find the area of □ABCD.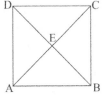

   A) 90   B) 49
   C) 98   D) 196

4. ABCD is a square. A(BEC)=21cm². Find the area of ΔDAB.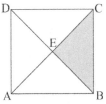

   A) 22   B) 88
   C) 40   D) 42

5. ABCD is a square. Δ(ABE)=98cm². Find the perimeter of □ABCD.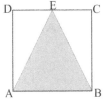

   A) 14 cm²   B) 56 cm²
   C) 49 cm²   D) 58 cm²

6. ABCD is a square. A(BEC)=100 cm². Find the perimeter of □ABCD.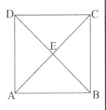

   A) 60   B) 80
   C) 128   D) 64

7. ABCD is a square. AL=LB=BK=KC. AD=18 cm. Find the sum of all areas of all squares in the figure.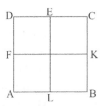

   A) 324   B) 81   C) 100   D) 648

8. ABCD and KFEL are squares. A(ABCD)=256cm², A(KFEL)=625cm². Find the ratio of the perimeters.

   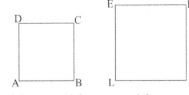

   A) $\frac{15}{16}$ B) $\frac{16}{25}$ C) $\frac{16}{15}$ D) $\frac{25}{46}$

   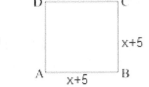

*

9. Find the perimeter of square. ABCD.

   A) 2x -25   B) x² - 25
   C) 4x+20   D) x²+25x

10. Find the area of square ABCD

    A) x²+10x+25   B) x²+5x+25
    C) 2x+10   D) x²+3x+9

* ABCD square perimeter is 10cm.

11. Find the side of the square.

    A) $\frac{5}{10}$ B) $\frac{5}{2}$ C) $\frac{2}{5}$ D) $\frac{5}{10}$

12. Find the area of square ABCD

    A) $\frac{25}{4}$ B) $\frac{5}{4}$ C) $\frac{4}{25}$ D) $\frac{5}{10}$

TEST – 148

Area and Perimeter of a Rectangle

1. ABCD is a rectangle. AB=x+7, BC=x+3 Find the perimeter.

    A) 4x+20
    B) 2x+10
    C) 4x+6
    D) 4x+4

2. ABCD is a rectangle. AB=7x, BC=6x, perimeter ABCD is 52 cm. Find the area of ABCD.

    A) 160   B) 42
    C) 168   D) 100

3. ABCD is a rectangle. AB=32, BC=11. Find the ratio A(ABCD):P(ABCD).

    A) $\frac{176}{43}$ B) $\frac{176}{42}$

    C) $\frac{100}{43}$ D) $\frac{100}{42}$

4. ABCD is a rectangle. Area of ABCD is 192 cm². AB=3x, find the perimeter of ABCD.

    A) 32
    B) 64
    C) 128
    D) 16

5. ABCD is a rectangle. BC=5, AC=13. Find the perimeter of ABCD.

    A) 48
    B) 34
    C) 100
    D) 64

6. ABCD is a rectangle. BC=10, AB=24. Find the perimeter of BAC.

    A) 240
    B) 100
    C) 60
    D) 68

7. AB=30, BC=11, A(ABCD):A(ABC)=?

    A) 1
    B) 2
    C) 3
    D) 5

    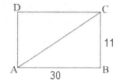

8. A rectangle has edges with lengths of 3 cm and 6 cm. Find the length of a diagonal of the rectangle in centimeters.

    A) 34   B) 17   C) $3\sqrt{5}$ D) $2\sqrt{5}$

9. The lengths of two sides of a rectangle are in the ratio 1:3. Find the area of the rectangle if its perimeter is 32 cm.

    A) 16   B) 48   C) 28   D) 22

10. AE=3, EC=12, ∠DEC=90°, Find DE.

    A) 6   B) 9
    C) 36   D) 18

    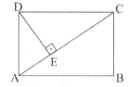

11. AB=6, BC=5, DC=7. Find the ratio A(ABD):A(ACDE)?

    A) $\frac{4}{7}$ B) $\frac{3}{11}$

    C) $\frac{1}{13}$ D) $\frac{2}{9}$

12. ABCD is the rectangle. AB=10, BC=6cm. Area of ABD=40cm². Find the area of A(ACDE)?

    A) 72 cm²
    B) 112 cm²
    C) 128 cm²
    D) 75 cm²

TEST – 149
Rectangular Prisms and Cubes

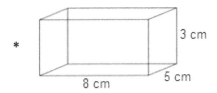

1. Find the base area.
   A) 120cm^2 B) 40cm^2
   C) 60cm^2 D) 66cm^2

2. Find the volume of the rectangular prism.
   A) 120cm^3 B) 130cm^3
   C) 40cm^3 D) 24 cm^3

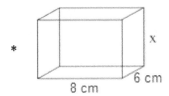

Volume is 384cm^3.

3. h=?
   A) 7cm   B) 8 cm
   C) 12cm   D) 10cm

4. Find the base area.
   A) 60cm^2 B) 64cm^2
   C) 48cm^2 D) 120cm^2

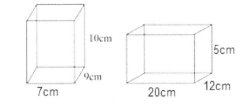

5. Find the ratio of volumes.
   A) $\dfrac{21}{80}$ B) $\dfrac{21}{40}$ C) $\dfrac{3}{40}$ D) $\dfrac{3}{20}$

6. Find the ratio of base areas
   A) $\dfrac{21}{80}$ B) $\dfrac{3}{40}$ C) $\dfrac{21}{40}$ D) $\dfrac{3}{4}$

7. Ones side of a cube measures 5 m. Find the volume of the cube.
   A) 25m^2 B) 125m^3 C) 50m^3 D) 5m^3

8. A cube's side is $\dfrac{3}{8}$ cm. Find the volume of the cube.
   A) $\dfrac{9}{64}$ cm^3 B) $\dfrac{27}{64}$ cm^3
   C) $\dfrac{27}{512}$ cm^3 D) $\dfrac{9}{15}$ cm^3

9. A cube's volume is 216cm^3. Find the surface area.
   A) 216cm^2 B) 36cm^2
   C) 64cm^2 D) 68cm^2

10. A cube's all face area is 96cm^2. Find the volume of the cube.
    A) 16cm^3 B) 4cm^3
    C) 27cm^3 D) 64cm^3

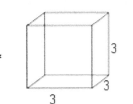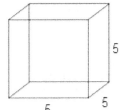

11. Find the ratio of base areas.
    A) $\dfrac{3}{5}$ B) $\dfrac{9}{25}$ C) $\dfrac{6}{10}$ D) $\dfrac{15}{10}$

12. Find the ratio of volume .
    A) $\dfrac{27}{25}$ B) $\dfrac{27}{125}$ C) $\dfrac{9}{125}$ D) $\dfrac{3}{5}$

TEST – 150
Similar Triangles

1. ΔABC~ΔDEC, DE=9 cm, AB=27, AC=54. Find DC.
   A) 6   B) 18
   C) 8   D) 12

2. The triangles shown are similar. Find x.
   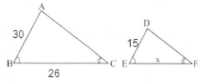
   A) 13   B) 2   C) 14   D) 16

3. AB∥DC and ∠A=82°, ∠CED=22°, ∠C=?
   A) 75
   B) 76
   C) 70
   D) 104
   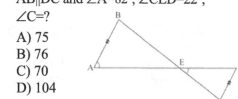

4. DE∥BC and AD=5, DB=9, EC=x+4, AE=x, x=?
   A) 9   B) 5
   C) 8   D) 10

5. AD=12
   BD=13
   AE=20
   EC=?
   A) $\frac{65}{3}$ B) $\frac{65}{4}$ C) $\frac{3}{20}$ D) $\frac{46}{3}$

6. AD=10, DB=6, AE=9, EC=?
   A) 5.2   B) 6.5
   C) 5.4   D) 3.2

7. x =?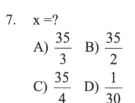
   A) $\frac{35}{3}$ B) $\frac{35}{2}$
   C) $\frac{35}{4}$ D) $\frac{1}{30}$

8. x =?
   A) 12.8   B) 13.5
   C) 14   D) $\frac{23}{2}$
   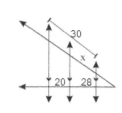

9. BC=15, EF=25, ABC~DEF. Find the ratio A(ABC):A(DEF).
   A) $\frac{3}{5}$ B) $\frac{9}{25}$ C) $\frac{5}{3}$ D) $\frac{25}{36}$

10. x =?
    A) $\frac{23}{2}$ B) $\frac{23}{3}$
    C) $\frac{52}{7}$ D) $\frac{27}{2}$
    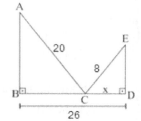

11. AD=16, DC=14, BC=20, DE=?
    A) 11   B) 14
    C) $\frac{32}{3}$ D) $\frac{20}{3}$
    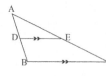

12. ABC triangle is similar DEF triangle. Perimeter ratio is 2/7. Find the area ratio?
    A) $\frac{7}{2}$ B) $\frac{4}{7}$ C) $\frac{4}{49}$ D) $\frac{4}{21}$

TEST – 151
The Pythagorean Theorem

1. Find the length of a hypotenuse, x=?

   A) $\sqrt{73}$ B) $\sqrt{77}$

   C) $\sqrt{69}$ D) $\sqrt{57}$

2. $\angle A=90°$, AB=15, AC=8, x=?

   A) $\dfrac{17}{3}$ B) 3.4

   C) 4.2 D) 17

3. $\angle B=90°$, AD=13, AB=5, BC=4, DC=?

   A) 12 B) 4

   C) 8 D) 15

4. AE=7, EC=5, BC=4, AB=?

   A) $\sqrt{10}$ B) $\sqrt{12}$

   C) $\sqrt{20}$ D) $\sqrt{58}$

5. $\angle B=90°$, AC=6x,

   AB=5x, BC=?

   A) 7 B) 5

   C) $5x^2$ D) $x\sqrt{11}$

6. $\angle B=90°$, AB=8x, BC=16x, A(ABC)=?

   A) 64x B) 8x+2

   C) $8x\sqrt{2}$ D) $2x\sqrt{10}$

7. Find the x?

   A) $\sqrt{13}$ B) $7\sqrt{27}$

   C) $\sqrt{27}$ D) $2\sqrt{22}$

   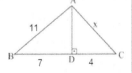

8. Find the area of ABC
   A) 18
   B) $33\sqrt{2}$
   C) 20
   D) $22\sqrt{2}$

   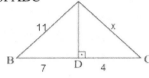

9. $\angle A=\angle D=90°$, BD=4, DC=9, A(ABD):A(ADC)=?

   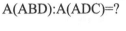

   A) $\dfrac{3}{2}$ B) $\dfrac{4}{9}$ C) $\dfrac{4}{13}$ D) $\dfrac{9}{4}$

   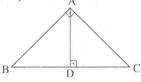

* ABC is a right triangle. AB=x, BC=x+7, AC=13.

10. x=?
    A) 12 B) 5 C) 4 D) 3

11. Find the perimeter of ABC triangle.

    A) 21 B) 23 C) 27 D) 30

12. Find the area of ABC triangle.
    A) 32 B) 30 C) 24 D) 26

TEST – 152
Special Right Triangles
(Theorem: 45º–45º–90º), (Theorem: 30º–30º–90º)

1. $\angle B=90º$, AB=BC=18, AC=?

    A) $13\sqrt{2}$ B) $18\sqrt{2}$
    C) 324   D) 8

2. $\angle B=90º$, $\angle A=\angle C=45º$,
    AC=$16\sqrt{2}$, AB+BC=?

    A) 34   B) 16
    C) $32\sqrt{2}$ D) 32

3. $\angle B=90º$, AC=14,
    $\angle A=\angle C=45º$,
    A(ABC)=?

    A) 98   B) 96
    C) 196   D) 49

4. $\angle B=90º$, AB=BC=3x, P(ABC)=?

    A) $6x + 3\sqrt{2}$
    B) $6x + 3x\sqrt{2}$
    C) $6x + 9x\sqrt{2}$
    D) 9x

5. $\angle B=90º$, $\angle A=\angle C=45º$, A(ABC)=8cm². Find the perimeter of ABC.

    A) $12 + 4\sqrt{2}$ B) $4 + 4\sqrt{2}$
    C) $8 + 4\sqrt{3}$ D) $12\sqrt{2}$

6. $\angle A=90º$, $\angle B=\angle C=45º$, BC=18cm,
    $\dfrac{(AB + AC)}{BC} = ?$

    A) $\sqrt{2}$ B) $\sqrt{3}$
    C) $18\sqrt{2}$ D) $6\sqrt{2}$

7. $\angle A=60º$, $\angle B=90º$, $\angle C=30º$, AC=14cm,
    $\dfrac{BC}{AB} = ?$

    A) 2   B) 3
    C) $\sqrt{2}$ D) $\sqrt{3}$

    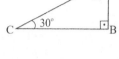

8. $\angle A=60º$, $\angle B=90º$, AB=10cm,
    Find the area of $\triangle ABC$.

    A) $10\sqrt{3}$ B) $20\sqrt{3}$
    C) $50\sqrt{3}$ D) $\sqrt{3}$

9. $\angle A=60º$, $\angle B=90º$, AC=6x,
    Find the area of $\triangle ABC$.

    A) $\dfrac{9\sqrt{3}x}{2}$ B) $9\sqrt{3} \cdot x^2$

    C) $\dfrac{9\sqrt{3}}{2}$ D) $\dfrac{9x^2}{5}$

10. $\angle B=90º$, $\angle D=30º$,
    DC=AC=3, BC=?

    A) 5   B) 1.5
    C) 4   D) 7.5

    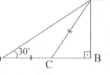

11. $\angle B=90º$, $\angle C=15º$, $\angle DAB=30º$,
    AB=7 AD=?

    A) 14   B) $7\sqrt{2}$
    C) $7\sqrt{3}$ D) $6\sqrt{2}$

    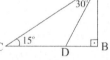

12. $\angle C=90º$, $\angle BAC=45º$, $\angle CAD=30º$,
    AD=10, BC=?

    A) 12
    B) $6\sqrt{3}$
    C) $6\sqrt{6}$
    D) $5\sqrt{3}$

    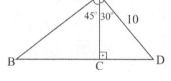

TEST – 153
Angle Measures in Polygons

1. How many sides does a polygon have if the sum of its interior angles is 720°?

   A) 8   B) 7   C) 6   D) 5

2. How many sides does a polygon have if the sum of its interior angles is 1260°?

   A) 7   B) 9   C) 10   D) 8

3. What is the size of one interior angle of a regular twelve–sided polygon?

   A) 120   B) 130   C) 150   D) 140

4. Each of the interior angles of a regular polygon is 140°. How many sides does the polygon have?

   A) 20   B) 9   C) 10   D) 12

5. What is the sum of the interior angles of a regular twelve–sided polygon?

   A) 1800   B) 1700
   C) 1840   D) 2160

6. ABC is a triangle. A=60, B=110, Find the C angle.

   A) 10   B) 15   C) 20   D) 25

7. What is the measure of each interior angle in a regular hexagon?

   A) 45   B) 60   C) 75   D) 120

8. Find the sum of the measures of the interior angles of a dodecagon (12 sides).

   A) 1160   B) 1060
   C) 1888   D) 1800

9. α=?

   A) 82
   B) 80
   C) 100
   D) 90

10. x=?

    A) 112
    B) 114
    C) 105
    D) 94

11. AB=BC=DC=DE=EF=FA=5cm,
    α=?

    A) 30
    B) 70
    C) 60
    D) 95

    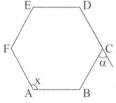

12. Find the x angle measure.

    A) 95^0
    B) 120^0
    C) 110^0
    D) 96^0

TEST – 154

Surface Area of Prisms and Cylinders

1. Find the surface area of the right prism.

   A) 408
   B) 204
   C) 200
   D) 208

   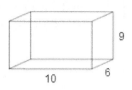

2. Find the surface area of a rectangular prism.

   A) 226
   B) 236
   C) 240
   D) 108

   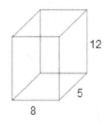

3. Find the surface area.

   A) 390
   B) 298
   C) 392
   D) 400

4. Find the surface area of a rectangular prism with sides of length 5, 7 and 10cm.

   A) 300   B) 310   C) 280   D) 392

5. Find the surface area of a rectangular prism if the base is square with edge length 9cm and height 6cm.

   A) 378
   B) 189
   C) 300
   D) 112

6. Find the surface area of a right rectangular prism with a height of 8cm, a length of 5cm and width of 4cm.

   A) 180
   B) 104
   C) 184
   D) 188

7. FC=6, DF=8, AD=12cm. Find the surface area.

   A) 336   B) 296
   C) 276   D) 96

   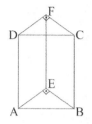

8. ∠E=∠F=90°, EA=10, BE=24, BC=5cm. Find the prism surface area.

   A) 336   B) 540
   C) 640   D) 350

   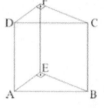

9. $\dfrac{1}{a}+\dfrac{1}{b}+\dfrac{1}{c}=4$ and $V=120cm^3$, Find the surface area of the rectangular prism.

   A) 960   B) 780   C) 420   D) 480

   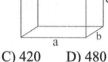

10. KL=8cm, LD=7cm. Find the surface area of the right cylinder.

    A) 208π   B) 50π
    C) 108π   D) 200π

    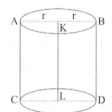

11. AB=12cm, BC=6cm. Find the surface area of the cylinder.

    A) 200π   B) 90π
    C) 216π   D) 44π

    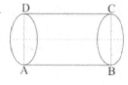

12. BC=14cm, AB=8cm. Find the surface area of the cylinder.

    A) 144π   B) 214π
    C) 140π   D) 72π

    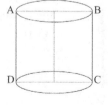

TEST – 155
Surface Area of Pyramids and Cones

1. Find the surface area of a triangular pyramid if the area of its base is 16cm^2 and each of its lateral faces has an area of 9cm^2.

   A) 43   B) 44   C) 46   D) 47

2. Find the base area of a square pyramid whose base has a side length of 12cm.

   A) 148   B) 144   C) 143   D) 140

3. The base area of a square pyramid is 225cm^2. Find the length of an edge of the base of the pyramid.

   A) 12   B) 13   C) 1   D) 15

4. This diagram shows a square–based pyramid with base length 16 cm and height 6cm. What is the surface area of the square base area?

   A) 126
   B) 132
   C) 220
   D) 256

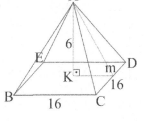

5. What is the surface area of the pyramid?

   A) 426   B) 526   C) 576   D) 580

6. AB=BC, EK=8, AB=6. Find the surface area of the regular pyramid shown.

   A) 96
   B) 102
   C) 122
   D) 132

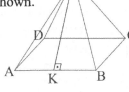

7. AB=4, EK=5. AB=BC. Find the surface area of the regular pyramid.

   A) 48   B) 50
   C) 54   D) 56

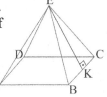

8. AB=BC=9, EK=12. Find the surface area of the regular pyramid shown.

   A) 280   B) 282
   C) 297   D) 300

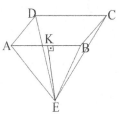

9. Find the surface area of the right cone shown.

   A) 48π   B) 49π
   C) 50π   D) 51π

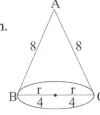

10. AC=13, BC=10cm. Find the surface area of the right cone.

   A) 90   B) 80π
   C) 90π   D) 100π

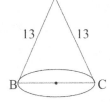

11. AB=16, AC=12. Find the surface area of the right cone.

   A) 132π   B) 132
   C) 144π   D) 144

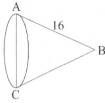

12. AB=24cm, CK=5cm, Find the slant height of the right cone.

   A) 10   B) 11
   C) 12   D) 13

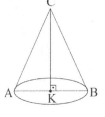

TEST – 156

Volume of Prisms and Cylinders

1. a=5cm. Find the prism's volume.

    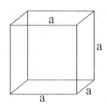

    A) 25   B) 75
    C) 125   D) 225

2. Find the prism's volume.

    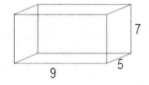

    A) 315
    B) 480
    C) 490
    D) 512

3. $V=210cm^3$. Find the x.

    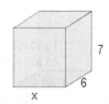

    A) 10   B) 8
    C) 6   D) 5

4. What is the volume of a prism where the base area is $25cm^2$ and which is 15cm long?

    A) 275   B) 250   C) 375   D) 512

5. $V=8000cm^3$. x=?

    A) 10   B) 8
    C) 7   D) 6

6) Find the volume of the right prism.

    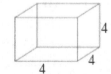

    A) 16   B) 64
    C) 24   D) 32

7. Find the volume of the right prism.

    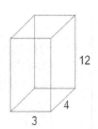

    A) 48
    B) 36
    C) 96
    D) 144

8. Find the ratio of the volume $(V_1:V_2)$.

    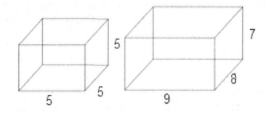

    A) $\dfrac{25}{81}$ B) $\dfrac{25}{63}$ C) $\dfrac{125}{504}$ D) $\dfrac{25}{504}$

9. r=5cm, h=7cm. Find the volume of the right cylinder.

    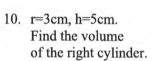

    A) 100π
    B) 125π
    C) 175π
    D) 130π

10. r=3cm, h=5cm. Find the volume of the right cylinder.

    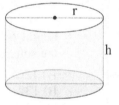

    A) 45π B) 45
    C) 15π D) 15

11. AB=8cm, BD=13cm. Find the volume of the right cylinder.

    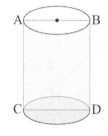

    A) 208π
    B) 64π
    C) 832π
    D) 104π

12. r=5cm, AB=9cm. Find the volume of the oblique cylinder.

    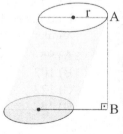

    A) 100π
    B) 120π
    C) 225π
    D) 360π

TEST – 157
Volume of Pyramids and Cones

1. EK=10, AB=6. Find the volume of the pyramid with the square base show the right.
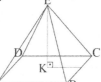
   A) 360   B) 120
   C) 600   D) 360

2. AB=BC=8cm, EK=13cm. Find the volume of the pyramid. Round your answer to the nearest whole number.
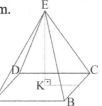
   A) 832   B) 900
   C) 277   D) 300

3. ∠B=90°, AB=7, BC=10, h=18. Find the volume of the pyramid.

   A) 630   B) 210
   C) 70   D) 420

4. AB=BC=AC=5cm, h=12cm. Find the volume of the pyramid.

   A) $25\sqrt{3}$ B) $60\sqrt{3}$
   C) $30\sqrt{3}$ D) $20\sqrt{3}$

5. ABCD is square. EK=9cm, AB=6cm. Find the volume of the pyramid.

   A) 54   B) 72
   C) 108   D) 121

6. AB=BC=11cm, EK=21cm. Find the volume of the pyramid.
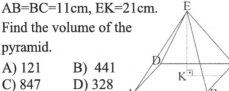
   A) 121   B) 441
   C) 847   D) 328

7. ABC is a right circular cone. KC=8cm, AK=12cm. Find the volume of the cone.
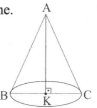
   A) 110π B) 256π
   C) 120π D) 64π

8. r=7cm, h=9cm, Find the volume of the cone.

   A) 147π B) 49π
   C) 63π D) 81π

9. DC=5cm, AD=9cm. Find the volume of the cone.
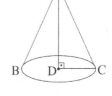
   A) 75π B) 150π
   C) 225π D) 180π

10. DC=3 cm. V=36πcm^3, h=?
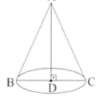
   A) 10   B) 11
   C) 12   D) 13

* DC=9cm, AC=15cm.
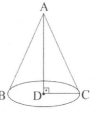

11. Find the AD=?
   A) 9   B) 10   C) 11   D) 12

12. Find the volume of the cone.
   A) 60π B) 324π
   C) 81π D) 243π

TEST – 158

Rectangular Prism and Cube

1. Find the surface area of a cube with edge length 5cm.
   A) 150   B) 250   C) 125   D) 100

2. Find the surface area of a cube whose volume is 343cm³.
   A) 125   B) 245   C) 180   D) 294

* A rectangular prism has side of length 5cm and 6cm and height 8cm.

3. Find the base area.
   A) 28   B) 30   C) 36   D) 40

4. Find the volume of the prism.
   A) 70   B) 80   C) 90   D) 240

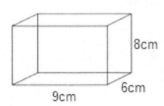

* **A rectangular prism has side of length 9cm and 6cm and height 8cm.**

5. Find the base area.
   A) 54cm²   B) 72cm²
   C) 52cm²   D) 48cm²

6. Find the volume of the prism.
   A) 384cm³   B) 486cm³
   C) 432cm³   D) 288cm³

7. Find the sum of right and left area.
   A) 120   B) 96   C) 144   D) 84

8. Find the sum of top and bottom area.
   A) 122cm²   B) 108cm²
   C) 126cm²   D) 120cm²

9. Find the sum of back and front areas.
   A) 72cm²   B) 96cm²
   C) 144cm²   D) 48cm²

10. Find the volume of a cube with side $\frac{3}{5}$ cm.
    A) $\frac{9}{25}$ cm³   B) $\frac{27}{125}$ cm³
    C) $\frac{9}{125}$ cm³   D) $\frac{27}{25}$ cm³

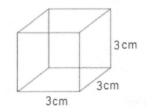

*

11. Find the volume of cube?
    A) 54   B) 27   C) 81   D) 2

12. Find the surface area.
    A) 27cm²   B) 36cm²
    C) 45cm²   D) 54cm²

TEST – 159
Mixed Problems

1. Find the domain and range.
    A) D(-8, 3)
       R(1, 3)
    B) D $(-\infty, \infty)$
       R $[4, \infty)$
    C) D $[-\infty, \infty)$ D) D $(-\infty, \infty)$
       R $(4, \infty)$ R$(-\infty, 4)$

2. f(x) = 4x + 6, find the domain.
    A) D $(-\infty, 6)$ B) D $(-4, \infty)$
    C) D $(-\infty, \infty)$ D) D $(-\infty, \frac{3}{2})$

3. f(x)= $\sqrt{x-12}$, find the domain.
    A) $(12, \infty)$ B) $(-\infty, 12)$
    C) $(-\infty, \infty)$ D) $[12, \infty)$

4. $f(x) = \dfrac{3x-9}{\sqrt{x+4}}$, find the domain.
    A) $[-4, \infty)$ B) $[-4, \infty]$
    C) $[-8, 3]$ D) $[-\infty, 9]$

5. Find the domain and range.
    A) {2, 4, 6}
       {8, 9, 7, 3}
    B) {8, 9, 7, 3}
       {2, 4, 6}
    C) {8, 4, 7, 2}   D) {2, 4, 8, 9}
       {2, 4, 8}   {8, 9, 4, 6}

6. Find the domain.
    A) {7, 1, 6}
    B) {7, -3, 6}
    C) {1, 6, 5}
    D) {7, 2, -3}

x	y
7	1
2	6
-3	5

7. Find the range.
    A) y < 3   B) y≥3
    C) y≤-2   D) y≥-2

    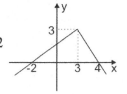

8. Find the domain.
    A) 0<x<9   B) 0≤x<5
    C) 0<x<5   D) 0<x<3

    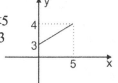

9. What is the range of the function?
    A) [0, -5)   B) [-4, 2]
    C) [-4, -5] D) [0, 5]

    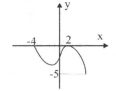

10. What is the range of the
    $f(x) = 5 + \sqrt{x-6}$?
    A) $(-\infty, 5)$ B) $(5, \infty)$
    C) $[5, 6]$ D) $[5, \infty)$

11. What is the range of the function?
    A) y>5   B) y<5
    C) y≥5   D) y≤ -5

    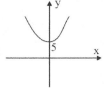

12. What is the domain
    the function?
    A) x≥-3   B) x>-3
    C) x≥3   D) x≤ -3

    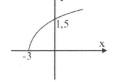

TEST – 160
Mixed Problems

1. If $6m + 9n = 24$, what is the volve of $2m + 3n$=?

   A) 6   B) 7   C) 8   D) 9

2. Solve the inequality for $-9 + 3n \geq 18$.

   A) n>9   B) n<9   C)n≥9   D) n≤9

3. What is the slope for the equation $9x + 6y = 24$?

   A) $\dfrac{3}{2}$ B) $-\dfrac{3}{2}$ C) $-\dfrac{2}{3}$ D) $\dfrac{2}{3}$

4. $\left(\dfrac{1}{2}m^2\right)^2 \cdot \left(4\dfrac{1}{m}\right)^2 = ?$

   A) $\dfrac{m^2}{4}$ B) $\dfrac{4}{m^2}$ C) m^2 D) $4m^2$

5. Solve the equation for $(x - 3)^2 = 14$.

   A) $14 + \sqrt{3}$ B) $3 \pm \sqrt{14}$

   C) $14 \pm \sqrt{3}$ D) $4 \pm \sqrt{14}$

6. Evalvate: x^2y^3z for x=1, y=2 and x=3.

   A) 12   B) 16   C) 18   D) 24

7. What is the quotient of $\dfrac{(x+3)^2}{\left(x^2 + 7x + 12\right)}$

   A) 1   B) $\dfrac{x+3}{x-2}$ C) $\dfrac{x+3}{x+2}$ D) $\dfrac{x+3}{x+4}$

8. Solve: $|2x - 2| = 14$

   A) $\{6, 8\}$ B) -6, 8}

   C) $\{-6, 8\}$ D) $\{-7, 2\}$

9. $\angle A$ and $\angle B$ are vertical angles. $\angle A = 80$ and $\angle B = 2x-20$. What is the value of x?

   A) 40   B) 45   C) 50   D) 60

10. The triangle has one side of 8 cm and another side of 12 cm. What is the maximum perimeter of the triangle?

    A) 30   B) 39   C) 42   D) 43

11. ABC and DEF are similar triangle. Find the x value.

    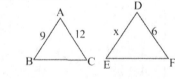

    A) 4   B) 4.5   C) 5   D) 6

12. New math book`s original price is $60. If is sold for $45, what is the discount percentage?

    A) 10%   B) 20%   C) 25%   D) 30%

TEST – 161
Mixed Problems

1. Ahmet and five friends are eating out of dinner. The bill was $124.24. How much did each person pay to share the payment equally?

   A) $20   B) $20.7   C) $22.7   D) $23

2. Simplify: $(8a^2 - 8a + 4) - (2a - 4)^2$

   A) $4a^2$ B) $4a^2+12$ C) $4a^2-12$ D) 12

3. Solve for x: $9x^2 - 4 = 0$

   A) $-\dfrac{2}{3}$ and $\dfrac{2}{3}$ B) $-\dfrac{2}{3}$ and $\dfrac{3}{2}$

   C) $-\dfrac{3}{2}$ and $-\dfrac{1}{3}$ D) $-\dfrac{9}{4}$ and $-\dfrac{9}{4}$

4. Evaluate the expression: $8 + (8 \div 8)^2 - 8$

   A) 1   B) 2   B) 16   D) 32

5. A={2,3,5,7,9}, B={5,7,9,11,12}.
   Find $A \cap B = ?$

   A) {7,9}   B) {2,3,5,11,12}
   C) {5,7,9}   D) {2,3,5,9}

6. A={1,3,5,7}, B={2,4,5}. Find $A \cup B = ?$

   A) {1,3,5,7}   B) {1,2,3,4,5,7}
   C) {1,2,3,5}   D) {2,4,5,7}

7. Which equation represents a linear function?

   A) $y=x^2+4$ B) $y=x^2-9$
   C) $y=x^3$ D) $y=3x+4$

8. The area of the square is $4x^2$ cm^2. What is the perimeter of the square?

   A) $8x^2$ B) $6x^2$ C) $9x$ D) $8x$

9. The equilateral triangles has a side length of 20 cm. What is the length of the altitude of the triangle?

   A) 10 cm   B) $10\sqrt{2}$ cm

   C) $10\sqrt{3}$ cm   D) $8\sqrt{3}$ cm

10. If AB = AC = BC, then $\angle A$=?
    A) 60^0
    B) right angle
    C) complementary
    D) 90^0

11. What is 20% of 30?

    A) 60   B) 6   C) 15   D) 0,6

12. Which of the following represent the wash time?

Cars (c)	5	10	20
Wash time	15	30	60

    A) C+3   B) C − 3   C) 3×C   D) C/3

TEST – 162
Mixed Problems

1. The sum of the ages of 3 siblings is 48. What was the sum of their age four years ago?
   A) 39   B) 38   C) 37   D) 36

2. The sum of three even consecutive integers is 42. What is the smallest number?
   A) 10   B) 12   C) 14   D) 16

3. What is the $\frac{3}{4}$ of 24?
   A) 18   B) 20   C) 21   D) 24

4. Solve for x: $3x + 4 = 34$
   A) 8   B) 9   C) 10   D) 11

5. Solve for x: $\frac{x+4}{2} = \frac{x-3}{3}$
   A) -18   B) -19   C) -20   D) -21

6. Solve for x: $\sqrt{3x+3} = 3$
   A) 1   B) 2   C) 3   D) 4

7. There are 6 green and 10 yellow marbles in a box. What is the probability or randomly selecting a marble that is green?
   A) $\frac{3}{5}$ B) $\frac{5}{3}$ C) $\frac{5}{8}$ D) $\frac{8}{5}$

8. What is the probability of selecting boys from the group of 8 boys and 12 girls?
   A) 0.4   B) 0.5   C) 0.6   D) 0.7

9. What is the x – intercept of the line that has the following $3x + 4y + 12 = 0$?
   A) (4, 0)   B) (0, 4)
   C) (0, -4)   D) (-4, 0)

10. What is the surface area of a cube if the length of a cube if the length of one side is 0.3cm?
    A) 54   B) 5.4   C) 0.54   D) 0.054

11. $\frac{36}{144}$ is equivalent to which fraction?
    A) $\frac{1}{4}$ B) $\frac{1}{3}$ C) $\frac{2}{3}$ D) $\frac{4}{7}$

12. $\left(\frac{0.24}{0.12}\right)^3 = ?$
    A) 1   B) 2   C) 4   D) 8

TEST – 163
Mixed Problems

1. $0.74 + 0.84 + 1.74 =?$
   A) 3   B) 3.22   C) 4   D) 4.22

2. Geometry book cost \$15. It is reduced to \$9 in a sale. How much is the percentage reduced?
   A) 30%   B) 40%   C) 45%   D) 60%

3. Find the percent decrease from 120 to 90?
   A) 10%   B) 15%   C) 20%   D) 25%

4. What is the percentage increase of a \$75 item on sale for \$100?
   A) 25%   B) 40%   C) 33%   D) 45%

5. Find the percent change from 40 grams to 60 grams.
   A) 50%   B) 40%   C) 30%   D) 70%

6. $|-7| + |-6| + |6| + |1/2| = ?$
   A) 19   B) 19.5   C) 4.5   D) 7

7. $\dfrac{|-70|+|60|}{|40|-|10|}=?$
   A) 13   B) $\dfrac{13}{3}$ C) $\dfrac{13}{5}$ D) 10

8. Which is prime number?
   A) 81   B) 61   C) 42   D) 32

9. Which is composite number?
   A) 97   B) 71   C) 61   D) 501

10. Set A={2,5,9,11,19,21,31,41,97}
    How many prime number is sat A?
    A) 5   B) 6   C) 7   D) 8

11. Set B={5,7,9,11,17,81,90,120}
    How many composite is a set B?
    A) 4   B) 5   C) 6   D) 7

12. $24 - (-24) + (4 - 6)^2 = ?$
    A) 4   B) 48   C) 52   D) -4

TEST – 164

Mixed Problems

1. $(4 - 6)^2 + 4(-2) - 7$

   A) 10   B) -10   C) 11   D) -11

2. Which are the prime numbers in the list?

   A) {2,3,5,7,21,31,41}
   B) {5,7,9,11,17,19,31}
   C) {3,7,11,13,19,21,41}
   D) {2,3,5,7,11,15,19,29}

3. Which are the composite numbers in the list?

   A) {4,6,9,15,21}
   B) {4,6,9,11,15}
   C) {9,11,21,24,72}
   D) {11,12,15,16,18}

4. 7, 6, 9, 12, 9, 21, 6, 9
   Which number is a prime number?

   A) 7   B) 6   C) 12   D) 9

5. 4, 2, 7, 11, 21.
   Which is the median number?

   A) 7   B) 2   C) 4   D) 11

6. Give A(-7,5) and B(3,7). What is the midpoint coordinate?

   A) (2,6)   B) (5,7)   C) (-2,6)   D) (-2,3)

7. What is the perimeter of triangle?

   A) 6m + 4   B) 6m + 6
   C) 4 + 4m   D) 7m + 6

8. What is the range of the data for: 7, -3, 6, 21, 5, 32 and 94.

   A) 94   B) 97   C) 37   D) 42

9. What is the median of the data for 6, 14, 20, 10, 6 and 4?

   A) 8   B) 7   C) 6   D) 10

10. Which is not function?

    A) 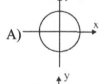   B)

    C)   D)

11. f(x)=2x + 3, f(2) – f(1) =?

    A) 1   B) 2   C) 3   D) 4

12. Simplity: 3(x + 2) – 4(2 – x)

    A) 7x+2   B) 6x+4   C) 7x-2   D) 6x-4

TEST – 165
Mixed Problems

1. Which is one of the factor for: $x^2 + 7x + 12$
   A) x+12   B) x+7   C) x+3   D) x+5

2. What is the average of the first 4 prime numbers?
   A) 5   B) $\dfrac{17}{4}$ C) $\dfrac{17}{5}$ D) 6

3. Ahmet ha $25 more than six times Jack. What equation best represents?
   A) A=25 – 6J   B) J=25 + A/6
   C) J=25 + 6A   D) J=25 + 6A

4. Given: 5, 7, 9, 12, 17, 19, 21, 29 and 31. What is the probability of selecting prime number?
   A) $\dfrac{9}{7}$ B) $\dfrac{3}{2}$ C) $\dfrac{2}{3}$ D) $\dfrac{7}{9}$

5. The length of a square is 20 cm. If the side reduced by 20% what percent is the area reduced?
   A) 36%   B) 32%   C) 25%   D) 20%

6. The length of a circle radius is 10 cm. If the radius reduced by 20% what percent is the area reduced?
   A) 30%   B) 36%   C) 40%   D) 45%

7. What is the solution: 6x+6 = 4x+14
   A) 8   B) 6   C) 4   D) 2

8. Which is the nonlinear function?
   A) 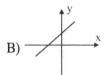   B)
   C) 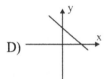   D)

9. If AB = 24 cm, what is the area of circle?

   A) 14π   B) 48π   C) 144π   D) 22π

10. R=7cm, r=3cm. What is the shaded area?

    A) 40   B) 40π   C) 16   D) 16π

11. What is the equation of the linear?
    A) 2x + 7y =1
    B) 2x + 7y=14
    C) 7x + 2y=-14
    D) 7x + 2y=14

12. What is the perimeter of the rectangular?

    ▭ x+1
    3x
    A) 8x   B) 6x+2   C) 4x+1   D) 8x+2

TEST – 166
Mixed Problems

1. Solve for x: $\dfrac{x+1}{2} = 7$

   A) 10   B) 11   C) 12   D) 13

2. Solve inequality: $6n+6 \geq 36$

   A) n>6   B) n≥-6   C) n≥5   D) n≤5

3. What is the equation of the graph?
   A) y=x²+5x
   B) y=x²+25x
   C) y=x²+25
   D) y=x²-25

4. f(x)=x²+4x. What is the value of the f(x+1)?
   A) x²+6x+5   B) x²+5x+6
   C) x²+6x+4   D) x²+4x+4

5. What is the 40% of 70?

   A) 30   B) 28   C) 24   D) 14

6. x=?
   A) 11   B) 12
   C) 13   D) 14

7. In a class of 30 children, 30% of the children are boys. How many girls are there in the class?

   A) 9   B) 19   C) 20   D) 21

8. There are Algebra, Geometry and Science books in the ratio 1:3:5. If there were 180 total, how many algebra books were there?

   A) 60   B) 40   C) 30   D) 20

9. Ahmet donated $7 to charity every week. How much did he donate in 420 days?

   A) $400   B) $420
   C) $430   D) $440

10. What is the ratio of 4x+4π to π+x?

    A) π B) x   C) π + x   D) 4

11. $\dfrac{14}{25}$ convert the fraction in the decimal.

    A) 0.28   B) 0.14   C) 0.42   D) 0.56

12. What is the least common multiply of 5, 10 and 25?

    A) 1   B) 5   C) 10   D) 25

TEST – 167
Mixed Problems

1. $\left(\dfrac{2}{3}\right)^{-3} = ?$

   A) $\dfrac{6}{9}$ B) $\dfrac{8}{27}$ C) $\dfrac{27}{8}$ D) $\dfrac{24}{7}$

2. What is the quotient of $(x^2+8x+7) \div (x^2+7x+6)$?

   A) $\dfrac{x+7}{x+6}$ B) $\dfrac{x+6}{x+7}$ C) $\dfrac{x+3}{x+6}$ D) $\dfrac{x+4}{x+7}$

3. Which equation represents direct variation?

   A) $y=3x + 7$ B) $y=6^x+7$

   C) $y= \dfrac{1}{x}$ D) $y=6x$

4. What is the solution of x^2+5x+6?

   A) (2, 3)   B) (-3, 2)
   C) (-3, -2)   D) (2, 3)

5. 9 is what percent of 72?

   A) 20%   B) 16%
   C) 15%   D) 12.5%

6. What is the greatest common divisor for 27 and 36?

   A) 3   B) 6   C) 9   D) 12

7. Convert to fraction in the simplest form for 0.24.

   A) $\dfrac{6}{20}$ B) $\dfrac{6}{25}$ C) $\dfrac{7}{25}$ D) $\dfrac{9}{20}$

8. What is the product of $\dfrac{1}{6}$ and the sum of 130 and 50?

   A) 30   B) 28   C) 25   D) 24

9. $A \cap B = ?$

   A) {6, 7}
   B) 6, 9, 7}
   C) {9, 8}
   D) {10, 11, 6, 7}

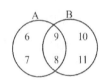

10. What is 30% more than 30?

    A) 39   B) 38   C) 36   D) 32

11. $|4^2 - 4| + |3^2 - 3| = ?$

    A) 18   B) 16   C) 14   D) 12

12. Find the surface area of a cube with edge length 6cm.

    A) 212cm^2 B) 216cm^2
    C) 218cm^2 D) 236cm^2

TEST – 168

Mixed Problems

1. Which are possible side lengths of a triangle?

   A) 5, 7, 9   B) 2, 7, 5
   C) 8, 4, 12   D) 12, 14, 26

2. What is $6\frac{2}{5}$ written as a decimal?

   A) 6.20   B) 6.30   C) 6.40   D) 6.60

3.

Item	Price	Discount	Sale price
Book	$40	20%	?

   A) $30   B) $31   C) $32   D) $33

4.

Item	Price	Tax	Total bill
Book	$30	3%	?

   A) $31.9   B) $30.9   C) $32.4   D) $33.3

5. What is the range of the data 32, 21, 10, 63, 95?

   A) 65   B) 55   C) 75   D) 85

6. $x - y = 4$, then $2|x - y| + 3|y - x| = ?$

   A) 10   B) 12   C) 16   D) 20

7. Solve equation: $\dfrac{n+7}{4} = 3$

   A) 6   B) 5   C) 4   D) 3

8. What is the supplement of an angle measuring 54?

   A) 120   B) 122   C) 126   D) 128

9. What is the complementary of an angle measuring 24^0?

   A) 60   B) 62   C) 66   D) 68

10. $0.32 \cdot 10^{-2} = ?$

    A) 32   B) 3.2
    C) 0.032   D) 0.0032

11. Write 0,00045 in scientific notation.

    A) 45×10^{-2} B) 45×10^{-3}
    C) 45×10^{-4} D) 45×10^{-5}

12. Which expression is the perfect square?

    A) $20x^2$ B) $36y$ C) $\dfrac{1}{9}x^2 y^2$ D) $81y$

TEST – 169
Mixed Problems

1. The sum of the ages of 3 siblings is 58. What was the sum of their age four years ago?

   A) 39   B) 38   C) 37   D) 46

2. The sum of three even consecutive integers is 48. What is the smallest number?

   A) 10   B) 12   C) 14   D) 16

3. What is the $\dfrac{3}{4}$ of 48?

   A) 36   B) 20   C) 21   D) 24

4. Solve for x: $4x + 4 = 44$

   A) 8   B) 9   C) 10   D) 11

CLEP – College Mathematics – Test Answers

Test No	Q1	Q2	Q3	Q4	Q5	Q6	Q7	Q8	Q9	Q10	Q11	Q12
Test – 1	B	B	C	D	A	B	C	B	B	A	D	D
Test – 2	C	D	A	B	B	A	C	A	A	A	C	C
Test – 3	A	B	D	A	C	A	A	B	A	D	D	B
Test – 4	B	D	B	C	C	A	B	A	A	C	B	A
Test – 5	B	C	C	D	D	D	A	A	A	A	A	A
Test – 6	A	B	A	D	B	A	B	B	D	C	D	A
Test – 7	B	A	C	A	B	B	A	A	D	A	C	A
Test – 8	A	A	B	D	C	D	B	C	A	A	A	C
Test – 9	A	C	D	A	A	C	C	C	A	A	D	B
Test – 10	B	B	C	A	C	A	D	C	C	A	A	D
Test – 11	B	B	C	D	A	D	B	C	B	C	A	D
Test – 12	B	C	A	D	D	D	B	C	A	C	A	D
Test – 13	B	A	D	A	A	B	A	B	A	C	B	B
Test – 14	C	B	A	C	B	C	B	C	A	B	C	D
Test – 15	B	C	D	D	C	D	A	A	D	A	C	C
Test – 16	A	C	D	D	B	B	A	C	B	B	A	A
Test – 17	D	D	A	B	A	D	D	C	D	D	D	D
Test – 18	B	D	D	A	D	B	A	A	B	C	C	B
Test – 19	D	B	D	A	B	A	B	C	D	C	C	B
Test – 20	B	B	A	C	D	B	B	B	D	C	B	A
Test – 21	A	A	D	B	A	D	B	D	C	D	A	B
Test – 22	A	B	D	D	A	C	D	A	C	D	A	C
Test – 23	A	D	A	A	D	D	C	D	B	C	A	B
Test – 24	B	D	B	C	C	A	B	C	A	D	A	B
Test – 25	A	C	D	A	D	D	C	B	A	B	C	D
Test – 26	A	B	C	C	D	A	C	C	B	A	A	C
Test – 27	B	C	D	B	C	C	D	C	A	B	A	B
Test – 28	D	B	A	B	D	B	C	D	A	A	B	B
Test – 29	A	A	A	B	C	B	C	D	C	C	D	A
Test – 30	C	B	C	A	C	B	D	B	D	B	C	C
Test – 31	D	C	A	C	D	C	D	D	A	B	B	D
Test – 32	C	C	B	C	C	D	C	A	B	C	B	D
Test – 33	D	A	B	C	D	C	C	A	B	C	D	C
Test – 34	D	D	C	B	D	A	B	C	D	B	C	B
Test – 35	D	A	C	C	C	D	B	D	C	D	B	B
Test – 36	D	C	D	C	D	B	D	C	D	D	A	A
Test – 37	C	C	C	A	D	C	C	C	A	B	D	B
Test – 38	C	B	B	C	D	A	D	C	C	B	B	A

Test – 39	C	B	C	D	D	B	B	D	D	A	C	D
Test – 40	B	D	C	A	B	C	D	B	C	B	B	C
Test – 41	B	A	C	C	D	D	C	A	A	C	D	C
Test – 42	B	B	A	D	A	D	C	A	C	C	D	C
Test – 43	C	D	C	D	A	B	C	D	A	A	B	D
Test – 44	A	B	B	C	B	C	D	A	B	A	D	B
Test – 45	B	D	C	B	C	A	D	D	A	B	A	C
Test – 46	D	C	B	A	C	A	D	C	C	D	C	A
Test – 47	C	A	B	D	A	D	D	C	A	C	A	D
Test – 48	B	B	A	C	C	B	C	B	D	A	C	D
Test – 49	B	D	C	A	C	D	C	B	D	C	D	B
Test – 50	C	C	A	D	B	B	A	C	D	D	D	A
Test – 51	D	C	B	B	C	A	B	C	B	D	C	D
Test – 52	B	C	B	C	D	D	C	B	A	B	A	D
Test – 53	B	C	D	A	D	C	D	D	A	B	C	D
Test – 54	B	C	D	A	C	D	A	C	C	B	A	C
Test – 55	C	C	B	C	B	C	C	B	C	D	D	A
Test – 56	C	B	A	A	A	C	D	B	C	A	B	D
Test – 57	D	C	B	A	B	C	A	B	A	D	C	D
Test – 58	B	A	D	C	A	D	D	B	A	A	D	B
Test – 59	B	B	B	C	A	A	B	D	B	D	C	D
Test – 60	A	B	C	C	C	C	D	B	D	A	D	C
Test – 61	B	D	C	B	A	A	D	D	C	C	D	C
Test – 62	D	C	D	B	D	B	A	B	D	C	A	C
Test – 63	A	C	C	A	D	A	A	C	A	C	A	C
Test – 64	D	B	C	A	B	A	D	B	A	C	B	B
Test – 65	D	C	C	C	B	B	D	D	B	B	B	C
Test – 66	B	C	B	B	D	D	C	B	D	C	D	A
Test – 67	C	D	D	B	A	D	A	B	B	A	D	B
Test – 68	A	D	C	D	B	B	D	C	C	D	B	C
Test – 69	B	A	B	B	D	A	C	A	D	A	A	A
Test – 70	B	A	D	A	B	D	C	A	B	A	C	D
Test – 71	A	C	D	B	C	C	B	C	A	A	C	A
Test – 72	B	C	C	D	C	A	B	B	A	A	B	B
Test – 73	B	D	C	A	B	B	C	B	A	C	A	C
Test – 74	D	A	B	A	A	A	C	C	D	A	C	D
Test – 75	B	C	D	C	D	C	B	A	C	A	C	A
Test – 76	D	B	A	D	C	A	D	B	A	B	B	C
Test – 77	A	C	B	B	B	B	D	A	B	A	C	A
Test – 78	C	D	A	C	B	B	A	A	C	D	B	C

Test – 79	A	B	D	D	D	C	D	A	C	A	A	C
Test – 80	A	D	D	A	D	D	C	D	B	D	A	B
Test – 81	C	D	C	A	B	D	B	A	C	D	D	A
Test – 82	A	B	C	B	B	A	C	A	D	A	C	C
Test – 83	B	A	B	A	C	A	A	C	D	B	B	B
Test – 84	A	D	A	A	D	D	D	D	B	C	C	B
Test – 85	A	A	B	A	C	A	D	A	B	A	C	D
Test – 86	B	C	D	B	C	C	A	A	A	C	D	A
Test – 87	C	C	C	C	C	A	C	A	C	B	C	C
Test – 88	B	A	B	B	D	D	D	A	A	A	C	A
Test – 89	B	A	C	A	A	A	B	B	C	A	D	C
Test – 90	B	D	B	C	B	A	D	D	B	A	C	D
Test – 91	C	A	D	C	A	C	D	C	C	D	D	B
Test – 92	D	A	A	C	D	C	C	D	B	D	B	A
Test – 93	B	A	C	D	D	A	B	B	D	C	A	C
Test – 94	B	B	C	B	A	C	A	D	B	A	D	C
Test – 95	B	C	A	A	D	C	C	A	D	A	B	D
Test – 96	B	A	C	D	D	B	A	B	C	D	B	B
Test – 97	D	A	B	B	B	A	D	D	B	A	A	B
Test – 98	B	C	C	D	B	B	D	C	D	D	B	A
Test – 99	C	C	D	A	D	C	A	D	A	A	B	D
Test – 100	D	B	B	A	C	A	D	D	C	C	D	A
Test – 101	B	C	A	C	D	B	D	D	B	A	C	A
Test – 102	A	B	D	D	C	D	A	D	D	C	C	B
Test – 103	A	D	B	B	B	A	D	A	B	D	C	D
Test – 104	D	C	D	D	A	B	A	D	A	A	B	A
Test – 105	B	D	D	D	C	B	A	A	C	C	A	B
Test – 106	A	A	A	B	B	C	B	A	B	B	B	A
Test – 107	A	D	D	C	A	A	D	B	A	C	D	A
Test – 108	D	A	D	B	D	D	C	B	D	D	A	D
Test – 109	C	B	B	A	B	B	B	B	C	D	B	A
Test – 110	D	C	C	D	B	A	A	A	B	D	D	C
Test – 111	A	A	A	C	C	D	A	B	A	D	B	A
Test – 112	B	C	C	B	D	C	D	B	D	A	B	B
Test – 113	B	D	D	B	D	D	A	D	D	B	C	C
Test – 114	D	B	B	D	C	C	C	D	A	C	D	D
Test – 115	C	D	A	C	A	A	C	B	C	B	D	C
Test – 116	C	B	B	B	A	A	C	A	C	C	C	D
Test – 117	C	A	D	C	D	D	A	B	A	A	A	B
Test – 118	B	D	D	A	C	D	A	A	D	B	A	D

Test – 119	D	C	D	D	C	C	B	A	B	D	C	A
Test – 120	D	A	B	A	D	D	A	C	D	B	B	D
Test – 121	D	C	C	A	A	B	D	B	D	C	D	C
Test – 122	A	B	B	C	D	B	D	B	A	B	A	B
Test – 123	D	C	D	B	C	A	D	D	B	C	B	C
Test – 124	A	C	A	A	B	C	A	C	C	D	A	D
Test – 125	D	C	C	A	B	B	D	B	B	C	A	C
Test – 126	B	A	D	A	C	B	C	A	D	C	B	B
Test – 127	D	A	C	A	D	A	C	D	C	A	C	D
Test – 128	B	C	C	D	A	D	C	B	A	D	A	B
Test – 129	D	B	C	A	B	A	D	A	C	D	C	A
Test – 130	C	C	D	D	A	D	C	B	A	B	C	A
Test – 131	C	B	D	D	B	B	D	C	C	C	C	A
Test – 132	C	C	D	A	B	D	B	B	B	A	C	B
Test – 133	B	B	C	A	C	D	B	D	A	C	D	D
Test – 134	B	A	A	D	B	A	C	D	B	B	B	A
Test – 135	D	A	B	B	D	D	A	B	B	C	A	C
Test – 136	B	D	B	D	B	D	D	B	B	A	B	D
Test – 137	A	C	B	D	A	C	B	C	A	D	B	A
Test – 138	B	B	D	B	C	A	C	D	D	B	C	B
Test – 139	A	B	C	C	C	A	D	A	D	A	C	D
Test – 140	A	B	C	A	B	A	C	A	C	D	B	A
Test – 141	B	B	D	D	C	C	D	D	D	B	A	A
Test – 142	B	A	A	D	C	C	D	A	C	C	D	D
Test – 143	A	B	D	C	B	B	B	A	A	B	B	C
Test – 144	A	C	C	A	A	C	A	A	D	D	A	C
Test – 145	B	A	C	C	B	B	D	D	D	D	A	C
Test – 146	D	A	D	D	A	B	A	C	C	A	D	D
Test – 147	A	A	C	D	B	B	D	B	C	A	B	A
Test – 148	A	C	A	B	B	C	B	C	C	A	B	C
Test – 149	B	A	B	C	B	A	B	C	A	D	B	B
Test – 150	B	A	B	B	B	A	C	A	B	A	C	C
Test – 151	A	B	C	D	D	A	D	B	B	B	D	B
Test – 152	B	D	A	B	B	A	D	C	A	B	B	D
Test – 153	C	B	C	B	A	A	D	D	A	D	C	B
Test – 154	A	B	C	D	A	C	A	B	A	D	B	A
Test – 155	A	B	D	D	C	D	D	C	A	C	A	D
Test – 156	C	A	D	C	A	B	D	C	C	A	A	C
Test – 157	B	A	D	A	C	C	B	A	A	C	D	B
Test – 158	A	D	B	D	A	C	B	B	C	B	B	D

Test – 159	B	C	D	A	B	D	A	C	A	D	C	B
Test – 160	C	D	B	D	B	A	D	B	C	B	B	C
Test – 161	B	C	A	A	C	B	D	D	C	B	B	C
Test – 162	A	B	A	C	D	B	A	A	D	B	A	D
Test – 163	B	B	C	C	A	B	B	B	D	D	A	C
Test – 164	D	B	A	A	A	C	B	B	A	A	B	C
Test – 165	C	B	C	C	A	B	C	A	C	B	C	D
Test – 166	D	C	D	A	B	D	D	D	B	D	D	B
Test – 167	C	A	D	C	D	C	B	A	C	A	A	B
Test – 168	A	C	C	B	D	D	B	C	C	D	D	C
Test – 169	D	C	A	C								

About the Authors

Tayyip Oral, M.Ed & MBA

Tayyip Oral is a mathematician and test prep expert who has been teaching in learning centers and high school test since 1998. Mr. Oral is the founder of 555 math book series which includes variety of mathematics books. Tayyip Oral graduated from Qafqaz university with a Bachelor`s degree in Industrial Engineering. He later received his Master`s degree in Business Administration from the same university. He is an educator who has written several SAT Math, ACT Math, Geometry, Math counts and Math IQ books. He lives in Houston,TX.

Sheryl Knight

Sheryl Russell Knight has a Bachelor of Science degree in Mathematics from Southern Nazarene University and a Master's degree in Educational Administration from Texas State University at San Marcos. She has taught ACT/SAT preparation courses. She has served in classrooms in elementary and secondary mathematics in Texas, Missouri and California. She served as a District Coordinator for Special Education in Texas. She is currently an IEP educator in central Texas.

Books by Tayyip Oral

1. Sheryl Knight, Mesut Kizil, Tayyip Oral, ACCUPLACER MATH PREP, (1092 Questions with Answers), 2018

2. Sheryl Knight, Mesut Kizil, Tayyip Oral, TSI MATH Texas Success Initiative, (1092 Questions with Answers), 2017

3. Tayyip Oral, Osman Kucuk, Hasan Tursu, Geometry for SAT & ACT (555 Questions with Answers), 2017

4. Tayyip Oral, Ferhad Kirac, Bekir Inalhan, Algebra for The New SAT, Level – 1, (1111 Questions with Answers), 2017

5. Sheryl Knight, Tayyip Oral, Servet Oksuz, Algebra for ACT, Level – 1, (1080 Questions with Answers), 2017

6. Kristin Alexander, Tayyip Oral, Sait Yanmis, 555 Gifted and Talented, Question Sets for the Mathematically Gifted Middle Grade Scholar (1111 Questions with Answers), 2017

7. Steve Warner, Tayyip Oral, Sait Yanmis, 1000 Logic&Reasoning Questions for Gifted and Talented Elementary School Students, 2017

8. Tayyip Oral, 555 ACT Math, 1110 Questions with Solutions, 2017

9. Tayyip Oral, 555 Math IQ for Elementary School Students (1270 Questions with Answers), Second Edition, 2017

10. Tayyip Oral, Ersin Demirci, 555 SAT Math, 2016

11. Tayyip Oral, Sevket Oral, 555 ACT Math - II, 555 Questions with Answers, 2016

12. Tayyip Oral, 555 Geometry (555 Questions with Solutions), 2016

13. Tayyip Oral, Dr. Steve Warner. 555 Math IQ Questions for Middle School Students: Improve Your Critical Thinking with 555 Questions and Answer, 2015

14. Tayyip Oral, Dr. Steve Warner, Serife Oral, Algebra Handbook for Gifted Middle School Students, 2015

15. Tayyip Oral, Geometry Formula Handbook, 2015

16. Tayyip Oral, Dr. Steve Warner, Serife Oral, 555 Geometry Problems for High School Students: 135 Questions with Solutions, 2015

17. Tayyip Oral, Sevket Oral, 555 Math IQ questions for Elementary School Student, 2015

18. Tayyip Oral, 555 ACT Math, 555 Questions with Solutions, 2015

19. Tayyip Oral, Dr. Steve Warner, 555 Advanced math problems, 2015

20. Tayyip Oral, IQ Intelligence Questions for Middle and High School Students, 2014

21. T. Oral, E. Seyidzade, Araz publishing, Master's Degree Program Preparation (IQ), Cag Ogretim, Araz Courses, Baku, Azerbaijan, 2010.

    A master's degree program preparation text book for undergraduate students in Azerbaijan.

22. T. Oral, M. Aranli, F. Sadigov and N. Resullu, Resullu Publishing, Baku, Azerbaijan - 2012 (3.edition)

A text book for job placement exam in Azerbaijan for undergraduate and post undergraduate students in Azerbaijan.

23. T. Oral and I. Hesenov, Algebra (Text book), Nurlar Printing and Publishing, Baku, Azerbaijan, 2001.

A text book covering algebra concepts and questions with detailed explanations at high school level in Azerbaijan.

24. T.Oral, I.Hesenov, S.Maharramov, and J.Mikaylov, Geometry (Text book), Nurlar Printing and Publishing, Baku, Azerbaijan, 2002.

A text book for high school students to prepare them for undergraduate education in Azerbaijan.

25. T. Oral, I. Hesenov, and S. Maharramov, Geometry Formulas (Text Book), Araz courses, Baku, Azerbaijan, 2003.

A text book for high school students' university exam preparation in Azerbaijan.

26. T. Oral, I. Hesenov, and S. Maharramov, Algebra Formulas (Text Book), Araz courses, Baku, Azerbaijan, 2000

A university exam preparation text book for high school students in Azerbaijan.

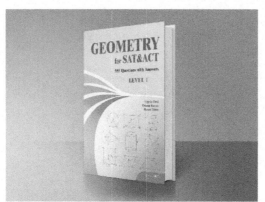

A very special thanks to Metehan Sancaktutar for his immense amount of contribution, foresight, and critical assistance to the book of CLEP College Mathematics - 1900 Questions with Answers

Tayyip Oral

555 Math Books Series Author

Made in the USA
Las Vegas, NV
23 February 2024